The Man Who Founded the ANC

The Man
Who Founded
the ANC

A Biography of Pixley ka Isaka Seme

BONGANI NGQULUNGA

PENGUIN BOOKS

Published by Penguin Books
an imprint of Penguin Random House South Africa (Pty) Ltd
Reg. No. 1953/000441/07
The Estuaries No. 4, Oxbow Crescent, Century Avenue, Century City, 7441
PO Box 1144, Cape Town, 8000, South Africa
www.penguinrandomhouse.co.za

Penguin
Random House
South Africa

First published 2017

1 3 5 7 9 10 8 6 4 2

Publication © Zebra Press 2017
Text © Bongani Ngqulunga 2017

PUBLISHER: Marlene Fryer
MANAGING EDITOR: Robert Plummer
EDITOR: Lynda Gilfillan
PROOFREADER: Bronwen Maynier
COVER DESIGNER: Ryan Africa
TYPESETTER: Monique van den Berg
INDEXER: Sanet le Roux

Set in 11 pt on 14.5 pt Minion

Printed by **novus print**, a Novus Holdings company

MIX
Paper from
responsible sources
FSC
www.fsc.org   FSC® C022948

Penguin Random House is committed to a sustainable future for
our business, our readers and our planet. This book is made
from Forest Stewardship Council ® certified paper.

ISBN 978 1 77022 926 6 (print)
ISBN 978 1 77022 927 3 (ePub)

This book is dedicated to two generations of Ngqulungas:
firstly, to my parents for the gift of life, and secondly,
to my children Mijelo, Kwande and Sakhiwe for the gift of love.

Contents

'I don't want to oppose the policy of Congress or to play solo in any shape or form. The President-General must be supported by all our people and I will do the same.'   – Pixley ka Isaka Seme

Introduction

The death of Pixley ka Isaka Seme on Thursday morning, 7 June 1951, at his legal practice in central Johannesburg came as a shock to black people in South Africa and neighbouring territories. Although Seme was close to seventy, his death took everybody by surprise, including his wife, Princess Phikisile, the eldest daughter of Dinuzulu ka Cetshwayo. When her husband died, she and their three children were not in Johannesburg; they had relocated to Mahhashini in the Nongoma district of Natal, where she had built a home not far from the royal homestead of Cyprian ka Solomon, her nephew and the Zulu king at the time. The first she heard of her husband's illness was an urgent message that she should travel to Johannesburg immediately. By the time she arrived Seme was dead; his body was already in a mortuary in Alexandra Township outside Johannesburg.

Seme's death followed closely upon that of Sefako Makgatho, just two weeks before, on 23 May 1951. Now, four of the first five African National Congress (ANC) presidents were deceased, John Dube and Josiah Gumede having died in 1946. Only Reverend Zaccheus Mahabane remained, and he would live on until 1971, eventually passing away at the age of ninety.

Although Seme had by then abandoned active politics, the news of his death nevertheless evoked a deep sense of loss, resulting in impassioned eulogies in black newspapers. *The Bantu World* captured the dominant sentiment of the time: '[If] today, Basutos, Zulus, Xhosas, Shangaans, Bechuanas and Vendas know themselves as Africans, and that Africa is the land of their fathers, they owe this to the inspiring foundation of African nationalism laid by Pixley ka Izaka Seme.'[1] *Ilanga lase Natal* echoed this in an editorial: '[T]he passing away of Dr Seme removes from our midst one of the pioneers of African nationalism. Indeed it might be said it brings to a close an important era in the political life of the African people.'[2] In a tribute, Jordan K. Ngubane, editor of *Inkundla Ya Bantu*, went so far as to suggest that Seme would go down in history as 'the greatest African of the first fifty years of the twentieth century – if not of the century as a whole'.[3]

Seme was buried at Newclare Cemetery in Johannesburg on 17 June 1951. The funeral service was held at two venues: the first part took place at the Bantu Men's Social Centre in Eloff Street, while the second was held at St Cyprian's Anglican Church in Anderson Street. Over two thousand people attended, including leading figures in the black community. Dr James Moroka, who was ANC president at the time, spoke at the funeral. Other speakers included Dr A.B. Xuma, a former president of the ANC; Chief Albert Luthuli, president of the ANC in Natal at the time, and soon to be national president; Richard V. Selope Thema, a former general secretary of the ANC and one of its founders; Levi T. Mvabaza, a veteran leader of the ANC and a member of the 1919 SANNC delegation to Great Britain; and Professor D.D.T. Jabavu, the first black professor at the University of Fort Hare, editor of the first black-owned newspaper *Imvo Zabantsundu* and president of the All-African Convention (AAC). The legal profession was represented by Advocate L.R. Dison. Leading traditional leaders attended or sent representatives to the funeral; among them were chiefs from Hammanskraal and Daggakraal. Chief Alpheus Hlope, who spoke at the funeral service, represented King Sobhuza II of Swaziland, while the Zulu royal family was represented by Prince Mshiyeni ka Dinuzulu, who also spoke on behalf of the Seme family. The apartheid government sent a spokesman for Dr W. Eiselen, the Secretary for Native Affairs. The service was presided over by Father Wood of St Cyprian's Anglican Church.[4]

The speakers lauded Seme for his role in bringing about the unity of black people. Dr A.B. Xuma called him 'an architect of our people', adding that Seme gave black people 'the inspiration of being a nation, he himself having laid the foundation of our freedom'. The speakers mentioned Seme's many achievements, including the fact that in January 1912, at age thirty, he had founded the South African Native National Congress (SANNC), which was renamed the African National Congress in 1923. He was the first treasurer general in 1912 and its fifth president from 1930 to 1937. He also served as the secretary for the chiefs in the ANC executive of President General Xuma. He was the second African to be admitted as a practising lawyer, after Alfred Mangena. Through his successful legal practice he became the first black person to argue a case in the British Privy Council. He was also a trusted advisor to various traditional leaders, and the Swazi and Zulu royal families in particular. He founded two newspapers: *Abantu-Batho*, the first national black newspaper, carrying reports in English as well as African languages; and *Ikwezi le Afrika*, which he established in 1928 and which was later incorporated into a newspaper called *African Leader*. He also founded numerous organisations, including the Native Farmers Association of South Africa (later renamed the Native Farmers Association of Africa), which bought land from white farmers for black settlement, and the Native Landowners Association of Africa.

What the speakers chose not to mention about Seme's life was equally significant, if not more so. Their tributes omitted the fact that by the time Seme died he had become a discredited public figure with a record of scandal and controversy. His presidency of the ANC from 1930 to 1937 had caused untold damage to his reputation and public standing. His leadership style was often described as authoritarian, undemocratic and arrogant. So widespread was the perception that he was intolerant of views differing from his own that the leading black newspaper at the time, *The Bantu World*, called Seme the *thulasizwe* of the black race – he who is never opposed and does not tolerate views other than his own. By the time Seme was voted out of office in December 1937 the ANC had almost collapsed and his reputation lay in tatters.

Though a pioneering lawyer with a reputation for successful litigation on behalf of black people, Seme was on more than one occasion found to have breached the law and the protocols of his profession. One particular case involved the small community of Waverley Township outside Pretoria, which faced eviction from a property it had occupied for decades. The community approached Seme, and though he agreed to represent it, he was accused of overcharging and leaving his clients in the lurch, which led to him being struck off the roll. The Waverley Township incident eroded Seme's reputation and resulted in the accusation that he was quick to take advantage of the desperation of vulnerable black people. It did not help matters that this was not the first time he appeared to have done exactly that. Alongside his reputation for being a political visionary grew a strong perception that he was an unscrupulous leader whose penchant for the finer things in life led him to exploit his people.

* * *

It is no wonder that by the time Seme died in 1951 he was an isolated political figure who was spoken about in the past tense, if at all. Perhaps nothing better captures his fall from grace than the epithet on his modest tombstone, the most notable feature of which is the simple inscription 'In loving memory of Dr P ka I Seme, BA LLD'. Underneath this are the words 'The stone has been erected by his family and Inkatha Yenkululeko Yesizwe', and below that 'Founder of African National Congress in 1912'. Although politics is full of surprises, it is nevertheless astounding that the tombstone of the founder of the African National Congress was erected by Inkatha Yenkululeko Yesizwe, a rival political organisation whose vision many would consider antithetical to that embraced by Seme throughout his adult life. And yet this seeming contradiction encapsulates the fundamental nature of Seme's life, with all its complexity and ambiguity.

These characteristics have made Seme a somewhat strange historical figure, a person whose imprint on the South African political stage, though significant, has received minimal recognition. Even basic information about his life remains unknown or is inaccurate. For instance, there are claims that his mother's name was Sarah Mseleku and that Seme completed a law degree; even though both assertions are incorrect, they have often been repeated.[5] Similarly, his brothers, especially Isaac Marsh and Mbekwana Isaac Seme, have been mistaken for his father.[6] It has also been erroneously claimed that his first wife, Frances Xiniwe, who is often referred to simply as 'the Xhosa woman', passed away while married to Seme, while she in fact died after their divorce.[7] Other claims have not been adequately interrogated. Richard V. Selope Thema, for instance, has suggested that Seme's Christian upbringing in the missionary community of Inanda, as a Zulu, had an influence on his life.[8] Jordan Ngubane claimed that Seme was not in fact Zulu, but rather a Tonga man, while Seme himself occasionally claimed to be related to the Zulu royal family or to be a blood relative of Reverend John Langalibalele Dube.

There is also confusion about Seme's educational history. While there is a general assumption that he received a law degree at the University of Oxford where he was a student in the early 1900s, this is in fact incorrect. His nephew, King Edward Masinga, believed that Seme had many more academic degrees than the only one he actually gained. At various points, Seme himself made false claims to having a master's degree as well as a doctoral degree in law. The gaps and confusion reflect, in part, the paucity of information about Seme's life, yet this has not deterred attempts to write about him.

Moss Mashamaite has written a biography, but it leaves substantial areas of Seme's life untouched,[9] and the brief sketch written by Richard Rive and Tim Couzens focuses on Seme's years as a student at the Mount

Hermon School for Boys in north-western Massachusetts.[10] Chris Saunders has addressed aspects of Seme's life, the most comprehensive of which is an article drawing largely on Seme's correspondence with Alain LeRoy Locke, a fellow student at Oxford University. An article by Rob Moore examines Seme's farm purchases in the former eastern Transvaal, in particular one in Middelburg. Peter Limb has edited an impressive volume that focuses on *Abantu-Batho*, the newspaper that Seme started in 1912.[11] In addition there are two masters dissertations: the first, by Marvin Faison in 1983, focuses on Seme's presidency of the ANC; the second, by Michael Ndlovu in 2014, examines Seme's political ideology.

The time has come for a more comprehensive account of a man who lived an unusual and interesting life long before the formation of the ANC and an even more storied and controversial life afterwards. Seme is described either as the founder of the ANC, or as the moving spirit behind its formation. For while others were involved in establishing the organisation, it was Pixley Seme who led the initiative and gave the inaugural address at the founding conference on 8 January 1912. Four decades later Richard V. Selope Thema, a conference delegate, wrote about Seme's remarkable achievement in bringing together 'tribes that had never met together before except on the battlefields'. Thema went on to say that the founding conference was a 'gathering of educated Africans who had never exchanged views before, it was [a] gathering, if I may say so, of departed spirits of the African race, among whom were such men as Sandile, Tshaka, Moshoeshoe, Cetyewayo, Moroka, Khama, Sekhukhune, Sotshangana and Ramapulana'.[12]

Seme's involvement extended to his relationship with the Zulu and Swazi royal families, including his marriages to a Zulu and a Swazi princess. But Seme's relationship with the two royal families went beyond the personal. For many years he was King Sobhuza II's lawyer, confidant and representative on matters affecting the Swazi nation. Seme was also intimately involved in the affairs of the Zulu royal house, beginning with the reign of King Dinuzulu ka Cetshwayo right until his death, when Cyprian ka Solomon became king. There is a strong indication that Seme played a decisive role in ensuring that Prince Solomon was chosen over Prince David, another claimant to the throne.[13]

In Seme's final years the ANC Youth League adopted African nationalism as its guiding philosophy. Indeed, it lay at the heart of the ANC's 1949 Programme of Action. A key figure behind the reassertion of African nationalism in the ANC was a young lawyer by the name of Anton Muziwakhe Lembede, who happened to have served his articles under the tutelage of Seme at his legal firm in Johannesburg. It is possible that Seme taught Lembede not just law, but also politics. It is easy to imagine the two men debating politics, although it has to be noted that Lembede's brand of African nationalism was decidedly more radical than Seme's. The important point is that African nationalism, and its pan-African variant, has been a golden thread throughout the ANC's century of existence. It is a crucial aspect of Seme's political legacy.

Six decades after his death, Pixley Seme and his contribution to South Africa are finally receiving recognition. In 2006 the Presidency of the Republic of South Africa awarded Seme the Order of Luthuli in Gold: this order is awarded to South Africans who have made a significant contribution to the struggle for peace, justice, democracy and human rights.[14] In awarding the order to Seme, the Presidency stated that his life 'is an outstanding example of a search for academic excellence running parallel with a commitment to a struggle for justice'. The government of Mpumalanga has erected a statue in his honour in the town of Volksrust, where Seme and his associates had bought a farm through the Native Farmers Association. The government of KwaZulu-Natal has likewise erected a statue at the homestead where Seme was born. Street names, a municipality and buildings have also been named after him. These are fitting tributes to a distinguished South African. But official honours and recognition tend to tell only half the story; they simplify a complex life into statues and monuments before which we are expected to pay our respects. There is obviously a place for hero worship in every society. But the role of a biography is different: it should examine the life of its subject in a multifaceted and complex manner. That is how life is, after all: multifaceted, complex – and ambiguous. The life of Pixley Seme was certainly no exception.

* * *

When mourners drove to Newclare Cemetery to bury Pixley Seme, they were not joined by the executive committee of the organisation Seme had founded. Instead, members of the committee attended a meeting with the Transvaal Indian Congress, the purpose of which was to plan for what became known as the Defiance Campaign of 1952. Present at that meeting were Dr J.S. Moroka, the president of the ANC at the time, Dr Yusuf Dadoo (who did, however, manage to attend Seme's funeral), Walter Sisulu, Oliver Tambo and several other leaders of the ANC. Given Seme's preference for non-confrontational forms of protest, or '*hamba kahle* politics' as the ANC Youth League derisively called it at the time, it is ironic that the turn to confrontational mass mobilisation against the apartheid state was planned while his funeral was taking place. That turn to the masses fundamentally transformed the character and trajectory of the ANC and brought to the fore new leaders such as Albert Luthuli, Oliver Tambo, Nelson Mandela and Walter Sisulu. If one were to ask any young South African today to name a few ANC leaders, they would probably mention Luthuli, Mandela, Tambo, Sisulu and their contemporaries, but most likely not Pixley Seme – as may be expected considering that Seme led the ANC during the first half of the twentieth century. Nonetheless, Seme's diminished status in the public consciousness should not detract from the contribution he made to South Africa, or discourage scrutiny of his life.

* * *

In the 1930s Dr A.B. Xuma, the sixth president general of the ANC, wrote a biographical pamphlet about Charlotte Maxeke titled 'Charlotte Manye (Maxeke) or What an educated African girl can do', to which W.E.B. Du Bois wrote a foreword. In his introduction, Xuma issued the following caveat:

> Biographers in whose society and group, thank God, I do not belong, are usually great enthusiasts about their subjects. Being artists they often create hero and heroine rather than relate true history and activity. They polish and gloss over the rough edges; they are sometimes so successful in their art, creating a picture or image which though perfect is so unlike the subject that he almost fails of recognition by those who knew him in life, and if living, himself is urged to ask, 'Whose life is this? Is this my life story?'[15]

Like many biographers, I began as an enthusiast about my subject – but I have tried as far as possible to write frankly about Seme's life and the context that shaped it. The complexity and ambiguity of Seme's life and legacy have served as a check against polishing or glossing over his rough edges. At the same time, I have tried not to fall into another temptation, which is to emphasise his failures at the expense of his many achievements.

The balancing act this entails may frustrate the reader who prefers a universe of saints and villains. Seme, like most human beings, was neither. He could be upliftingly brilliant, but also depressingly disappointing. I have sought to capture his highs and lows, and to do so honestly. Whether I have successfully avoided the biographers' pitfalls that Xuma so eloquently identified is for the reader to judge.

1

The bustard hunters

King Edward Masinga, popularly known as K.E. Masinga, was the first black person to be appointed by the South African Broadcasting Corporation (SABC) as a radio announcer in December 1941. There is a story, probably apocryphal, that is often told about how he came to be appointed in the first place. It is claimed that one day he was walking down Aliwal Street in Durban when he noticed a building and decided to walk inside. Lo and behold, he discovered that the building was the Durban home of the SABC, which was the only institution at the time that did radio broadcasting in South Africa. Upon making the discovery, Masinga decided to ask for a job as a radio announcer and was appointed on the spot.

The decision by the SABC to appoint Masinga was a manifestation of the South African government's strategy to popularise its participation in the Second World War. It had identified the black population as one of the key constituencies whose support for its involvement in the war had to be won. Thus it was that Masinga was appointed to broadcast the news from the battlefields to the black population. As Masinga would later relate, he was given a few minutes a day, at most three, to read his news broadcast about the war. From those humble beginnings the seed of black radio broadcasting was planted. When the apartheid government decided in 1960 to establish Radio Bantu, Masinga became the face and anchor of its isiZulu section. This section later became Radio Zulu, today known as Ukhozi FM, which has the largest listenership on the African continent.

Masinga is rightly recognised as a pioneer of radio broadcasting in South Africa and has received many accolades, including having a main road in Durban named after him. The public acclaim that Masinga enjoyed was, however, not new to his family. Another widely known family member was his maternal uncle, Pixley ka Isaka Seme. So integral and close was Masinga to the Seme family that he became its historian. The record of the Seme family history that Masinga left after his death in 1990 is likely the only reliable source of information left by any family member about the origins of the Seme family and how it ended up settling at Inanda Mission outside Durban.[1]

* * *

How the Seme clan acquired its name is the stuff of legend. According to Masinga, the Semes were part of the Mthethwa tribe who were scattered between the Black and White Mfolozi rivers during the reign of King Dingiswayo ka Jobe. After the death of his father, Dingiswayo sent a group of strong young men selected from his army on a lion hunt; he wanted certain body parts to use as *umuthi* to strengthen him. When Dingiswayo's hunting party came face to face with a lion, a hunter tried to kill it by stabbing its left shoulder. But the lion did not die. A second hunter left only a scratch on the lion's body when he tried to stab it, after which others used their sticks to kill the creature. On the way back the hunters struggled to find food, which forced some members of the party to resort to eating bustard birds.

When the hunters arrived at Dingiswayo's homestead they handed him the dead lion. When Dingiswayo looked at it and asked who had stabbed it on the left shoulder, the man responsible was pointed out to him. Dingiswayo was pleased with the hunter's efforts and he rewarded him with cattle and gave him a place to build himself a big homestead. Dingiswayo said that the hunter and his followers would henceforth be known as *abakwaNxele* (the Nxele clan) for the man's role in stabbing the lion. The king then asked what had caused the scratch on the creature's body. He was informed that one of the hunters had tried to stab the lion but missed his mark. The king was happy for his efforts and rewarded him with cattle and a place to build his homestead. He called the second hunter and his followers the Msweli clan (those who missed). The king was also told about the difficulties his hunting party experienced trying to get food. He was informed that some of the hunters had even resorted to eating bustards (*amaseme*). Dingiswayo named the group that hunted and ate these birds *abakwaSeme* (the Seme clan). Thus, from that single hunting episode emerged the Nxele, Msweli and Seme clans, who all originated from the Mthethwa tribe.

It is of course difficult to ascertain the veracity of the story told by Masinga. The similarities it shares with Alfred T. Bryant's version in *Olden Times in Zululand and Natal*, published in 1929, are nonetheless striking.[2] Like Masinga, Bryant states that the Seme clan belongs to the broader

Mthethwa tribe and is related to the Nxeles and Mswelis. Bryant's explanation of how the Seme clan acquired its name is, however, different from Masinga's. For Bryant, it started with a conflict that arose in the Mthethwa tribe when an unnamed Mthethwa king decided to marry Msweli's daughter or sister. Perhaps as a reward, or to distance the Mswelis from the Mthethwas, the king then gave the Mswelis a clan name of their own: *abakwaNxele*. With his newfound royal favour, Msweli, with the assistance of the king, attacked his senior brother, driving him and his followers to the marshes along St Lucia Bay. The land was not conducive to pastoral or agricultural pursuits, so, owing to the concentration of bustards in the area, they resorted to bustard hunting. As a result they came to be known as *abakwaSeme* (the bustard people).

It was from these bustard hunters that Isaka Seme, father of Pixley and his siblings, originated. By the time he migrated south to Inanda, it appears that certain sections of the Seme clan had already moved from St Lucia Bay and settled in the Mtubatuba and Hluhluwe areas. Some went as far south as the Hlabisa and Nongoma districts. According to one of Isaka's sons, Ponqela Lindley, Isaka's family did not move very far from St Lucia Bay. Isaka's father, Sinono, appears to have settled in what is today known as Mtubatuba, where he married a daughter of Duma ka Mseleku ka Lwandle. Sinono was a son of Mbuyazi of Njonjo of Khuwana of Mqumbela of Sokoti of Seme. From that marriage were born children, one of whom was a boy whose original name is unknown, although he became known as Isaka Seme when he settled at Inanda Mission outside Durban.

The circumstances that led Isaka to leave his home and travel to faraway Inanda are murky. A story that has gained currency is that when Sinono, Isaka's father, died in one of the wars, probably between the Ndwandwes and the Mthethwas, his wife gave up her son, Isaka, to missionaries who were passing by. The story goes that Isaka had acquired the skill of driving horse-drawn carriages. Upon learning this, the missionaries hired him to be their driver as they travelled around South Africa.

This story of how Isaka ended up at the Inanda Mission of the American Board of Missions (ABM) seems improbable, however. Firstly, there is no evidence that any of the ABM missionaries travelled as far as the Mtubatuba area in the early to mid-1800s. The missionary who went furthest up the north coast and into Zululand was Reverend George Champion. Yet even in his case, nothing suggests that he reached the Mtubatuba/ St Lucia area. The only mission station in the vicinity of Mtubatuba was the Entumeni Mission, built by Bishop Hans Schreuder of the Norwegian Missionary Society in 1843. No claim has been made that Isaka Seme worked with the Norwegian missionaries, and there is no evidence to that effect.

Masinga upends the claim that Isaka left his family in Mtubatuba/ St Lucia in order to work for missionaries. After Sinono ka Mbuyazi died, his family fell victim to the dispossession and displacement that generally accompanied the migration of white people into the interior of South Africa. Family members were forced into working for white farmers in what Masinga calls slave-like conditions. It was while he was a farm labourer that Isaka became proficient in the Dutch language. Isaka was also given a Dutch/Afrikaans name, Isaak. So intolerable were the working conditions, however, that Isaka, together with his kinsman Slykom Mthethwa, decided to run away. Both men ended up at Inanda Mission. There, either he or the American missionaries changed his name to Isaac, the English version of Isaak. When Reverend Daniel Lindley, founder and head of the mission at Inanda, decided to work as a missionary among the Boers, who spoke Dutch, he took along Isaka Seme as a translator, and also to assist with transportation. According to Masinga, Isaka Seme was not taken from Mtubatuba/St Lucia because he was a skilled transporter; rather, he became a skilled transporter while at Inanda Mission.

No other sources corroborate Masinga's version of Isaka's arrival at Inanda. Indeed, as Masinga's cousin George Seme suggests, it is possible that Isaka left home in search of Christianity. Whatever the reason for his migration, when Isaka arrived at Inanda he was assimilated into the community and soon became a prominent member. He married Eliza Bhulose, whose family were related to the Ndelus, the Mselekus and the Dumas. It has been suggested that Isaka's wife was in fact Sarah Mseleku, though Seme and his siblings always recorded their mother's name as Eliza. Masinga, her grandson, recorded her surname as Bhulose, not Mseleku. There is no historical record of how Isaka and Eliza met. Her Christian name suggests that she was, or became, part of the community of the converted. Eliza and Isaka had eleven children: five boys – Marsh, Nompondo, Mbekwana Isaac, Ponqela Lindley and Pixley – and six girls, Lucy, Loti, Sannah, Speke, Dalitha and Martha. They named Marsh, their eldest child, after Reverend Samuel Marsh, founder of the American Zulu Mission at Thafamasi in Natal. They named another son Lindley after Reverend Daniel Lindley, while Pixley was named after Reverend Stephen Pixley, also of

Inanda Mission. The girls too were named after prominent members of the Inanda mission station.

Although active in the community life of Inanda Mission, Eliza and Isaka appear not to have been leading figures, unlike the Dubes or the Gobas. They did not occupy any prominent positions, either in the church or the community. Nor were they materially wealthy; they were a simple family that eked out a living through subsistence farming. Their children, however, did make a name for themselves. The girls became closely associated with Inanda Seminary, a girls school built by the American Board of Missions. Dalitha, the eldest of the sisters, was a pupil at Inanda, and also taught there for a while before becoming a missionary of the ABM at Inhambane in Mozambique. Lucy also taught at Inanda, while Loti, Sannah, Martha and Speke were pupils there. The boys were educated at Adams College in Amanzimtoti. The girls seem to have spent most of their adult lives teaching at schools around Natal, especially in the Durban area (with the exception of Dalitha, who became a missionary). The Seme boys, however, pursued various other options. Marsh and Nompondo followed in the footsteps of their father and became farmers. Nompondo owned a large herd of cattle – so large, in fact, that the grazing area allocated to black people in the Inanda area became inadequate for his herd, forcing him to request permission for the cattle to graze at Springfield. His request was denied, and his brother Marsh left Inanda to farm in the eastern Transvaal (now Mpumalanga). There, Marsh worked with his younger brother, Pixley, who eventually bought farms in the Wakkerstroom district.

Ponqela, mostly known by his second name Lindley, followed an altogether different career path. After passing Standard Five at Adams College he left for the United States of America, where he studied at various universities. He spent six years at Benedict College in South Carolina doing an agricultural course. He then went to Virginia Theological Seminary where he spent four years. From there he left for Shaw University in North Carolina, where he studied medicine for three years. After a year at Battle Creek Sanatorium in Michigan, he moved to McGill University in Canada where he studied for four more years. When the First World War broke out he joined the American Medical Corps as a medical assistant, and returned to South Africa in 1921.[3] He then applied for financial support from the government to start an agricultural project, but nothing much seems to have come of this. Ponqela died in Swaziland. Pixley followed

Ponqela to the United States where he distinguished himself as a student. Their brother Mbekwana became a pastor of the American Board of Missions, and for many years served at various mission stations in Natal.

In many respects, the other boys at Inanda Mission were no different from the Seme boys. Born mostly of parents who did not have formal education, they went to school and followed careers that were unimaginable to their elders. They also sought certain privileges that were not available to their parents. One was to be exempt from the obligations of Native Law. Those 'natives' who sought such exemption had to petition the Governor of the colony of Natal. The Seme brothers filed petitions, duly motivating why government authorities should exempt them from Native Law. When, as a twenty-five-year-old in 1898, Mbekwana Seme applied for exemption, his motivation was that he was about to practise as a minister of religion and he needed 'freedom of movement and comfort under English Law as applied to Europeans'. Like his brother Marsh, who had previously filed a petition, Mbekwana mentioned in his application that his parents, whose names he gave as Isaac and Eliza, were deceased. The use of the English version of his father's name, Isaac, is interesting because both Marsh and Pixley gave their father's name as Isaka. In any event, Mbekwana's petition was turned down. In a letter he wrote in January 1899 he complained that his application had been refused without reasons being given. It took several petitions over a ten-year period for the authorities to finally grant exemption.[4]

A few weeks after his return in 1910 from his studies overseas, Pixley Seme also applied to be exempted from Native Law. His motivation was that he wanted to 'acquire testamentary rights over my future property and in the meantime to be able to enjoy and exercise the freedom of locomotion which the practice of my profession requires'.[5] Seme's reference to testamentary rights over *future* property was apt because he did not own much property at the time; in fact, he said the only property he had was a horse and 'a few law books'.[6] He also mentioned that his parents were dead. The authorities were reluctant to grant Seme the exemption he sought because he had left Inanda to live in Johannesburg where he planned to practise as a lawyer. In a letter dated 7 June 1911, the Acting Chief Native Commissioner of Natal informed Seme that his application could not be granted because he was no longer resident in that province.[7]

Seme mentioned in his application that he was twenty-nine years old, which suggests that he was born in 1881. This detail is important as there is some confusion about the actual year of his birth. The source of confusion is in fact Seme himself. When, in October 1906, he filled in an admission form (also called a matriculation form) to study at Oxford University, he recorded his birthday as 2 October 1882, not 1 October 1881, the date given on his application to the Mount Hermon school. He also claimed that his late father's name was Sinono Isaka, not simply Isaka, as his brothers had previously recorded. In the same form, Pixley Seme claimed that his late father was a member of the Tribal Council, a new claim that cannot be supported by facts. He also claimed to be the fourth son of Isaka, not the fifth.[8] So the information contained in the matriculation form contradicts much of the available information on Seme's early life.

Masinga's record of the family history states that Pixley Seme had five brothers, as mentioned previously, and that his father's name was not Sinono, but Isaka. Sinono was his grandfather's name. In adulthood, Seme's six sisters went on to start families: Loti married into the Ntshiba family of New Germany, Lucy married into the Mbambo family, Dalitha married into the Hlantis, and Masinga's mother, Sannah, married into the Masingas (all these families were from Inanda), while Speke married into the Madonelas from Mzimkhulu, and Martha married into the Mfekas from Mzumbe. Like their brothers, the Seme women went on to have successful careers. There is, however, no doubt that the most accomplished of the whole Seme clan was Pixley, the family's last-born son. It is doubtful that his parents or his siblings would have predicted that the youngest Seme would go on to achieve what he did. The first step towards that journey began at a small primary school at Inanda Mission.

2

The education of an African patriot

On 12 December 1962 Kwame Nkrumah, the founding president of the Republic of Ghana and an iconic figure in Africa's struggle for independence from colonial rule, gave the opening address at the First International Congress of Africanists held in Accra, Ghana. Towards the end, he said he felt it was his 'duty to place on record at this first Africanist Congress taking place here in Africa, the oration of Isaka Seme, which although made some fifty years ago, is still relevant to the postulates of our present situation in Africa'. Nkrumah then read a speech that Pixley Seme had given as a student at Columbia University in April 1906: 'The Regeneration of Africa'. It had won him the university's Curtis Medal and was widely reported in newspapers in the United States and abroad. Nkrumah's quoting of the speech some five decades later underscored its enduring inspiration to successive generations of African nationalists and Pan-Africanists. By invoking Seme at the first congress of Africanists to be held on the African continent, Nkrumah was linking the Pan-Africanist ideals of his time to the vision Seme had espoused five decades before.

Over a century has passed since Seme first gave the speech and still, scores of scholars and politicians pore over it for insight, inspiration, analysis and debate. What is remarkable about the speech is not only its powerful oratory, but also the depth of its vision for the African continent and its pride in African people. This speech, together with the formation of the SANNC in 1912, is generally regarded as a high point in Seme's life. The fact that he delivered it as a twenty-four-year-old about to graduate has amplified the admiration surrounding its reception. Understandably, it has drawn attention to Seme's education and other circumstances at the time, with questions being posed as to whether there was anything in his educational history that might account for its award-winning quality. This chapter traces Seme's footsteps from the time he was a young student at Inanda Mission outside Durban, to a brief stint at Adams College in Amanzimtoti, to high school in Massachusetts in the United States, right through college at Columbia University where he earned his degree, to his four-year period studying law in the United Kingdom, part of which was spent at the University of Oxford.

The early school years[1]

Information about Seme's early school education is scant. What little is known comes largely from his admission form for Mount Hermon School for Boys in Massachusetts. Seme's education began at the Inanda Mission school. In 1895, at the age of fourteen, he moved to Adams Training School for Boys to further his studies. Adams College, as the school was later renamed, had been established in 1853 by an American missionary, Reverend David Rood, at Amanzimtoti, outside Durban, in honour of Reverend Dr Newton Adams, who had founded the mission in the 1830s when he arrived in Natal. There is no record of Seme's time at Adams, and the only information available from Mount Hermon is that he did a bit of photography and participated in some farming activities while there. His farming stint would later lead Reverend Stephen Pixley, a missionary at Inanda and one of Seme's benefactors, to call him a 'cowboy'.[2]

Seme did not stay long at Adams. He spurned the opportunity to study teaching and opted instead to further his studies abroad. His decision was not surprising. A group of black people, some of whom were his neighbours, had gone overseas, to the United States in particular, for study purposes. One of these was John Langalibalele Dube, whom Seme knew well, although Dube was ten years his senior. What is perhaps surprising is that Seme left at a relatively young age, not yet out of his teens. Seme sailed the ten thousand miles to the United States and arrived in Brooklyn, New York, where he stayed with Dube, who was at the time a student at a theological seminary in Brooklyn. After a few months, Seme, assisted by Dube and Reverend Pixley who was in Boston at the time, applied for admission to Mount Hermon.

The application form reveals interesting details about young Seme's life. The first concerns his name, which he gave as Pixley I. Seme – as did Dube, acting as his guardian. Reverend Stephen Pixley, however, called him Seme Isaac, omitting the name Pixley. In a letter dated 1 September 1898, Reverend Pixley again referred to him as Seme Isaac, however adding 'alias Pixley Seme'. In another letter, dated 25 September, addressed to Professor Henry F. Cutler, principal of Mount Hermon, Reverend Pixley again wrote 'Seme Isaac', though noting that he (Seme) preferred to be called Pixley I. Seme. Seme's name was evolving: Reverend Pixley may have been reluctant to use Seme's first name, Pixley, out of modesty; and it is possible that Seme gave himself the name in gratitude for assistance provided by the reverend.

There are other interesting bits of information in the application form. One is that Seme appears not to have had any substantial formal education prior to moving to the United States. In answer to the question regarding number of years of schooling completed, Seme answered three. This suggests that the only schooling which was counted was the time he spent at Adams, which may mean that the education he received at the Inanda Mission school was rather informal. The subjects Seme studied during his schooling in South Africa were arithmetic, grammar and analysis, geography, and history. The form also reveals that Seme's parents had died by the time he left for the United States and that Reverend Pixley supported his admission application as his priest rather than his guardian. The religious link to Reverend Pixley is evident where Seme gives his church as the Lindley Mission Church (the Congregational Church) at Inanda Mission outside Durban.

Some of the information in the form is incorrect. For instance, Reverend Pixley stated that Seme had one married sister who was at Gaza Mission in present-day Mozambique. It is true that one of his sisters was a missionary and spent some time doing mission work in Mozambique. But, as stated previously, Seme had more than one sister. It is possible that, because Reverend Pixley knew the missionary sister through her involvement in the church, he chose only to mention her. Another interesting nugget is that Reverend Pixley explained that Seme's goal was to become a 'teacher of a high type of piety and ultimately a missionary to the Zulu people'. The following year, Reverend Pixley returned to the objective of Seme's Mount Hermon education: to prepare him to 'return to South Africa to aid in the elevation and Christianization of the Zulus'.[3] As things turned out, Seme became neither a teacher nor a missionary, and as for piety, this was an especially high expectation.

One tricky issue about Seme's overseas study was the funding. There is nothing to suggest that he received financial support from his family. Reverend Pixley did, however, commit to pay part of his fees for the first year of his schooling. In addition, Dube stated that a Mr Louis Stoiben of New York would carry part of the fees and the rest would be carried by Seme himself. Evidently, there was no dependable source of support for either his living expenses or his schooling. As Reverend Pixley stated in his motivation letter to the principal of Mount Hermon, all they had was faith that Seme's bills would somehow be paid.

When Seme was admitted to the school in late 1898, Reverend Pixley met his obligation by paying $50 for the first half of the academic year, and sending Seme some clothing. John Dube also contributed $50 in September that year, and another $50 in 1900. These contributions seem to have covered tuition and living expenses for Seme's first year. However, the next academic year remained unsettled, which concerned Seme. In a letter addressed to the principal in August 1899, Seme revealed that he had only managed to save $45 from temporary employment during the summer. He did not know where the fees for the following school term would come from, and he could not count on his benefactor, Reverend Pixley, to provide the money. Seme simply said: 'But the Lord has done so much for me that it is impossible for me to loose [sic] faith in him, and so I because I believe I hope.'

Seme's faith appears to have been rewarded as other benefactors came to the fore. Reverend Pixley paid another $50 for the second academic year. Mrs Eliza Smith from Massachusetts donated $100 for the 1900–1901 academic year, stating that, at the request of Reverend Pixley, Seme should not be informed of the donation. Mr A.J. Breinig of Maryland paid for his final term, stating that the Lord had put it in his heart to support Seme. This would not be the only time Mr Breinig assisted Seme. In the summer of 1902 he employed Seme to work on his farm, a job Seme described as hard but healthy. A Mrs Beals also contributed $5 towards Seme's education. And Mrs Harriett Doubleday of Rutherford, New Jersey, made a donation in the form of clothes; in her letter to the principal, she requested that Seme be measured up by a tailor. The tailor, Mr Garl W. Kettler, provided Seme's measurements (he had a 32 waist). There was an expectation that Seme would find work during school holidays to fund his education – which he did. Throughout his time as a student he worked during the summer months, thereby contributing towards the payment of his fees.

Seme underwent a transformation at Mount Hermon. He grew increasingly assertive during his four years there, and became a polished communicator. This was especially evident in his correspondence with the school. In a letter to the principal in late August 1898, he asked for the school catalogue to be sent to him. What is noteworthy is Seme's description of himself: 'the Zulu boy for whom both Rev. S.C. Pixley and Dube asked the prof. to receive as a student in the school'.[4] But by August 1901 he had shed this meekness. Writing to Professor C.E. Dickerson – probably the teacher responsible for allocating rooms to boarders – Seme indicated his preference for the following year, beginning: 'Good morning, Sir! I suppose it makes no difference with you where I sleep anyway – I don't believe it – so I guess I better write anyway.' He then added a request: 'For my room-mate put in the best new coloured fellow if there is one, or else leave the place blank until 29th August, 6 p.m.'[5]

This letter suggests a remarkable degree of assertiveness, as well as a hint of petulance. Here was a young man who was confident enough to write to his professor in a forthright manner. He had abandoned a begging posture, and had assumed a more confident attitude. His request for a 'coloured' roommate is also revealing. It demonstrates a measure of politicisation, a race consciousness, which had not been evident on his arrival in America. The full transformation would be splendidly revealed four years later, in 1906, when he delivered his famous speech, 'The Regeneration of Africa'.

In his final year at Mount Hermon, Seme started applying to tertiary colleges. The correspondence suggests that he was especially interested in Yale or Columbia. Yale was particularly taken with his story, as well as the possibility that Seme might be the first black person from South Africa to enrol. Its interest was further piqued at the suggestion that Seme's admission might provide an opportunity to extend its influence in South Africa. Accordingly, Yale reacted by promising to remit Seme's fees owing to his financial situation.[6]

Seme's dream of going to Yale was not realised, however. He failed the admission examination, with the university informing him that he did not quite make the grade. He was encouraged to try again, but Seme was reluctant. With a whiff of despair, he said he would try his best to get to college, though the dream of Yale seemed to have eluded him. Fortunately for Seme, Columbia University accepted his application, and in the autumn of 1902 he enrolled as a first-year Bachelor of Arts (BA) student at Columbia College, the undergraduate liberal arts college of Columbia University.

'His face dark, but his mind brilliant'
Columbia University set certain requirements for prospective students. For those, like Seme, who applied to be admitted as a freshman, the requirements included submitting a certificate of good character from a teacher or citizen in good standing. Equally important was for candidates

to write entrance examinations on two appointed dates a few months before the start of the academic year. The examinations cost $5, payable in advance, and were conducted by Columbia's College Examination Board. Prospective students had to pass a combination of subjects with a collective numerical value of fifteen points. Two subjects were compulsory: English and elementary mathematics, with each of these subjects contributing three of the fifteen points required. For Seme's 1902 freshman class, there were several additional subjects from which prospective students had to choose. These included elementary Latin, elementary Greek, elementary German, elementary French, history, elementary physics, botany, chemistry, physiography and zoology. In addition to the required English and mathematics, Seme took exams in Latin, German, Greek and history.

Seme's performance seems to have been satisfactory, as his name appeared on the list of those recommended for admission to the first year of a Bachelor of Arts degree in 1902. Seme was then informed of the requirements for the successful completion of the degree. Students had to pass a group of subjects, each of which had a numerical value, which had to total sixty points. Although students were allowed to choose any available course, certain courses were prescribed and had to be taken by all those studying for a BA degree. The prescribed subjects included English, Latin, Greek, French, German, mathematics, history, psychology, economics, and either botany or physics.

Seme joined the cohort of newly admitted freshmen[7] in October 1902. He was one month short of twenty years old. He gave his New York address as 19 West 135, Harlem, and his home address as Port Natal, Durban, South Africa. Curiously, he gave his late father's name, Isaka Seme, in the section of the student record form requiring the name of a parent or guardian; when he had applied for high-school study in Massachusetts, Seme stated that his parents were deceased. In a possible attempt to cultivate a separate identity, Seme did not mention Reverend Stephen Pixley, or any of his financial benefactors. Interestingly, it was while he was at Columbia that he added 'ka' (son of) to his name, so that it became Pixley ka Isaka Seme.

Seme enrolled for five subjects: English A, German 2, French A, Latin B and mathematics A. English A covered rhetoric and composition; German 2 included grammar, reading and composition, and students were required to attend classes for at least three hours a week throughout the academic year; Latin B covered prose and verse illustrative of Roman public and private life, and here too students had to spend at least three hours a week in class; mathematics A covered geometry, algebra and trigonometry.[8]

All students, especially freshmen, were expected to spend at least two hours a week at the gymnasium doing physical exercise. They were entitled to a physical examination, and, based on the outcome, a training programme suited to the individual's needs was developed.

In addition, Seme busied himself in other student activities. His main extramural interest was debating. Two months into his first year, he was already active in the Freshman Debating Society. One debate in which he participated related to the question of whether small colleges were preferable to large colleges. He and his partner, C.A. Stewart, argued against the motion, and won the debate.[9] In January 1903 the student newspaper, *Columbia Daily Spectator*, reported that Seme and two other first-year students had been chosen to organise a debate between first-year and second-year students in April 1903.[10] Seme and his two fellow students were also mandated to arrange a debate with freshmen from Yale University, as well as New York City's Patria Club. As if that were not enough for a first-year student who had barely settled in, Seme and the other two students were appointed judges of a debate on the topic of whether the United States government should interfere in the 'disenfranchisement of Southern negroes'.[11] Seme also put his name forward as a candidate for the freshman team that would take on the sophomores in April, though he was not selected.[12] He was, however, elected vice president of the Freshman Debating Society. He was also the chairman of the Freshman-Sophomore Debate Committee. These extramural activities extended to the university's Philharmonic Society, as well as the Christian Association.

For four years he was a member of the Barnard Literary Association, a debating society established at the university in 1877. The *Columbia Daily Spectator* regularly reported on the activities of the association, and Seme's name was mentioned on several occasions. In a report of 1 October 1903, for instance, Seme is named as one of seven debaters at the association's first meeting that year. In the same month he debated whether 'National or State legislation should be enacted declaring criminal any organization, public speaking or writing in favour of annihilation of all government by revolutionary means'. Seme and his partner, W.H. Pollak, argued for the motion, but lost the debate.[13] His participation in the association's affairs seems to have increased with seniority. In October 1904 he was reported to have given an extempore speech at a meeting, while in November he debated the topic of whether the federal government should impose a graduated tax on income.[14] The edition of 15 March 1905 reported that Seme would address a meeting where there would be a debate as to whether the thesis requirement for the BA degree at Columbia College should be abolished. In April the same year, Seme, together with another student, E.B. Merrill, opposed a debate motion that Columbia should have a general athletic association to direct all branches of athletic sport at the university. The pattern of participating in debate activities continued until the last weeks of his final year.[15]

Seme was also involved in extracurricular studies such as stenography, typing, photography and auto mechanics.[16] The university provided many outside amenities to its students, which Seme is likely to have made full use of and enjoyed. These included access to institutions such as the American Museum of Natural History, the Metropolitan Museum of Art, and the New York Botanical Garden. Seme used the gymnasium and presumably the library too; he was fully immersed in university life, which he was clearly enjoying. It is no wonder that in a letter to Professor H.F. Cutler, principal of his former high school in Massachusetts, Seme described Columbia as 'a very fine college' and stated that he could not have chosen a better one. He also mentioned that the 'students as well as the professors make it very pleasant' to study at the university.[17]

Seme's extracurricular activities did not interfere with his academic studies. He passed his freshman courses, and took even more subjects in his second year: English 4, French 1, economics 1, economics A, history A, psychology A, psychology 10, and gymnasium, of course. In his junior year (third year), Seme took eight courses: history 7, economics 603, philosophy A and philosophy 2, botany 1, English B, and anthropology 1. In his final year he took three history courses, two economics courses, French, English and public law. By the end of the fourth year he was deemed to have taken all the prescribed courses, which included economics, history, French, English, Latin, German, mathematics, natural science, psychology, and two courses of rhetoric.

How Seme funded his studies is unclear. The material found at Mount Hermon by Richard Rive[18] shows that some of Seme's Mount Hermon benefactors continued to support him at Columbia. One such benefactor was S.A. Beals, who was related to Reverend Stephen Pixley. Beals gave Seme $5 in January 1903, a few months after he had started at Columbia. It is unclear who else supported his studies, and it seems that he did not enjoy sufficient financial support. At the end of his first académic year Seme was looking for work to pay for his second-year studies. A story appeared in the *Boston Journal* of May 1903 with the headline 'Royal Zulu Willing to Become Valet' and the sub-heading 'Oka Seme, Student at Columbia, Looks for Work'.[19] The story is extraordinary in many respects. It describes Seme as a 'full blooded Zulu of royal lineage' who 'distinguished [himself] as an unusually bright scholar' in his first year at Columbia. It then states that he wished to work as a valet on a yacht during the American summer of 1903. In the article, Seme's alleged royal lineage is linked to a claim that he is a nephew of Mqhawe, the chief of the amaQadi at the time. Seme is also said to be a cousin of Reverend John Langalibalele Dube. Although the report does not reveal whether the claims about his relationships with Mqhawe and Dube originated with Seme himself, it is inconceivable that the reporter would have known about Chief Mqhawe without Seme informing him. Whatever the case, the claims are not supported by evidence, and it is likely that Seme was embellishing his story in an attempt to find work.

In the same article, Seme describes his financial position as rather dire: 'My brother is studying for the ministry at Benedict College, and to keep us both here is very hard for our family. It is by getting something to do in the summer that I have been able to defray expenses. One summer I worked as a gardener in Massachusetts and another summer I worked as a bellboy'. This brother was of course Ponqela Lindley Seme, who, as stated previously, spent six years studying agriculture rather than the ministry, as Seme claimed. There is no evidence that the Seme family ever supported any of the brothers studying in the United States. Here again, Seme adds colour to his story in a probable attempt to get work or financial support for his studies.

His aim of working as a valet on a yacht was not realised. He did, however, secure a summer job with a Mr Kent, whom he described as 'one of the finest men' he had ever worked for. After making coffee in the morning, his job entailed the following: 'drive for the mail, attend to the general flood supplies of the house such as meats and groceries, freeze ice cream and keep my store room tidy'.[20] He had three hours free each afternoon. There is no evidence he worked anywhere else while at Columbia. His university record states that he was, at some point, a recipient of the university student scholarship, though there is no information about its value or duration. H. Selby Msimang, Seme's one-time secretary at his legal practice and a prominent leader of the ANC in the 1930s, later claimed that Seme had told him about an American benefactor who supported him with an annual allowance of $200 in addition to paying for his studies at Oxford.[21] The claim is in all likelihood false. Seme struggled financially while at Oxford, as will become clear later on. The support he received from donors while at Mount Hermon and Columbia involved very small sums, most of which were used to pay for his studies. A $200 annual living allowance would have been out of kilter with any other donation he received. The only conclusion that can be reached is that a combination of the university scholarship, a few donations and earnings from piece jobs probably took Seme through his studies at Columbia.

Seme completed his BA degree in 1906 and it was conferred in June of the same year. A group photo of the 1906 class shows a sea of white faces with one black face in the left-hand corner. That face was Seme's. *The Columbian*, the official yearbook of Columbia College, carried brief profiles of the 1906 class, including one for 'P. Ka Isaka SEME'.[22] He has a confident, purposeful gaze, and is dressed in a black jacket, white shirt and a tie. The yearbook describes him thus: 'His face dark, but his mind brilliant.'[23] It is uncertain whether Seme described himself in this way, or whether his fellow students did. Dark indeed he was, and his brilliance was also beyond question. If his skin colour had been juxtaposed against his brilliance to suggest some kind of incongruence, Seme and his four years at Columbia had proved that there was none.

In a profile of Seme in the *New York Times*, he said: 'My ambition has been to study the broad features of American life. I have tried to learn those things that will benefit my people and enable me to help them as I should.' Turning to the subject of why he chose to study at Columbia, Seme stated:

> I enjoy hard work, and I have always desired to be in the centre of things. This is why I came to Columbia. New York City is the cynosure of all American life: the greatest interests of the country are directed from this centre. A glance through the city's records is enough to convince any mind that Columbia is a force behind the throne in the greater movements of New York life.[24]

These are the words of a thoughtful young man who had clearly enjoyed his stay both at Columbia and in New York City. They suggest that he had learnt more than what he had been taught in class. It is no exaggeration to suggest the experiences alluded to fundamentally transformed Seme's outlook of life and set him on a course that eventually led to the formation of the African National Congress in 1912. That transformation was especially evident in his decision to change his name from Pixley Isaac Seme to Pixley ka Isaka Seme – an assertion of his identity as the son of Isaka, and an early indication of his embrace of a pan-African outlook. His award-winning speech on the regeneration of Africa, delivered a week before the *New York Times* profile, confirmed Seme's transformation.

'The Regeneration of Africa'

Seme's speech, 'The Regeneration of Africa', was his contribution to an annual public-speaking competition run by Columbia University. Two Curtis medals, one in gold and another in silver, were awarded for excellence in public speaking. The Curtis medals originated in 1902 through an anonymous gift in honour of George William Curtis. It was later revealed that the donor was Samuel P. Avery, who wished to establish a memorial to his deceased friend. Described as a master of English who wrote and published on political subjects, Curtis was also considered an eloquent orator. Students competing for the medals were judged on the substance of their speeches, their literary quality and also their delivery. The competition was open to all junior and senior students at Columbia. In December 1905 a preliminary list of students who had entered for the 1906 competition was announced, which included Seme. Students could speak on any topic of their choice, and the ones Mr W.B. Parker of the English department revealed ranged from Seme's 'The Regeneration of Africa' to 'The Future of Russia', 'Reform in American Politics', 'Optimism and Pessimism', 'The Labor Question' and 'The Negro Problem', to mention a few.[25] At the preliminary trials held in March 1906 the list of fifteen competitors was reduced to four finalists: H.K. Bell ('The Future of Russia'); M.G. Ellenbogen ('John Marshall's Influence on the Federal Constitution'); B.A. Rosenblatt ('Reform of American Politics'); and P.I. Seme ('The Regeneration of Africa').[26] April 5 1906 was set down as the date on which the four students would compete for the two Curtis medals, with the winner to be awarded the medal in gold, and the runner-up receiving the silver.

The competition was held on a Thursday afternoon in Earl Hall at the university. The *Columbia Daily Spectator* reported that the event was well attended. Among those present was the dean of Columbia College, Professor J.H. Van Amringe, who presided over the proceedings. As judges, three professors were appointed – Brander Matthews, Franklin H. Giddings and George W. Kirchwey. The four finalists had been coached by Parker, and expectations were high. First to speak was Bernard Rosenblatt, who delivered what the *Columbia Daily Spectator* described as a studied oration on 'Class Rule in America'. He was followed by Harold Bell, who spoke on 'The Public Services of Edward M. Stanton'. Seme spoke next.

'I am an African, and I set my pride in my race over against a hostile public opinion,' Seme began.[27] He argued that Africa should not be compared to Europe or any other continent. The basis of his plea was not because such a comparison might 'bring humiliation upon Africa', but rather because there was no single standard for comparison. To support his contention that Africa was as great as any other continent, he listed several achievements, starting with Thebes, the ancient capital of Egypt, known as the city of one hundred gates. Of Thebes, Seme said: 'The grandeur of its venerable ruins and the gigantic proportions of its architecture reduce to insignificance the boasted monuments of other nations.' From Thebes he moved to the pyramids, which, he argued, are incomparable. All the glory of the Egyptian monuments, Seme said, belongs to Africa and her people, and they serve as an indestructible memorial to the genius of Africans. From Egypt he went on to the pyramids of Ethiopia, which, though not as large as those of Egypt, far surpass the latter in architectural beauty. Clearly moved by the brilliance so evident in the beauty of Africa's creations, Seme uttered words which, more than a century later, have lost none of their inspirational force:

> Oh, for that historian who, with the open pen of truth will bring to Africa's claim the strength of written proof. He will tell of a race whose onward tide was often swelled with tears, but in whose heart bondage has not quenched the fire of former years. He will write that in these later days when Earth's noble ones are named, she has a roll of honor too of whom she is not ashamed. The giant is awakening! From the four corners of the Earth, Africa's sons who have been proved through fire and sword, are marching to the future's golden door bearing the records of deeds of valor done.

Seme then approached a subject that was perhaps closer to home. He directed his oratory at Mr John C. Calhoun, a deceased former vice president of the United States, whom he described as having been the most philosophical of slave-owners in the American south. Calhoun had said that if he could be shown a black person who understood Greek syntax he would change his mind and consider black people a human race. In reaction to this, Seme said he regretted that the moment was lost to prove Calhoun wrong. He could have shown him many black people with extraordinary accomplishments, black men of pure African blood who 'repeat the Koran in memory, skilled in Latin, Greek and Hebrew – Arabic and Chaldaic'. He could show him men of African descent who possessed great wisdom and profound knowledge, such as a black professor of philosophy at a celebrated university in Germany. Seme argued that there 'are many Africans who have shown marks of genius and high character sufficient to redeem their race from the charges which I am now considering'.

Moving southwards, Seme extolled the bravery of the people of the Congo who 'fought like men and died like martyrs'. He praised the system of governance in Bechuanaland (Botswana) that valued the wisdom of ordinary people. But Seme did not focus solely on the past glory of Africa. He ended by looking towards the continent's regeneration – the subject of his speech:

> The brighter day is rising upon Africa. Already I seem to see her chains dissolved, her desert plains red with harvest, her Abyssinia and her Zululand the seats of science and religion, reflecting the glory of the rising sun from the spires of their churches and universities. Her Congo and her Gambia whitened with commerce, her crowded cities sending forth the hum of business and all her sons employed in advancing the victories of peace – greater and more abiding than the spoils of war.
>
> Yes, the regeneration of Africa belongs to this new and powerful period! By this term regeneration I wish to be understood to mean the entrance into a new life, embracing the diverse phases of a higher, complex existence. The basic factor which assures their regeneration resides in the awakened race-consciousness. This gives them a clear perception of their elemental needs and of their undeveloped powers. It therefore must lead them to the attainment of that higher and advanced standard of life ...
>
> The regeneration of Africa means that a new and unique civilization is soon to be added to the world. The African is not a proletarian in the world of science and art. He has precious creations of his own, of

ivory, of copper and of gold, fine, plated willow-ware and weapons of superior workmanship ... The most essential departure of this new civilization is that it shall be thoroughly spiritual and humanistic – indeed a regeneration moral and eternal.

Seme ended with a flourish, reading a rousing poem in which he extolled the grandeur and virtue of the African continent:

> O Africa!
> Like some great century plant that shall bloom
> In ages hence we watch thee; in our dream
> See in thy swamps the Prospero of our stream;
> Thy doors unlocked, where knowledge in her tomb
> Hath lain innumerable years in gloom.
> Then shalt thou, waking that morning gleam,
> Shine as thy sister lands with equal beam.

The next day, the *Columbia Daily Spectator* reported on the outcome of the contest. It stated that the judges did not take long to decide on the winner, and that they 'unanimously awarded the first prize, a gold medal, to Pka Isaka Seme'. The silver medal was awarded to Maurice G. Ellenbogen, who had addressed the issue of John Marshall's influence on the American constitution. The report went into some detail about the subject of Seme's speech, describing Seme as being inspired by his topic. The news of Seme's triumph was widely reported in various newspapers in the United States, from the *New York Times* on the east coast to the *San Francisco Chronicle* on the west coast, with both newspapers carrying the story the very next day. The news also reached South Africa and was reported in various black newspapers such as *Ilanga lase Natal*, with its isiZulu edition headline 'IZulu Elidumileyo' ('A Famous Zulu'), though the English edition simply stated 'A Zulu Wins A Prize'.[28]

A great deal of praise has since been heaped on the speech, which in many respects was a product of its time. The period straddling two centuries was one of serious political debate and awakening concerning the rights of black people both in the diaspora and on the African continent. That political awakening crystallised in the convening of the first Pan-African Conference by the Trinidadian lawyer Henry Sylvester Williams, which took place at Westminster Hall in London from 23 to 25 July 1900.

In a pamphlet advertising the conference, Williams stated that it would address the '"Native Races" Question' and would be attended and addressed by those of 'African descent from all parts of the British Empire, the United States of America, Abyssinia, Liberia, Hayti [sic], etc.'[29] Williams also explained that the conference would provide the first opportunity for black men to meet in England where they could speak for themselves about their interests and seek to influence public opinion. The political situation of black people in South Africa was one of the issues on the agenda. The conference was attended by thirty-seven delegates from Africa, the West Indies, the United States and the United Kingdom, and included several observers from India as well as a smattering of white delegates from Britain. Among the speakers was Henry Sylvester Williams himself and W.E.B. Du Bois – a thirty-two-year-old African American who would later organise several iterations of the Pan-African Conference. It was at the first conference that Du Bois delivered a sensational closing address titled 'To the Nations of the World', where he argued that 'the problem of the twentieth century is the problem of the colour line'. In a rousing conclusion that would find echoes in Seme's own seminal address at Columbia in 1906, Du Bois made the following call to the nations of the world:

> Let the nations of the world respect the integrity and independence of the free Negro states of Abyssinia, Liberia, Haiti, and the rest, and let the inhabitants of these states, the independent tribes of Africa, the Negroes of the West Indies and America, and the black subjects of all nations take courage, strive ceaselessly, and fight bravely, that they may prove to the world their incontestable right to be counted among the great brotherhood of mankind. Thus we appeal with boldness and confidence to the Great Powers of the civilized world, trusting in the wide spirit of humanity, and the deep sense of justice and of our age, for a generous recognition of the righteousness of our cause.[30]

Du Bois's closing address, together with other speeches and deliberations at the conference, received wide media attention not only in the United Kingdom but all around the world. In the conference aftermath, Williams travelled to the Americas and the Caribbean to spread the message of the conference and to establish branches of the Pan-African Association. For his part, Du Bois published *The Souls of Black Folk*, a work that unflinchingly positions race at the centre of American society.

Although Seme did not directly refer to either the first Pan-African Conference or Du Bois's book in his 1906 address, there are echoes of both in the speech. They constituted a background to the address itself, the context in which it was conceived and framed. But its context extended beyond the immediate past. In order to understand Seme's argument in 'The Regeneration of Africa', one needs to take into account the debates among African-American intellectuals at the time regarding their relationship with the African continent. In large measure, Seme's speech makes sense and is better understood in the context of those debates. The title itself suggests that Seme conceived of it as a contribution to them. In 1861 Alexander Crummell, an influential African-American missionary and intellectual who had spent sixteen years in Liberia, delivered an address with the same title. However, Crummell's address differed fundamentally from Seme's in terms of its conception of Africa's regeneration.

To understand the difference in approach, it is useful to look at another address Crummell delivered, also in 1861, titled 'The Progress of Civilization along the West Coast of Africa'.[31] Crummell's view of Africa's past is startlingly different from Seme's. Where Seme saw in Africa's past not only grandeur but also valour and achievement, Crummell saw only their antithesis:

> ... we have to observe the sad and startling fact, that mental and moral benightedness has enshrouded the whole of the vast continent of Africa, through all the periods of time, far back to the earliest records of history ...
>
> And then, standing at the very start of the Christian era, if we strive to penetrate the long lapse of ages, which anticipated the coming of the Lord, we meet vista upon vista of the deepest darkness, stretching out to the earliest dawn of the world's being. So far as *Western* Africa is concerned, there is no history. The long, long centuries of human existence, there, give us no intelligent disclosures. 'Darkness covered the land, and gross darkness the people.'[32]

Crummell explained Africa's 'benightedness' partly in terms of its exclusion from the influence of European civilisation because of the Sahara Desert. In his view, the Sahara 'served to effectually cut off [Africa] from the ancient civilisations'. The consequences of this isolation, Crummell argued, led to the following:

Thrown thus back upon herself, unvisited by either the mission of letters or of grace, poor Africa, all the ages through, has been generating,
and then reproducing, the whole brood and progeny of superstitions, idolatries, and paganisms through all her quarters. And hence
the most pitiful, the most abject of all human conditions! And hence
the most sorrowful of all histories! The most miserable, even now, of
all spectacles![33]

At one time, Crummell had believed that Africa was on the cusp of regeneration – as did Seme some five decades later. In Crummell's sermon of
1853, 'Hope for Africa', he argued that there was evidence that Africa had
entered a period of regeneration. Speaking specifically of the African west
coast, he observed as a sign of progress and regeneration that the slave
trade had been uprooted and replaced by what he called 'legitimate' trade.
He stated that 'industrious communities [were] springing up, civilization
introduced, and a trade commenced which already has swelled up, in
exports alone to Europe and America to more than two million pounds
per annum'.[34] The regeneration was also evident in the number of black
people who were distinguishing themselves in various fields. Some of the
names he referred to were identical to those that Seme would mention in
1906, suggesting a direct connection between Crummell's views and Seme's
celebrated speech. Crummell cited 'philanthropists like Howard; scholars,
classical and mental; scientific men – one, a Doctor of Philosophy in a
German university [later cited by Seme]; distinguished painters and art-
ists; officers well known in Europe'.[35] As further signs of the black race's
progress, Crummell mentioned the black government of Haiti, the black
republic of Liberia, and the establishment of the colony of Sierra Leone.

While Seme saw this as evidence of the capabilities and creativity of
Africans and the black race generally, in Crummell's view the progress
was driven by forces external to the African continent. Among such external
forces were the leading European powers at the time, which he described
as having been merciful in 'scattering darkness from her [Africa's] agon-
ized brow, and her hastening the day of her final relief and regeneration'.
Another force driving Africa's regeneration was Christian missionaries
whose endeavours in the continent had, in Crummell's view, 'helped to
change to hopefulness the condition of Africa'.[36] Equally important was
the introduction of commerce on the continent, which, together with
Christianity, had brought about the development of the resources of the

continent, thereby conveying to 'its rude inhabitants the aids and instruments to civilization, to active industry, to domestic comfort, and to a budding social refinement'.[37]

While Crummell extolled the virtues and benevolence of European expeditions in Africa, Seme declared: 'the day of great exploring expeditions in Africa are [sic] over!' For Seme, contact between nations was mutually beneficial, and not a matter of one nation showing another the superiority of its knowledge or tradition. What is significant about 'The Regeneration of Africa' is its silence concerning the work of missionaries on the continent. This is especially so since Crummell and other African-American intellectuals placed much emphasis on missionaries as a force for good, for civilisation. Here then was a product – indeed, a beneficiary – of missionaries completely ignoring, if not dismissing altogether, the contribution of missionaries to the 'regeneration of Africa'. The omission was undoubtedly a consequence of Seme's politicisation as an Africanist which took shape at Columbia.

So, where Crummell saw the Sahara as isolating the African continent from the influence of 'ancient civilizations', Seme invited his audience to cast its 'eyes south of the desert Sahara' to marvel at the bravery of the Congolese people, the brilliance of Bechuanaland's system of governance, the wonder of Abyssinia under Menelik, and the promise of Zululand. Where Crummell perceived Africa and the black race as needing to benefit from Western civilisation, Seme envisioned a new and unique African civilisation which 'would soon be added to the world'. Where Crummell saw in Africans a 'whole brood and progeny of superstitions, idolatries, and paganisms', Seme's vision was hopeful and triumphant. He declared that 'the African is not a proletarian in the world of science and art. He has precious creations of his own, of ivory, of copper and of gold, fine, plaited willow-ware and weapons of superior workmanship'.[38]

As stated previously, crucial to an understanding of 'The Regeneration of Africa' is placing Seme's speech in the context of a broader debate among African-American intellectuals and other black leaders in the African diaspora at the time concerning the predicament of the black race generally and the African continent in particular. African-American intellectuals involved in the debate included Martin Delany, Edward Wilmot Blyden, Henry Turner, Henry Garnet, Frederick Douglass, and of course Alexander Crummell. W.E.B. Du Bois was an important contributor too. Another figure whose ideas and work influenced Seme was Booker T. Washington.

Even though Washington's 1895 Atlanta compromise speech was hotly contested by intellectuals such as Du Bois, he remained an influential figure during Seme's time at Columbia. A few years before Seme delivered his own speech, Washington had published his memoir, *Up from Slavery*, which was well received. It is no wonder that, soon after delivering his speech at Columbia, Seme visited Atlanta where he attended the conference of the National Negro Business League, which was addressed by Washington. In later correspondence with Washington, Seme would describe what he saw at the conference as 'the great vision of national power', praising also Washington and his industrial school at Tuskegee in Alabama.[39]

A few weeks after Seme delivered his acclaimed speech, Columbia University organised another competition to decide who should represent the university at the annual contest of the Central Oratorical League to be held at Ohio Wesleyan University on 11 May 1906. The league comprised four universities: Columbia, Cornell, Chicago and Ohio Wesleyan. The four contestants in the debate won by Seme were once again considered, though this time Seme was not selected. Somewhat strangely, a speech that had won hands down a few weeks before lost when it came to selecting a university representative for the regional oratorical competition. The outcome probably did not matter much to Seme, however, as he was invited by the New York Board of Education Public Lecture Bureau to deliver a series of free public lectures on 'Life in Zululand'.[40] Also, he was on his way to Oxford University in England where he was eventually admitted to study law.

The prince of Oxford

Four months after his graduation from Columbia University with a BA degree, Seme left for Oxford University.[41] The matriculation form which he filled in on 13 October 1906 indicates that he was first admitted as a 'non-collegiate' student. It was common at the time for students, especially foreign and mature students, to matriculate or be admitted as members of Oxford University without necessarily being members of a college or hall. The purpose of this arrangement was to broaden access to the university because becoming a member of a college required substantial amounts of money, connections or both. Non-collegiate students such as Seme lived in approved lodgings in the city of Oxford; this option was cheaper than living in a college or hall.[42] Non-collegiate students were enrolled under a scheme called the Delegacy for Non-Collegiate

Students, which was established in 1868 and was eventually transformed into St Catherine's College in 1962.

Seme moved to Jesus College on 22 January 1907. Migrating from the Delegacy to a college was common at the time. There were several reasons for such migration: students received a scholarship from a college; they wanted to gain access to college networks or improve their connections; and in some cases, they perceived being attached to a college as being more prestigious. Seme was admitted to Jesus College in January, though the minutes of the board of the Faculty of Law show that his application to do the Bachelor of Civil Law (BCL) degree was only approved some five months later, on 19 June 1907.[43] This too was not unusual; students were not required to register for a particular degree with the Delegacy, which made it possible for Seme to be registered as a university student for several months before actually enrolling for a degree.[44]

Jesus College's tutorial lists show that Seme was a student there from Hilary (Easter) term in 1907 until Trinity (summer) term in 1909. He is described as a 'Foreign Senior Student' and he lived outside the college.[45] Seme's tutor throughout his period at the college was Alfred Ernest William Hazel, who held a fellowship in law and was a member of the British Parliament for West Bromwich from 1906 to 1910. Hazel later became the principal of Jesus College, serving from 1925 to 1944.[46] There is not much information about the classes or academic courses that Seme took while a student at Jesus College. He does not appear to have spent much time at the college or at the university generally. Jesus College's Buttery and Buttels Books, which contain a daily record of charges to members of the college for bread, cheese, milk and beer (the staple food and drink at the time) for the period Seme was enrolled, reveal that Seme's expenditure was minimal. He spent two or three shillings a week on bread, which is likely to have been a minimum charge imposed even if a student had not consumed anything. Christopher Jeens, the college archivist, reveals that Seme's name appears in the Buttery and Buttels Books, though he was on occasion recorded as being absent.[47] Though he only formally left the college in July 1909, records suggest that Seme's relationship with it was for some time rather distant.

For a considerable period of time, Seme lived outside the university. For the 1906 Michaelmas term (first term of the academic year) he lived at 7 Iffley Road in the city of Oxford. For the whole of 1907 and large parts of 1908 his address is given as Walton Street, also in Oxford. Towards the end of 1908 he is recorded as living at 3 Black Hall Road, Oxford. He went back to Iffley Road in his final term as a registered student.[48] What the records do not show is that Seme spent a lot of time in London, at one point living in the same apartment as Alfred Mangena, a black South African studying law at Lincoln's Inn at the time. Seme also visited several countries in Europe.

Much of the information about Seme's activities while a student in Britain is sourced from letters he exchanged with Alain LeRoy Locke. An African-American graduate from Harvard University, Locke gained public attention when he became the first African American to win the prestigious Rhodes Scholarship, which took him to Oxford University. He had graduated magna cum laude from Harvard for his BA degree. It was the publicity that followed the awarding of the scholarship that brought Locke to Seme's attention. On 14 March 1907 Seme wrote to Locke congratulating him for what he had 'done for our race by taking so high a rank among American scholars'. Having himself arrived at Oxford just a few months before, Seme informed Locke about the university, remarking that it had twenty-six very old colleges, telling him also that he would find at Oxford 'others of your race who have carried first class honours'. Locke would also meet the 'best blood of India, Japan and of the whole world'.[49] From that first contact, the relationship between the two men blossomed.

Seme seems to have been aware of Locke's academic prowess, praising him for honouring the black race at Harvard. Writing that Locke's achievements filled his heart 'with genuine pleasure', he informed Locke that 'old Oxford is already filled with your fame et cetera'. Then, in news that may have alarmed Locke, Seme mentioned that he had heard about a group of American students who were displeased that Locke would be studying at the university. He however assured him that the university authorities were aware of the issue and supported Locke. He implored Locke not to be troubled by the news. In any event, he said, 'if the American Southerners try such things here' they would be 'violently opposed and looked down upon'. Seme revealed that he had faced similar opposition when he was admitted to Oxford. In his case the source of opposition was the Governor of Natal, whom the university had made to 'feel very small' because it 'stands high above these small ideas'.

In the same letter, Seme recommended several colleges to Locke: Christ Church, Magdalen, New College and University College. He did so despite acknowledging that Locke was likely to go to Hertford College – as indeed he eventually did. A few years older than Locke (who was born in Phila-delphia in September 1885), Seme seems to have assumed the role of an older brother. He may have taken this role a step too far, however – he was still trying to persuade Locke to choose a college other than Hertford as late as June, even though by then it had become evident that Locke had chosen Hertford.[50]

In the summer of 1907, Seme went to Brussels, writing to Locke that his visit was partly a vacation but also to study the French language. He described his time in Brussels as enjoyable. Taking up the role of older brother, Seme advised his 'dear friend' (at this stage they had only exchanged a few letters and not in fact met) on the best route from New York. He also recommended places Locke could stay once he arrived at Oxford. One such place was 21 Beaumont Street, where Locke should ask for a Mrs Norburn and inform her that he was Seme's friend. He also mentioned that Mrs Norburn 'has four beautiful daughters and will make nice and restful home for you'. If Locke chose to travel via London, Seme recommended a visit to Dr Theophilus Edward Samuel Scholes, who he described as a great Negro scholar. Scholes, born in Jamaica in 1858, had made a name for himself through various contributions as a medical doc-tor, missionary and political commentator. He was best known, however, as a critic of British imperialism, writing two acclaimed works, *The British Empire and Alliances: British Duty to Her Colonies and Subject Races* (1899), and *Chamberlain and Chamberlainism: His Fiscal Policies and Colonial Policy* (1903). Although it is unclear how Seme became acquainted with so revered a public figure as Scholes, it is likely that his 1906 speech brought him to the other man's attention. In any event, their relationship was sufficiently close that he had already told Scholes about Locke and was willing to act as an intermediary in the introductions. Although Locke did not immediately act on Seme's offer, soon afterwards he wrote to Scholes introducing himself, to which the latter replied, thanking Seme for his role.[51]

Locke's decision not to visit Scholes en route to Oxford may be attrib-uted to a letter he had received from Seme relating an incident involving himself, Scholes and a Sierra Leonean medical doctor, William Awuner Renner, also resident in London at the time. According to Seme, Renner and Scholes wanted to be introduced, and since Seme was acquainted with both, it fell upon him to do so. The three men met at the British Museum (at the 'mighty columns', as Seme put it), and from there they went to the Trocadero restaurant for lunch. To Seme's surprise, the two doctors brought 'mighty appetites with them to the expensive and attractive table'. Instead of lunch, they 'sat for dinner', and a lot of expensive food and beverages were consumed. Unfortunately for Seme, he was seated at the head of the table, which meant that the bill would be presented to him. The only money he had was a borrowed seven shillings and six pence, which was inadequate to settle the bill. What happened next revealed Seme's humorous (and perhaps mischievous) side. He told Locke that God inspired him to ask the two doctors to excuse him so that he could visit the lavatory. He asked a waiter to show him the way, and when they were a safe distance from the two distinguished men Seme told the waiter to give the bill to Dr Renner; then, tipping the waiter six pence, he left, leaving the two doctors with a huge bill to settle.

Whatever the effect on his relationship with the two doctors in the aftermath of the restaurant incident, Seme continued to enjoy his stint at Oxford where he was part of a large network of black students and scholars at the university and beyond. In April 1908 he wrote to Booker T. Washington to inform him that he was trying to recruit African students in Britain to form a union or society for the exchange of ideas – Seme was of the view that in Britain were to be found the future leaders of the African continent.[52] He corresponded with another famous African American too, W.E.B. Du Bois.[53] Seme befriended Henry Sylvester Williams, organiser of the first Pan-African Conference, who claimed to have a 'close friendship with Pixley Seme, a Zulu then studying at Oxford', as well as a large number of other Zulu acquaintances and friends. Though there is no mention of who those Zulus were, Williams was apparently well known to Alfred Mangena. Indeed, there is a suggestion that Mangena may have influenced Williams to write about the condition of Zulus in Natal in the aftermath of the Bhambatha Rebellion.[54]

Locke appears to have been Seme's closest friend at Oxford. As soon as he arrived at the university, Seme sent him invitations to lunch meetings, dinners and many other activities. In one undated invitation, Seme invited Locke to 'come and take coffee with me next Thursday at 8:15'. He informed Locke that he had invited a party of his friends, including three Americans who were students at Jesus College and whom he wished to introduce to Locke.[55] Among others regularly invited to Seme's parties were a Mr Downs and a Mr Harley.[56] Seme's friendship with Locke blossomed, to the extent that Locke informed his mother that Seme was in his room almost every day.[57] Together, they participated in various extramural activities, including

French lessons – on 7 October 1908 Seme wrote a full letter in French addressed to Locke. Their closeness was also evident in other areas. A photograph shows the two young men on horseback, dressed as if they were on their way to a polo tournament. They were also instrumental in establishing a student society called the Cosmopolitan Club, with Seme serving as treasurer and Locke as secretary. Locke wrote for the club's publication, the *Cosmopolitan Magazine*, and on one of the articles by Locke, Seme commented that it was 'interesting and instructive'.[58]

In mid-1908 Seme left Oxford to live in London. He did not tell Locke that he was leaving. In a letter written in June 1908, Seme apologised for not informing his friend, but expressed satisfaction about the location of his lodgings, which he described as nice and cheap. He mentioned the pleasures of living in London, such as visiting Parliament to listen to members' debates. He tried to persuade Locke to join him, saying that he might find a similarly cheap abode. But Locke did not follow Seme to London – which had its conveniences, as Seme occasionally asked Locke to run errands for him in Oxford, for example going to his jeweller, Carfax, to buy him a wrist watch.[59] He also asked Locke to pack up his belongings, remarking that he was 'awfully worried over the fact that I left so many of my things in such a state'. Included in the things he left behind were his cushions, a tobacco pouch, 'god forsaken pipes', a brass kettle and gas stove, bottles of wine, and books. He requested his friend also to empty his desk and to put everything into a large trunk. There was also the piano in his room, which he asked Locke to take to the shop above Magdalen Bridge (its name was written on the piano, he said); Locke should ask the shop owners 'to take back their piano now'. Seme pledged to pay the money he owed for the use of the instrument.[60]

The items that Seme left behind suggest that he lived a rather extravagant life for a student. It is no wonder that he got entangled in serious financial woes during his stay in Britain. In one of the letters he wrote to Locke from London, Seme said that he had been hiding from 'an overzealous Oxford tradesman'. So afraid was he of his creditors that he avoided picking up his post – but he mustered some courage and ordered that everything in his postbox 'except summons orders' be forwarded to the place where he was hiding.[61] In typically humorous vein, Seme subsequently said that when the post was eventually delivered he discovered that £200 had been waiting for him for three weeks and 'had nearly suffocated' in the envelope. He then declared that he was still a millionaire![62]

Of course he said that in jest. His financial troubles followed him. He was fending off one creditor after another. Oxford booksellers Joseph Thornton & Son sent Seme a letter on 27 January 1909 reminding him about an unpaid account and threatening him with litigation if he failed to settle it immediately.[63] Another letter of demand soon followed from another Oxford bookseller, Hubert Giles, demanding that Seme settle outstanding debt. Seme's financial troubles persisted when he visited Amsterdam in late 1909. He told Locke that he had been advised to visit Holland in order to 'renew my acquaintance with the Dutch language' in preparation for work in South Africa. Seme informed Locke that there were two official languages in South Africa and that he had been told that 'the boers regard it a great compliment to talk the pure accent [Dutch] as known in Holland'. He said it was imperative that he learn Dutch because it was the language of the court and the clergy.[64]

Once in the Netherlands, Seme expressed satisfaction to Locke about his progress in the language. His tutors said that he could read with a good accent and at times managed to speak fluently. In the same letter, Seme proposed that he and Locke work on a project he described as 'The Vision of Africa'. He did not elaborate on what this might entail, and merely said that he would explain the details when he returned to Oxford. Having dispensed with the niceties, Seme came to the main subject of the letter. He needed money, urgently. He pleaded with Locke to lend him the money so that he could settle his 'last accounts' in Amsterdam. He asked for £5 and promised to pay it as he would be receiving a 'comfortable sum after the 20th of this month [February 1910]'. In this rather desperate letter, he told Locke he needed to return to England but had to settle the accounts first. He also asked Locke to inform him as soon as possible if he would be able to help him.[65]

It is unclear whether Locke gave him the money or not. But Seme did go back to London, and he returned to South Africa in October 1910. He left England without the Oxford law degree he had hoped for. His name appears on the list of examination candidates for the degree of Bachelor of Civil Law for the 1909 Trinity term,[66] but it is not in the subsequently published class list of those who passed the examination.[67] Furthermore, Seme is not recorded as having passed any of the university examinations, and no degree was conferred on him.[68]

It is unsurprising that Seme did not earn a degree from Oxford. Although university records suggest that he spent the duration of his stay in the city of Oxford, the reality was different. Seme left quite soon to live in London. It is unlikely that he paid as much attention there to his studies as might have been the case had he stayed in Oxford. At some point he shared an apartment with Alfred Mangena, who stayed in the attic of the lodgings. Seme told Locke that he once found Mangena 'contemplating on his past and future dignity in an attic chamber', complaining that he 'couldn't sleep on account of the pigeons'.[69] This seemed to amuse Seme, whose room was reportedly more spacious.

Interestingly, a few months after arriving at Oxford, on 12 February 1907, Seme was admitted to the Middle Temple to train as a lawyer. He was called to the bar some three years later, on 8 June 1910. It is hard to fathom what motivated Seme to seek admission to Jesus College to study for a BCL degree when he had already been admitted to train as a lawyer. One possibility is that he did not realise at first that he did not need a university degree in order to qualify as a lawyer, but could study in a law inn such as Middle Temple – or Lincoln's Inn, where Mangena was doing his training. But Seme may simply have been enamoured of the idea of being an Oxford University student. It is evident from his correspondence with Locke that he held the university in high regard. He became increasingly nostalgic whenever he made reference to Oxford, and in one of his letters he wrote: 'Well Locke I miss you and Oxford.'[70] Then in early 1910, while in Amsterdam, he told Locke that he intended to return to Oxford 'in order to spend my last days abroad in that city of dreams "with its enchanted gardens" which poor Manchester has not'.[71] Clearly, Seme held a deep affection for the university, though it seems not to have been strong enough to keep him at Oxford. Offering an alternative route to becoming a lawyer, the pull of London was apparently greater. Nevertheless, while Seme opted for London, he kept before him the mirage of being a student at Oxford.

In later years, reflecting on Seme's life, H. Selby Msimang spoke about the former's time as a student at Oxford. Msimang noted that Seme was called a Zulu prince while there; moreover, associating with high society, Seme was a person on whom money was lavished, with an American benefactor who paid him an annual allowance of £200. While there are no records to corroborate this latter claim, it could refer to the £200 that Seme had himself mentioned in a letter to Locke as 'suffocating' in the envelope. What *is* evident, however, is that Seme's financial troubles paint a picture of a person who was certainly not wealthy.

* * *

In October 1910, Seme sailed back to South Africa. He had left as a teen-aged 'Zulu boy' hoping to be educated as a teacher and missionary to the Zulu people. But he returned as a Pan-Africanist whose deep and broad concerns extended beyond his small community of Inanda and his tribe. He had become a leader in his own right who was internationally respected for his intellect and his vision for the African continent. He was at the forefront of a global political movement that sought the regeneration of the continent and the affirmation of the humanity of the black race. His name was mentioned in the same breath as the likes of Henry Sylvester Williams, W.E.B. Du Bois, Theophilus Scholes, Booker T. Washington, Alfred Mangena, and other Pan-Africanists and black leaders across the globe.

The extraordinary tale of transformation of this young boy from Inanda is often overlooked in the larger story of Seme's life. It attests to his amazing intellectual skills, his ability to connect with people from diverse backgrounds, and the world-class education he received both in America and Britain. Seme was also fortunate in many ways. His political conscious-ness was forged during a period of political ferment in the world. There were fiery debates among African-American intellectuals regarding their condition and their relationship with the African continent; indeed, Seme's famous speech, 'The Regeneration of Africa', was a contribution to that debate. It also helped that Seme lived in cities such as New York and London, which were the epicentre of the political debates and the political move-ments of the time. At Oxford he met and interacted with students from many countries who shared his worldview and concern for the political upliftment of the developing world. Outside the university setting he was in close contact with important political leaders such as Williams, and he corresponded with the likes of Du Bois and Washington. Seme also had the opportunity to travel the European continent, thereby broadening his political outlook. From all these experiences an African patriot emerged. He would use the broad education he had received to attempt to transform a newly formed South Africa whose vision seemed at odds with his own: the restoration of African greatness as well as the dignity of the black race.

3

The moving spirit

After a twelve-year absence, Seme returned to South Africa on Sunday 2 October 1910. Having set sail from England on a Royal Mail steamer, he arrived in Cape Town. He did not stay, however, as his eyes were fixed on his birthplace, Inanda. Upon arrival in Durban, he found a large group of his friends waiting to welcome him back. Newspaper reports at the time noted his academic achievements, especially the fact that he had earned a BA degree from Columbia University in the United States, studied at prestigious Oxford University in England, and had been admitted as a barrister-at-law at Middle Temple in London. *Ilanga lase Natal* made special note of the fact that Seme was the only black person in South Africa who not only had a BA degree, but was also a barrister-at-law.[1] Reverend John Langalibalele Dube, founder and editor of *Ilanga lase Natal*, wrote the story about Seme's return; he remarked that although Seme made the occasional slip, he could still speak isiZulu well, despite having left Inanda as a teenager.

Seme did not stay at Inanda, thereby dashing Dube's hopes that he would settle in Natal. For the short while he was there he did, however, participate actively in the Inanda community's civic life. One of the first things he did was to visit Dube's Ohlange Institute, where he reportedly marvelled at Dube's achievement. He was involved in other community activities, including membership of a reception committee to prepare for Dr Walter Benson Rubusana's visit to Durban. Other members of the committee were Reverend Makanya, Reverend Goba and Reverend Nyawo, as well as Charles Dube (John Dube's younger brother) and Elka Cele. Rubusana had been invited to Durban by eminent leaders such as Dube to celebrate his election as a member of the Cape Provincial Council, the first black person to hold such a position. Rubusana's election had been widely celebrated in black newspapers across the country. The Durban reception was part of these celebrations and the dinner that took place at the Beatrice Street Congregational Church was the highlight of Rubusana's visit.[2]

Seme soon became involved in the hurly-burly of politics. Towards the end of October 1911 he issued a broad call to black leaders throughout the country and the neighbouring protectorates to unite and form what he called the South African Native Congress, or simply the Native Union. Seme pleaded: 'it is conclusively urgent that this Congress should meet this year, because a matter which is so vitally important to our progress and welfare should not be unnecessarily postponed by reason of personal differences and selfishness of our leaders'.[3] He proposed that the inaugural meeting be convened before the end of December 1911 and suggested a two-part programme. The first part would deal with the formal establishment of the South African Native Congress, followed by the adoption of its draft constitution and the election of office bearers. The second part would comprise presentations on a variety of subjects: native marriages and divorce, native schools and churches, land ownership by black people, native labour, and even a debate as to whether native beer was a national beverage.[4]

In terms that were clearly aimed at stirring the passion and conscience of black people across the land, Seme issued his now iconic plea for black unity:

> The demon of racialism, the aberrations of the Xosa-Fingo feud, the animosity that exists between the Zulus and the Tongaas [sic], between the Basutos and every other native must be buried and forgotten; it has shed among us sufficient blood! We are one people. Those divisions, those jealousies are the cause of all our woes and of all our backwardness and ignorance today.[5]

Seme's call for black unity and for the formation of the South African Native Congress was the culmination of several initiatives since his return. For instance, on 17 June 1911 he convened the executive committee of the South African Native Convention (SANC) – an organisation formed in 1909 to campaign against the exclusion of black people from negotiations for the establishment of the Union of South Africa. The president of the SANC was Dr Walter Rubusana, with Reverend John Dube serving as vice president. Seme convened the executive committee in Johannesburg to discuss, among other matters, resolutions of the last SANC conference and government responses to those resolutions, as well as the organisation's constitution.[6] It is not clear which members of the executive committee attended the meeting other than the secretary Cleopas Kunene, S. Nyongwana, and Seme himself.[7] There is no evidence that either Rubusana or Dube attended. What is noteworthy about that June meeting was the involvement of Seme at such a high level, an especially remarkable fact considering that he had returned to South Africa only months before. There is a suggestion that Seme was convening the meetings in an official capacity as treasurer of the SANC.[8]

The June 1911 meeting was to be the beginning of Seme's vigorous involvement in local political affairs, especially in agitating for the formation of Congress. On 7 August 1911 he convened another meeting at Nancefield Location on the outskirts of Johannesburg. The August meeting was well attended, and among those present were John Mocher and Thomas Mapikela, chairperson and secretary respectively of the Orange Free State Native Congress; S.J. Molema (representing Paramount Chief Lekoko) and Chief Silas Molema from Mafikeng; S.B. Mpama from Potchefstroom; Z.B. Makgothi from Winburg; J.T. Moloi from Harrismith; J.S. Noah from Krugersdorp; W. Letseleba, chairperson of the Transvaal Native Union; T. Fakazi and Seme from Johannesburg; J.K. Sephaphate from Randfontein; J. Mobela, secretary of the Transvaal Native Union; S. Gompo from Nancefield; and Kunene, as secretary of the SANC.[9] Also present were Levi Mvabaza and Messrs Fuku, Mqabi, Magqoki, Natana, Mahlamvu, Ntlebi, Cili, Ngema, Gozongo, Wauchope, Folobeni and Sibiya.[10]

The August meeting started at 11:45 a.m. and in the chair was W. Letseleba. On the agenda were various SANC matters, including correspondence received by its secretary, Cleopas Kunene, and resolutions of its last conference, as well as its constitution. Topping the list of correspondence received was a letter from the Secretary for Native Affairs, Edward Dower, responding to a letter that had been sent to him by the executive conveying the resolutions of its last conference, which had taken place in Bloemfontein in March 1910. The Bloemfontein resolutions related to a variety of issues: a proposal that fees charged by lawyers be regulated; the poor treatment of black people on trains; ownership of land by black people, especially in the Orange Free State where there were restrictions; and the working conditions of black workers. In the letter to Dower, Dr Rubusana had also raised the matter of a new requirement, especially in the Orange Free State, that black women should also carry pass books. Dower was dismissive of the conference's resolutions, and he did not regard the objection to the pass books as worthy of consideration.[11]

The August meeting was, however, preoccupied with two matters that proved contentious. The first was a proposal, most likely originating from Seme, for the SANC to establish its own newspaper. This proposal was strongly opposed by newspapermen such as Mvabaza, who argued that any such publication would be in competition with existing black newspapers. The second matter was political disunity in the Transvaal. The province had two rival organisations, the Transvaal Native Union and the Transvaal Native Organisation. The meeting proposed that a special committee be established to mediate between the two rival organisations. However, this special committee seems only to have been appointed at the next meeting, in November 1911, with Seme as convenor (its members would comprise several prominent leaders, including Reverends Tsewu, Ngcayiya, Nochula, Tywakadi and Mvabaza, and Messrs Makgatho, Makhothe, Kawa, Letseleba and Sokopo).[12] It was then left to Rubusana, as president, to convene the next meeting of the executive committee.

However, the next caucus meeting was not convened by Rubusana. Instead, it was convened by Seme on the night of 13 November 1911. In the letter he sent to various prominent black leaders inviting them to the meeting, Seme described the purpose of the meeting as twofold: to 'consider the date of the first meeting of the proposed Congress'; and to 'consider [its] draft Constitution which shall later be sent to the various Societies and Organisations in order that they may have ample time to criticise it before the matter comes before the General Congress for adoption and amendment'.[13] Though convened at short notice, the meeting drew numerous prominent leaders of various black organisations, including Sefako Makgatho (whom Seme proposed as interim chair), Solomon Plaatje and Edward Tsewu.[14]

Makgatho opened the meeting by remarking that the Union of South Africa, which had recently been established by white people, had given black people what he termed 'the finest lesson on Union'.[15] It was a lesson that they should emulate, he said. He then turned his attention to the convenor of the meeting, Seme, and commended him for his role in effecting black unity, especially through his efforts to bring about the formation of the proposed Congress. As Seme rose to address the meeting, 'the house vigorously applauded him'.[16] He began by observing how well represented the Transvaal was, and argued that, considering past divisions, this was a mark of progress towards black unity. He contrasted Transvaal's attendance with that of the Cape. While admitting that the Cape had not

been invited to the meeting in a fair manner, with some invitations arriving late, he nevertheless bemoaned what he called its failure to take a
'leading part in this movement for Union'.[17] Seme then explained that
political divisions in the Cape were contributing to its weak participation
in efforts to form a united black organisation; he pointed to the divisions
between Rubusana's Ingqungqutela (as the South African Native Congress
was popularly known) and D.D.T. Jabavu's Imbumba Ye Zizwe (Races'
Congress).

In order to illustrate the depth of those divisions, Seme referred to his
correspondence with Reverend B.S. Mazwi, a leading figure in Imbumba
Ye Zizwe, regarding the proposed South African Native Congress and the
terms under which his organisation might affiliate. Imbumba Ye Zizwe
suspected that the proposed organisation was merely an extension of the
SANC led by Rubusana; its antipathy to Rubasana, as well as its suspicions
regarding affiliation to the proposed Congress, were evident in three questions posed by Reverend Mazwi:

- 'Is your Congress not under the auspices of the Bloemfontein Convention established in 1909'?
- 'Has your proposed Organization got any connection with the Ingqungqutela (Native Congress in the Cape Colony)'?
- 'What terms of amalgamation with the Imbumba would you suggest'?[18]

Two of the questions related directly to Rubusana, since the two organisations mentioned were led by him. Seme's subsequent denial that the
proposed Congress was related to the Bloemfontein Convention (the SANC)
is telling, since it was effectively being organised under the auspices of the
SANC. In point of fact, from the time of the June 1911 meeting the understanding had been that it was the SANC which was being strengthened,
rather than a new organisation being formed. The first public declaration
of plans to form a *new* organisation – the proposed Congress – was only
forthcoming a few months later, when Seme issued his call in October 1911.
The language Seme used when making that public call for the proposed
Congress is revealing. While he had been mandated by meetings of the
SANC executive committee to perform tasks such as drafting a constitution, on the matter of forming a new organisation – the Congress – he
seems to have changed his tune: 'I have been requested by several natives,
leaders and chiefs to write a full and concise statement on the subject
of the South African Native Congress, so-called.' He continued: 'I feel.

however, that I shall better meet their desires as well as more properly treat this subject if I disregard the pretentious title and write on the simple subject of Native Union, for after all, this is what the Congress shall be'.[19] Meeting the 'desire' of 'several natives, leaders and chiefs' had replaced his previous urge to get a democratic mandate from the executive of the SANC.

This shift needs to be understood in the context of apparent opposition by Jabavu's faction in the Cape to any organisation associated with Rubusana. Viewed in that context, it makes sense that Seme's answer to Reverend Mazwi's second question was also to disavow any association with Rubusana's Ingqungqutela, even though he was vigorously campaigning for its support. Seme's answer to the third question was to flatter, reassure and cajole Jabavu and his followers. He began by stating that he did not have the power to offer Imbumba any terms of amalgamation. He suggested instead that 'Imbumba Ye Zizwe has an opportunity to make its own terms with the people'. What he was calling for was Imbumba's 'patriotic and united support', and if it answered the call it had 'nothing to fear in the hands of a grateful people'. In any event, Seme observed, 'Imbumba Ye Zizwe being no doubt as it shall be the stronger Native Society in South Africa ought to wield influence in this proposed union, not only in matters affecting the election of officers but also in shaping the policy of the Union and therefore of the Natives of South Africa as a whole'.[20] Despite all the assurances and flattery, Jabavu's Imbumba chose not to join with other black organisations to form the Congress. Instead – and despite being disavowed by Seme in pursuit of Jabavu's support – it was Rubasana who attended the founding conference on 8 January 1912.

At the same November meeting, Seme presented the draft constitution of the proposed Congress. In addition to a preamble, the constitution had three articles. Article 1 dealt with membership of the proposed South African Native Congress, the name Seme suggested at the time. There were to be three classes: ordinary members, honorary members and auxiliary members. Ordinary membership would be open 'to all men who belonged to the so-called negro or aboriginal African races South of the Zambesi'. Honorary membership would be 'composed of two classes': the 'Ruling Chiefs and Hereditary Princes of African blood', and 'men and women who shall have rendered eminent service to the native races of South Africa'. As far as auxiliary membership was concerned, 'all the wives of the members of any affiliated branch or branches and other distinguished African ladies where Congress or Committee therefore shall be holding its sessions shall ipso facto become auxiliary members of the Congress during the period of such session'. The gender discrimination was extended to the duties of members. While it was the duty of every member to join a local branch or organisation of the proposed Congress or attend in person its annual sittings, it was solely the duty of auxiliary members (i.e. female members by virtue of being wives of ordinary members) 'to provide suitable shelter and entertainment for delegates to the Congress'.[21] Article 2 dealt with officers of the proposed Congress, which included the president, honorary senior treasurer, seven vice presidents, the honorary secretary, junior treasurer and corresponding secretary, the executive committee, and the sergeant-at-arms. Article 3 dealt with modalities for convening meetings of the new organisation.

The November meeting decided that the draft constitution would be sent to all black organisations in South Africa. Mr Molefe, a participant at the meeting, further proposed that the draft constitution be translated into all 'Native languages'.[22] It is unclear whether that proposal was implemented. The meeting passed four more resolutions: it resolved to hold the inaugural conference of the proposed Congress on 8 January 1912 in Bloemfontein; it instructed the Transvaal province to convene a special meeting on 4 December 1911 to work out its position on the proposed Congress (there were still divisions in the Transvaal at the time); following Reverend Tsewu's suggestion, papers would be read at the January conference, with each province preparing a paper to stimulate discussion and debate; finally, the meeting recorded its appreciation for Seme and his role (his 'mission') in the formation of the proposed Congress, and passed a vote of confidence in him. The stage was now set for the founding of the South African Native Congress (thus described in the draft constitution). And Seme was to play a pivotal role.

After the November resolutions, the march to the inaugural conference seemed inexorable; however, the way things developed is noteworthy. At its March 1910 Bloemfontein conference, the SANC had re-elected Rubusana and Dube as president and vice president respectively, with Plaatje, Masisi and Makgothi being elected to the executive.[23] The sense from the 1910 conference was that the SANC should be established as a permanent organisation, which explains why the meetings in June and August 1911 were called under its auspices, and why their agenda dealt with the business of the organisation. The switch to establishing a new organisation only occurred after Seme's call in October 1911, though it remains unclear why the change occurred. One probable explanation is the division in the Cape Province. It is obvious from Seme's correspondence with Reverend Mazwi that black unity under the auspices of the SANC was not acceptable to Jabavu and his followers. Jabavu would not be party to an organisation established by Rubusana, his rival in Cape politics.

The second likely explanation is a shift that took place in black politics, from the Cape to the northern provinces, especially the Transvaal. The SANC had been established in 1909 at the instigation of the Orange Free State Native Congress, and was supported principally by the South African Native Congress, which was Rubusana's organisation. Though represented at the SANC founding conference by T. Moeletsi and Z. More, both of the Transvaal Native Union, the Transvaal membership was at the time hampered by divisions.[24] The Cape, however, was extremely active owing to its concern that it might lose the black franchise. But when the Union of South Africa was proclaimed and the Cape franchise was maintained, the Cape's active interest in efforts to establish a united black national organisation waned. The enfranchised group at the Cape continued to believe that its political fortunes lay in participating in the Cape electoral system, and not in the black nationalist movement that Seme and his colleagues in the north were calling for.[25] This is partly why Rubusana, for instance, was not a prominent figure in any of the SANC executive committee meetings leading up to the formation of Congress; indeed, for a full year, while planning was at its height, Rubusana chose to take a back seat. So inactive was he that in mid-1911 he left for Europe, where he spent three months with Chief Dalindyebo of the abaThembu who had gone to seek medical treatment.[26]

The northern provinces' interest in organising for a united political front lay in the fact that black people in those provinces had been major losers when the Union of South Africa was established. Unlike in the Cape, the black franchise had not been extended to them. In fact, the main white opposition to a black franchise had come from the Transvaal, Orange Free State and Natal.[27] It was into this environment of heightened political awareness in the Transvaal that Seme was thrust in late 1910. And it was the active political base in the Transvaal that would initiate and organise the inaugural conference of 8 January 1912.

'Trees of one and the same forest'

Once the decision was taken that the proposed Congress would be founded on 8 January 1912 in Bloemfontein, invitations went out to all black leaders in all the provinces and protectorates. The leading organiser of the conference was the Orange Free State Native Congress. In a circular dated 26 December 1911, the Orange Free State Native Congress publicised the programme of the upcoming conference as follows: the first session of the conference was scheduled to begin at 3 p.m. on 8 January 1912. Seme was to move for the formation and establishment of the South African Native National Congress, and Alfred Mangena, Seme's partner in their law firm, would second the motion. This would be followed by a consideration of the draft constitution, the election of office bearers, and a discussion of several papers which leaders drawn from different provinces had been tasked to prepare. A concert and a farewell reception would also be arranged.[28]

The day of the conference was a Monday, which dawned overcast but calm.[29] Some delegates had arrived the day before. Among them was Chief Maama, who was representing Paramount Chief Letsie II of Basutoland. He was accompanied by twelve Basutoland delegates, as well as his personal secretary, Philip Molise. Other Sunday arrivals were Chief Joshua Molema and B. Samson who represented Chief Lekoko and the Barolong. Paramount Chief Gaseitsiwe and the Bangwaketse nation from Bechuanaland were represented by chiefs Mokgalagadi and Chelenyane. More delegates arrived on the morning of the conference. They included newspaper editors such as Plaatje (editor of *Tsala ea Becoana*), Charles Dube (then editor of *Ilanga lase Natal*) and E. Monyakoane (editor of the *Basutoland Star*). D. Dwanya from Middledrift in the Cape was present, as were Chief Mohlaba from Soutpansberg and Chief Ramagube from Middelburg in the Transvaal. Other Transvaal representatives arrived, including Sefako Makgatho, Edward Tsewu, D. Tyakwadi, H.R. Ngcayiya and E. Chake.

The host province, the Orange Free State, was also well represented. The president of the Orange Free State Native Congress, John Mocher, was present, and so was its secretary, Thomas Mapikela. Natal was represented by Charles Dube, Chief James Majozi and Levi Mvabaza.[30] Rubusana arrived late, but he made it nonetheless, which probably came as a relief to the conference organisers considering that the Cape was poorly represented and Jabavu and his followers had boycotted the conference altogether (Reverend Mazwi had been put on the programme in the hope that

Imbumba's leaders would attend). All in all, more than sixty delegates attended, the majority of whom were from the Transvaal.[31] Some four decades after the conference was held, Richard V. Selope Thema observed:

> It was a gathering of tribes that had never met before except on the battlefields. It was a gathering of Chiefs who had never seen each other before. And they had come from the four provinces and the High Commission territories. It was a gathering of educated Africans who had never exchanged views before. It was a gathering, if I may say so, of the departed spirits of the African race, among whom were such men as Sandile, Tshaka, Moshoeshoe, Cetyewayo [sic], Moroka, Khama, Sekhukhune, Sotshangana and Ramapulana.[32]

The proceedings started at 11:40 a.m. In the chair was Mocher, who officially declared the conference open and welcomed all the chiefs and delegates. The next order of business was the appointment of Sol Plaatje to record as well as publicise conference proceedings through newspapers. A committee comprising three delegates from each province was appointed to look into the draft constitution. The conference adjourned at 1 p.m. and resumed at 3 p.m., but still there was no consensus. The sticking point was the financial contributions from local branches to the parent body.[33] This prevented the conference from adopting a final constitution; instead, what was settled on was a draft constitution and a decision that a final constitution would be adopted at some later point. The draft constitution contained a preamble, as well as the main aims of the SANNC: to 'promote unity and mutual cooperation between the Bantu races'; to establish a 'centre of communication between the government and the aboriginal races of South Africa'; to 'promote the educational, social, economic and political elevation of the native people in South Africa'; and to promote 'better understanding between the native Chiefs of South Africa, and to encourage in them and their people loyalty to the British Crown and all lawfully constituted authorities'. A further aim was for the SANNC to 'bring about mutual understanding between the White and Black inhabitants of South Africa'. Finally, the Congress would strive to 'safeguard generally the interest of the inhabitants throughout the native races of South Africa and to obtain redress of any other just grievances'.[34]

One point on which the conference did reach agreement was the name of the organisation. Certain influential leaders such as Sol Plaatje favoured an African name, with Plaatje's own preference being Imbizo YaBantu. He was supported in this by Chief Joshua Molema and also Cleopas Kunene, both of whom argued that too many organisations, run by various races, had the name 'congress' in some form or another. They contended that the name Imbizo YaBantu would give the new organisation a distinctly African identity.[35] Their proposal was defeated, however, and the South African Native National Congress it became.

When the proceedings resumed in the afternoon, Reverend Tsewu read from the scriptures, while Reverend Jacob Monyatsi of the Wesleyan Church in Bloemfontein said a prayer. In welcoming back the delegates, Reverend Rose of the local St Patrick's Anglican Church decried the fact that the draft constitution did not permit white people to become members and pleaded that it be duly amended. Seme later responded by saying that while membership was not open to white people they were nevertheless welcome to provide assistance to the new organisation.[36]

With formalities out of the way, Seme stepped up to give the keynote address. He opened with the following declaration:

> Chiefs of royal blood and gentlemen of our race, we have gathered here to consider and discuss a scheme which my colleagues and I have decided to place before you. We have discovered that in the land of their birth, Africans are treated as hewers of wood and drawers of water. The white people of this country have formed what is known as the Union of South Africa – a union in which we have no voice in the making of laws and no part in their administration. We have called you, therefore, to this conference, so that we can together devise ways and means of forming our national union for the purpose of creating national unity and defending our rights and privileges.[37]

Seme also acknowledged the difficulty of establishing a united organisation which drew its support from different elements representing 'different tongues and tribes'. While similar attempts had previously been made, these had failed, he said. Also, various associations formed in different provinces had been ineffective, did not cooperate, and often failed to per-suade the white authorities. Seme used a colourful metaphor to argue for united action: 'when a man drove a swarm of locusts from his mealie fields the swarm would invade the neighbour's lands, but by concerted action there was a chance to exterminate the pest, and a Congress of this nature would unite the separate bodies to work for the good of all concerned'.[38] With a typical rhetorical flourish, Seme said that he could read from the countenances of delegates that they were determined to forge a closer union among black people, and that the hour had come when 'Ethiopia would stretch forth her hands unto God, and when princes shall come out of Egypt'. In a possible attempt to reassure the white authorities, Seme declared that it was not the aim of the conference (neither the delegates nor black people in general) to cause trouble or offend anybody; the intention was only to help themselves, 'to seek and redeem the lost and neglected millions of this land, to point out to them the way of truth in this life, to urge and teach them to develop the victories of peace'.[39] He completed his rousing address by officially proposing the establishment of the SANNC. His colleague Alfred Mangena rose to second this proposal. Chief Joshua Molema also rose to express his support, as did chiefs Mohlaba, Mopedi and Mokgaladi, and Rubusana, who supported Seme's motion in a passionate speech that was loudly cheered.[40] This was followed by the delegates singing 'Lizalis'idinga Lakho, Thixo Nkosi Yenyaniso' (Fulfil Thy Promise, Faithful/Truthful God).[41]

Seme's speech would later be described as eloquent, and he would forever be known as the moving spirit behind the formation of the SANNC.[42] The conference then moved on to the delicate business of electing a president and office bearers. The stakes were high, given the fragility of the union being forged. It was therefore important that the executive be constituted in such a manner that it reflected different regional interests as well as constituencies represented by delegates.[43] To secure the support and participation of traditional leaders, George Montsioa, another overseas-trained lawyer and Seme's associate, proposed that prominent chiefs be appointed as honorary presidents of the SANNC. His proposal was accepted and the following traditional leaders were appointed: Lewanika of the Barotse, Letsie II of the Basotho, Lekoko of the Barolong, Marelane of the Pondo, Dalindyebo of the Thembu, Dinuzulu of the Zulu, and Makgatho of the Bakgatla; chiefs who were appointed included Mohlaba, Matlala, Sekhukhune, Matlaba, Mamogale, Mpahlela, Hekana, Dinguanyane, Namaube, Molepo, Mahlambiso and Tuliwamahashi. The only non-traditional leader elected as honorary president was the respected Rubusana, probably to compensate for not electing him president, despite expectations to the contrary.

How Rubusana lost out is one of the least understood aspects of the inaugural conference, with part of the explanation lying in the election pro-cedure. Unlike other office bearers, in the case of the president a special committee was appointed: consisting of three representatives from each province, it had to oversee the running of the conference, discuss pivotal matters such as the draft constitution, and also propose three names from which delegates would choose the president. The three nominees were John Dube (from Natal), Tsewu and Makgatho (both from Transvaal), though the selection criteria remain unknown. Dube was overwhelmingly elected despite being absent from the conference,[44] and his election was met with enthusiastic applause that for a few minutes brought proceedings to a standstill.[45]

Following the election of Dube, a motion was passed that other office bearers be nominated. Seven vice presidents were duly elected: Sefako Makgatho, Philip Molise, John Mocher, William Setsiliba, Thomas Zini, Simon Kambule and Chief Silas Molema. Seme was elected treasurer, with Mapikela junior treasurer, while George Montsioa was elected corre-sponding secretary and Plaatje secretary. The conference decided that the president, treasurer and secretary would in the meantime constitute the executive committee.[46]

There have been different explanations as to why forty-two-year-old Dube was preferred over Rubusana, who was thirteen years his senior. It may have been an expression of solidarity with Natal Africans who had suffered brutal suppression after the Bhambatha Rebellion, as well as subsequent harassment of leaders such as Dube.[47] However, a more compelling explanation relates to the prevailing politics of the Cape: rivalry between Rubusana and Jabavu, and the divisions this caused in Cape politics, ran deep. Considering the conference's emphasis on unity, it would have been untenable to elect Rubusana as president, especially because Seme still harboured hopes that Jabavu and his supporters would join the SANNC. That lingering hope was evident when Reverend Mqolobi, a well-known Jabavu supporter in Imbumba, was elected in absentia as chaplain-in-chief, with Reverend Ngcayiya as his assistant.[48]

The election of Dube also demonstrated a further shift in black politics from the Cape to the northern provinces: 'Dube was acceptable as president of Congress because the majority of delegates at its inaugural conference wished to emphasise that African political activity would in future no longer be centred in the relatively privileged Cape'.[49] It should be added that the majority of delegates came mainly from the northern provinces, with the Transvaal and Orange Free State dominating. It is no wonder, then, that two of the three nominees for the presidency were from the Transvaal.

After the election process was over, delegates listened to papers read by speakers from the different provinces. Reverend Ngcayiya addressed the topic of native schools and churches, which was followed by a brief general discussion. Levi Mvabaza focused on male hostels and passes for native women. Sefako Makgatho spoke on 'black and white peril', while Thomas Mapikela led the discussion on the Squatters Bill. Delegates were of the opinion that the bill would destroy 'native thrift', and its effect would be to 'turn the native population of South Africa into wanderers and pariahs in the land of their birth'. A committee of five was elected to meet with the Minister of Native Affairs to protest against the bill; if unsuccessful, the conference mandated the committee to take up the matter with the Governor General with the aim of persuading him not to assent to the bill.[50]

Decisions taken regarding the Squatters Bill formed part of a set of resolutions prepared by a special committee of eight: Rubusana (convenor and chair), Plaatje, Seme, Charles Dube, Moutshumi, Makgatho, Tsewu, Pathlane, Chief Silas Molema and Prince Solomon. Among the resolutions taken was a proposal for the establishment of 'two or more native colleges for giving higher education to natives so as to remove the necessity of our young men having to go abroad for their education'. A related resolution was for the establishment of a 'Central Agricultural College' to train 'the natives in modern methods of agriculture'. The conference expressed concern about the actions 'of certain alarmists who spread rumours about alleged native risings from time to time which are to endanger the peace of the country'. It resolved that the government should establish a commission of inquiry consisting of two well-known 'Europeans and two Natives' to investigate 'these charges with a view to re-assure the public of the loyalty of the natives'.[51] The conference registered its strong objection to black women carrying passes and having to undergo medical examinations prior to their being employed. On the matter of passes for women, the conference argued that such a law 'is degrading to our women'. Accordingly, the conference resolved to 'respectfully urge upon the Government the desirability of immediate withdrawing of all laws in the four provinces which compel native women to carry passes'. Finally, the conference declared that it was not opposed to the building of hostels especially designed for black miners as long as those hostels were managed by 'competent and sympathetic people'. The conference also resolved to 'respectfully point out to the Government the smallness of the compensation awarded to miners who are either killed or maimed in the Rand mines, and would respectfully urge that the workmen's compensation act be extended so as to include the native workmen'. Furthermore, the conference expressed alarm 'at the appalling death rate among the native labourers in the mines and would urge to see that this is reduced to a minimum'.[52]

With the SANNC established, important resolutions taken and office bearers elected, the conference drew to a close. Philip Molise was in the chair at the closing session in place of John Dube, the absent newly elected president. Molise noted in his closing remarks that the idea of uniting black people was not new, claiming that some fifty years before, King Moshoeshoe of the Basotho had met with Shaka of the amaZulu and Faku of the amaMpondo, and later with Sekhukhune of the baPedi, with the purpose of uniting their people. Moshoeshoe did not live to see his dream come true, however, but the establishment of the SANNC was the realisation of that dream. Molise urged the delegates to go back to their communities and preach the message of black unity, urging them to explain to their people that 'they are identified with different tribal names and dialects just as the different trees in the woods were known by different names; some were eatable and some were not, but the delegates could safely claim that they were now trees of one and the same forest'.[53] Inspired by this rousing message of African unity, the delegates rose to sing John Knox Bokwe's 'Plea for Africa':

> Give a thought to Africa
> Beneath the burning sun.
> There are hosts of weary hearts,
> Waiting to be won.
> Many lives have passed away,
> And in many homes
> There are voices crying now
> To the living God.
> Tell the love of Jesus
> By her hills and waters.
> God bless Africa
> And her sons and daughters.[54]

Hasten slowly

John Langalibalele Dube accepted the presidency of the SANNC in an open letter published in many black newspapers and addressed to the 'Chiefs and Gentlemen of the South African Native National Congress'. He began by expressing gratitude for the confidence and dignity bestowed on him through his election as first president of the SANNC. He described its formation as a momentous event in the history of black people in South Africa, a 'red-letter day' of their hopes and the birthday of their political renaissance. As 8 January 1912 was their political birthday, they were therefore still politically 'very young and inexperienced'. Dube used the 'youth and inexperience' of the SANNC to argue for a cautious approach in the manner in which it pressed its political claims. He cautioned that the path was thorny and steep; they had to tread 'softly, ploddingly'. In keeping with that approach, his motto, which he hoped would be adopted by the SANNC, was 'Festina lente', or 'Hasten slowly'. He declared his 'patron saint' to be Booker Washington, who he described as a 'great and edifying man'.

Dube went on to propose a policy that the SANNC might adopt in its relations with white authorities. He argued that the SANNC should pursue a policy of 'deep and dutiful respect for the rulers whom God has placed over us; a policy of hopeful reliance in that sense of common justice and love of freedom so innate in the British character'. If this approach of 'respectful and reasonable' dialogue with the white rulers was followed, the 'inherently religious and magnanimous British people would not refuse them a hearing nor their rights'. After all, Dube observed, 'the British had taught black people to seek and to strive'. He concluded by assuring the white authorities that while black people waged 'their little war, it shall always and only be along the constitutional way of peaceful endeavour and patient pegging away. An honest, manly fight every British admires.'[55] Dube's public acceptance statement, with its outline of a political approach, marked the inauguration of the SANNC as a working, functioning organisation.

Crowning moment

The formation of the SANNC was the realisation of a dream Seme had pursued ever since returning to South Africa; it was also his crowning moment. In just over a year, he had achieved what many before had failed to do. For that, he has been variously called the moving spirit behind the formation of Congress, or simply the founder of the ANC and African nationalism in general. But why did Seme succeed where others had failed? The answer requires an understanding of the character of the man as well as the circumstances in which he acted.

His contemporaries often observed that Seme was a man with a strong character complemented by a broad vision and a singular focus in achieving a goal once he had set himself a task. Later reflecting on Seme's life, Thema, a fellow founder, collaborator and frequent adversary, stated: 'That Pixley ka Isaka Seme was a man of action and a patriot no sane man can deny.' Thema also noted that Seme was ambitious, restless and 'believed in his mind only, and therefore could not listen to the advice of other men'.[56] Seme certainly had a 'strong sense of mission to bring about the political unity of the African people' – though the other side of this singlemindedness was a tendency to be 'overambitious, arrogant and rather hot-headed'.[57] His driving spirit, impatience and sense of mission enabled Seme to rally black leaders to the cause of forming a united black political organisation, eventually known as the African National Congress.

There was, however, more to Seme's success than these qualities of character. He returned to South Africa in late 1910, at a time of profound political change. The formation of the ANC in 1912, and Seme's leading role in it, is inconceivable without taking into account the context. In October 1910, when Seme returned, the Union of South Africa was barely six months old; two former colonies (the Cape and Natal) and two former Boer republics (the Transvaal and the Orange Free State) now formed one unitary state. Black people had been excluded from that political union. As part of the settlement, the black franchise had been retained in the Cape. But it had not been extended to black people in the three other provinces. As if the political exclusion of black people were not enough, the white government under the leadership of General Louis Botha began to pass and implement a slew of laws that were entirely against the interests of black people. For instance, the Native Labour Regulation Act tightened 'controls upon African labour'; the Mines and Works Act 'reserved certain categories of work for whites, the first time such a principle was actually embodied in government legislation'; and the Dutch Reformed Church Act 'prohibited full African membership' in the church.[58] Afrikaner nationalism was on the ascendance and the future of black people looked increasingly bleak.

It was this political context that spurred black leaders, especially in the northern provinces, to come together to form the SANNC. As many of them commented at the time, the coming together of the previously warring white people to form the Union of South Africa was a major lesson for black unity. There was an increasing realisation that the disunity of black people was preventing them from effectively pressing their political claims. Seme addressed this point directly in his October call for unity, stating that Africans were the 'last among all the nations of the earth to discover the precious jewels of cooperation and for this reason the great gifts of civilisation are least known among us today'. He then declared:

> The South African Native Congress [later the SANNC] is the voice in the wilderness biding all the dark races of this sub-continent to come together once or twice a year to review the past and reject therein all those things which have retarded our progress, the things which poison the springs of our national life and virtue; to label and distinguish the sins of civilisations and as members of one household to talk and think loudly on our home problems and the solution of them.[59]

Seme's effort was of course not the first: the South African Native National Congress was built on the shoulders of the South African Native Convention which had been established in March 1909 in Bloemfontein to fight for the rights of black people during negotiations for the Union of South Africa. When it was first established, the SANC was not meant to be a permanent structure. But that changed in 1910 when it became clear that its political claims had not been favourably considered by the white powerbrokers. The founding of the SANC was itself rooted in a tradition of formation of political organisations that originated around the end of the nineteenth century – a strategy that followed various military defeats. The first such organisation was the Native Educational Association (NEA), formed in the late 1800s.[60] While not an exclusively political organisation, the NEA addressed political matters, and it included eastern Cape leaders such as Jabavu, Rubusana, Elijah Makiwane, P.J. Mzimba, William Ntsikana, Paul Xiniwe, W. Soga, H. Maci and W. Gqoba.[61]

Being a newcomer to the political scene meant that Seme did not carry any political baggage; moreover, he came equipped with legal training and the prestige of being an overseas-trained attorney.[62] Other organisations formed in the late 1800s were Imbumba yama Nyama, established in Port Elizabeth in 1882, the South African Native Association, and the Thembu

Association.[63] Alongside these were emergent newspapers such as *Isigidimi samaXhosa*, originally a missionary newspaper based in Lovedale in the 1870s, edited by Elijah Makiwane.[64] Soon afterwards, in 1884, Jabavu founded *Imvo Zabantsundu*; in competition with this Rubusana, together with Meshach Pelem, A.K. Soga, S.D. Soga and R. Mantsayi, formed *Izwi Labantu*.[65] Although based mainly in the eastern Cape, *Izwi Labantu* had branches in Kimberley and some Transvaal towns.

The end of the Anglo-Boer War in 1902 brought disappointment to black people who had expected the British to reward them for their support by improving political conditions, particularly as a plethora of black organisations began to emerge across the land. It was in this context that the Cape Native Congress and the Transvaal Native Vigilance Association were formed, while 1904 saw the emergence of the Orange River Native Vigilance Association.[66] In Natal, *Funamalungelo* had been formed in 1888,[67] while the Natal Native Congress was formed in 1900; John Dube established *Ilanga lase Natal* in 1903, and another newspaper that was established around the turn of the century was *Ipepa lo Hlanga*, edited and published by Mark Radebe.[68] Political organisations and newspapers tended to be established by the same group of people, which in Natal included Martin Lutuli, Mark Radebe, Stephen Mini, Josiah Gumede, Cleopas Kunene, John Kumalo, James Majozi, and of course John Dube.

Most of these leaders were at the forefront of attempts to prevent the exclusion of black people from negotiations for the Union of South Africa. Some were founders of the SANC in Bloemfontein in 1909. Others joined up with a new cohort of young leaders such as Seme in the establishment of the SANNC in 1912. Black leaders from the Transvaal such as Makgatho, and Orange Free State leaders such as Mocher and Mapikela, together with newspaper editors such as Plaatje, deserve special mention for their role in establishing the SANNC. In a sense, the SANNC was an heir to earlier efforts by these leaders to organise themselves in order to advance their political claims. This is not to suggest that there was a direct link between the NEA, for instance, and the eventual establishment of the SANNC. Instead, there are zigzags and discontinuities between the period of black political awakening at the turn of the century and the formation of the SANNC in 1912. What is, however, indisputable is that earlier organisations paved the way for the formation of the SANNC.

Seme tapped into this rich tradition, creating a network of leaders and organisations – and ironically it was a help rather than a hindrance that he

was new to the political scene in South Africa. Indeed, Seme's 'contribution was that of a newcomer to the political scene, equipped with the
training and prestige of an attorney'.[69] Seme's admission by the Transvaal
Supreme Court and his impressive performances as an attorney received
broad newspaper coverage. This undoubtedly assisted him in persuading black leaders, and the chiefs in particular (many of whom were legal
clients), to support the SANNC.

Moving on

Seme had for a while been interested in founding a national newspaper,
as evidenced by his unsuccessful proposal at the June 1911 meeting, where
it was argued that the existing papers were adequate to the task. Soon after
the formation of the SANNC, Seme agitated for the establishment of a
newspaper that would propagate its views – even informing his friend,
Alain Locke, about his plan.[70] The SANNC executive eventually acceded,
and he named the newspaper *Abantu-Batho*.[71] Its headquarters were in
Johannesburg, and it was published in Zulu, Sotho, Xhosa and English.
Seme was appointed managing editor, with Cleopas Kunene as first editor
for the English and Zulu sections, and Daniel S. Letanka editor of the Sotho/
Tswana section. Letanka would later succeed Seme as managing editor.
Among other ANC luminaries who edited the paper were Saul Msane,
Levi Mvabaza, T.D. Mweli Skota and Richard V. Selope Thema. For a short
while in the early years, Robert Grandon was editor. Seme received financial
support for establishing the paper from the Swazi royal family, in particular Queen Labotsibeni. It is unclear what the sum was precisely, though
several scholars claim it was £3 000.[72] *Abantu-Batho* fulfilled its promise,
chronicling black political struggles until the early 1930s when it closed
down mainly owing to financial problems.

After establishing *Abantu-Batho* Seme moved on to another project. He
started a company called the Native Farmers Association of South Africa.
Its purpose was to buy land for black settlement. This was an extremely
important issue, and through the company Seme bought the farms
Daggakraal and Driefontein in the Wakkerstroom district of the eastern
Transvaal. To this day, the descendants of families who were settled on
those farms live on that land.

Soon afterwards, Seme began to withdraw from active participation
in the affairs of the SANNC. Despite being treasurer, he was not at the
forefront of fundraising efforts for the 1914 deputation sent to Britain to

protest the Natives Land Act of 1913. Considering its impact on the lives of black people, as well as Seme's own interest in land ownership, his failure to involve himself was extraordinary. So inactive was Seme in the affairs of the SANNC that he was eventually removed from his position as treasurer.

Seme provided no explanation for his withdrawal from the political scene, though it is likely that he was becoming increasingly preoccupied with his other endeavours, including his legal practice, the Native Farmers Association and *Abantu-Batho*. In addition, he was acting as legal advisor to both the Swazi and Zulu royal families. After his return to South Africa Seme became close to Dinuzulu ka Cetshwayo, to the extent that when Dinuzulu died in 1913 Seme became involved in the succession battle. His involvement in Swazi affairs was even more extensive. There were also developments in Seme's personal life, and so it is hardly surprising that his attention was deflected from the SANNC. Thema's observations concerning Seme's unsuitability for building an organisation such as the SANNC, which required time and attention, are valid. Had Seme curbed his youthful ambition and restlessness, Thema contended, he would not have lost interest in the SANNC. Thema also criticised Seme for his inability to cooperate with others and for his failure to make compromises necessary for teamwork. In a reference to the failure of Napoleon, Thema claimed that Seme's plans for building institutions that would uplift the African race were 'wrecked by the extravagance of his own genius'[73] – a trait that would drive the ANC to the brink of collapse during Seme's term as president in the 1930s.

The same flaws would push Seme to play a destructive role when he briefly resurfaced in the SANNC in 1916 and 1917. Using the platform of *Abantu-Batho*, which was edited by Saul Msane at the time, Seme began to attack Dube's leadership. The confrontation reached a climax at the fifth annual general meeting of the SANNC in Bloemfontein, which discussed mainly the SANNC's attitude to government's proposed policy of territorial segregation. Citing correspondence between SANNC secretary general Thema and the British-based Anti-Slavery and Aborigines' Protection Society, Seme, backed especially by Alfred Mangena and Saul Msane, charged that Thema and Dube had expressed support for the principle of territorial segregation, thereby contravening the position of the SANNC. When the matter was discussed and Thema was asked to read the letter in question, it turned out that the charge against him and Dube was baseless. Despite this, Seme and Mangena (together with Msane and Stephen Mini) pushed ahead with their demand for Dube and his executive to step down;[74] Mangena accused Dube of doing nothing since his election as president in 1912. The debate became heated, with Plaatje admonishing Seme and his supporters for unduly attacking Dube, to the extent that Seme and other delegates, in particular Makgatho and Thema, almost came to blows. With the atmosphere having become so toxic, Dube, Thema and other members of the executive resigned their positions. This left the SANNC leaderless.

Dube's ousting from the presidency of the SANNC and Seme's instrumental role in it underscored their unpredictable and sometimes fractious relationship. Seme had played an enormous part in Dube's election as SANNC president in January 1912, but by 1913 their relationship had begun to sour mostly due to their respective influence over prominent members of the Zulu royal house. Distrustful of Seme, Dube told Alice Werner, his mutual friend with Harriette Colenso, that Seme was 'very ambitious'. In a letter to Colenso, Werner warned that Seme's ambition would lead to a Lucifer-type fall.[75] By 1916 there was open hostility between the two men from Inanda, with Seme and his supporters using the platform of *Abantu-Batho* to attack Dube, and Dube and his supporters using *Ilanga lase Natal* to attack Seme. Seme's antipathy towards Dube went as far as leading him to offer Plaatje the SANNC presidency while Dube was still president.[76] Writing a short while after his ousting by Seme and his associates, Dube expressed his conviction that he still held 'the confidence of the people and if I cared to stand again I have no doubt as to my success'.[77] He added that what prevented him from standing again was his decision to focus on the affairs of Ohlange school, which he confessed to have neglected.

A committee was then appointed to elect an interim leadership to take over until the following conference. The committee met at Newcastle in Natal. The meeting was well attended and among those present were Msane, Letanka, Mvabaza, R.W. Msimang and Reverend Ngcayiya, all from the Transvaal, and Stephen Mini, W. Makanya, J.T. Gumede, Elka Cele, W.W. Ndlovu and P.T.B Mtembu, all from Natal. Alfred Mangena was present, as was Chief Nkabane. The discussion focused on nominations for interim president. Seme's supporters were opposed to Sefako Makgatho on the grounds that he had followed Dube, Thema and Twayi in resigning at the tempestuous Bloemfontein conference. A heated discussion then ensued as to whether Makgatho's name should be considered for the presidency. A vote was taken, and Seme's supporters lost. S. Mabaso then proposed Makgatho, who was seconded by Ndlovu and Cele. Msane nominated Chief Stephen Mini, who was seconded by Gumede. Votes were cast, and Makgatho received ten against Mini's three. When the time came for nominations for secretary general, Seme's supporters lost heart and hope: no one was prepared to second Msane's proposed candidate, Gumede. This meant that Mr Machochoko from Winburg in the Orange Free State was elected unopposed. For the position of treasurer, Mr Ndhlovu of Vryheid was also elected unopposed.[78] After the failed bid to take over the SANNC, Seme went into the political wilderness, and it was only when his luck turned in the late 1920s that he would resurface.

* * *

Seme's role in the establishment of the ANC and his subsequent behaviour, including his ambitious attempt to oust Dube, inevitably bring to mind Thema's image of a leader whose plans were 'wrecked by the extravagance of his own genius'.[79] And Pixley Seme was undeniably a genius. At just thirty years old and without political experience, he succeeded where older and more experienced men had failed by initiating the formation of the ANC. Not only that, but in a short space of time he established a growing legal practice, founded a newspaper, started a company to buy land, became a confidant and advisor to kings and queens, and much more besides. Within a few months he succeeded in achieving what most people fail to achieve in a lifetime. The greatest of these achievements, of course, was to plant a mustard-seed idea among black people: they were far more than mere ethnic fragments incapable of working together. They could become – indeed they were – one united black nation. The African National Congress, which Seme founded on 8 January 1912, continues to be a living monument to the depth and breadth of his vision. That fact alone more than compensates for his many flaws.

4

The Swazi nation's attorney

Running parallel with Seme's political involvement was his burgeoning legal career. On 22 November 1910 Mr I. Lapin, a lawyer acting on behalf of Seme, lodged an application with the registrar of the Supreme Court of South Africa for his client's admission as an attorney. The matter was placed on the roll, and on Thursday 22 December Seme appeared before Justice Wessels in the Transvaal Provincial Division of the Supreme Court. Seme presented his credentials, which included the fact that he had been called to the bar of the Honourable Society of the Middle Temple on 8 June 1910, and that he continued to be a member of that society. Since a law degree was at the time not required for admission as an attorney, Seme's three years of study at Middle Temple sufficed.

Seme's appearance at the Supreme Court was covered by various newspapers. Contrary to the norm, he appeared before the judge without legal representation because, as *Imvo Zabantsundu* would later report, he 'could find no one to represent him'.[1] His appearance drew a large crowd of white people who came to witness a black person applying for admission as an attorney, a rare sight at the time. Seme did not disappoint his onlookers. *Imvo Zabantsundu* reported that Seme was 'immaculately dressed in the best of tailor-made garments'.[2] *Ilanga lase Natal* remarked that he spoke polished English and comported himself respectfully.[3] Seme's style and attention to his appearance would frequently be remarked upon in future years, with H. Selby Msimang, for instance, describing Seme as clean shaven and well groomed, with 'an appearance of an aristocrat'.[4] At the start of the proceedings Justice Wessels asked Seme whether the Transvaal Law Society was aware that he was lodging an application to be admitted as an attorney. Replying in the 'clearest English', Seme stated: 'All the papers are in perfectly good order, my Lord.' Justice Wessels then 'curtly' instructed Seme to take his orders, and Seme, 'having been duly sworn in, bowed politely and withdrew'.[5]

The question as to whether the Transvaal Law Society was aware of Seme's application is significant. A few months before, on 14 July 1910, another black person had appeared in the same court to apply for admission as an attorney. That person was Alfred Mangena – the first black person to be admitted as an attorney by a South African court. Like Seme, Mangena was born in Natal, though in the Midlands town of Estcourt. In the late 1890s he went to Cape Town, where he completed his schooling. From there he sailed to England to study law at Lincoln's Inn in London, where he was admitted into the Honourable Society of Lincoln's Inn on 5 October 1903; five years later, on 1 July 1908, he passed his law exams.

Upon his return to South Africa, Mangena applied to the Transvaal Provincial Division of the Supreme Court for admission to practise as an attorney. However, in the affidavit signed by its president, Hendrik Lodewyk Malherbe, the Transvaal Law Society fiercely opposed Mangena's application. The society stated that there was no possibility that a black attorney would find legal work from members of the white population in the Transvaal. Thus, a black attorney would have to find legal work from black people. But this, in the view of the Law Society, went against government policy, which encouraged black people to approach the Minister of Native Affairs and his native commissioners to assist them in settling disputes instead of taking them to the courts. The Law Society expressed agreement with government policy, declaring that from time to time it had 'used its influence and disciplinary powers to discourage members of the Society from interfering with the said Policy'. It argued furthermore that 'it would not be in the interests of the natives of the Transvaal to create among them a class of Native Practitioner' and that 'such Native Practitioner would be beyond the control of the Society who would find it difficult to exercise its discipline over him'.[6]

Mangena's application came before Justice Smith of the Transvaal Provincial Division of the Supreme Court. He ruled that Mangena was entitled to be admitted as an attorney, arguing that where 'an applicant possessed the statutory qualifications the Court would not be justified in refusing to admit him merely because he belonged to one of the native races'. In addition, the judge disputed the Law Society's contention that Mangena would encourage litigation among black people, and that he would be guilty of professional misconduct. The judge concluded by suggesting that if, for any reason, it was not desirable for black people to be admitted as attorneys, it was not for the courts to make that call. That responsibility fell with the legislature. He dismissed the Law Society's application and admitted Mangena as the first black attorney in South Africa.[7]

The judge's decision paved the way for Seme to apply for admission without opposition from the Law Society. It is likely also to have reaffirmed Seme's admiration of Mangena, which he had expressed in a glowing biographical profile published in August 1908, calling Mangena his hero.[8] The admission of Mangena and Seme as attorneys greatly pleased black public opinion. In late 1911 *Ilanga lase Natal* published an extensive article singing the praises of Mangena, Seme and George Dixon Montsioa – the third black person to be admitted. Mangena was referred to as *ingqwele* (leader), with Seme being described as *inkunzana egwebayo* (the prosecuting bull).[9]

An impressive beginning

Seme joined forces with Mangena, and the two young attorneys established a law firm. Mangena ran the firm's main office in Pretoria, while Seme opened an office on the corner of Joubert and Anderson streets in central Johannesburg. While Seme's office administration was poor, with his clerk not being paid for six months at a time, this did not hamper Seme. He got off to a remarkable start, and one of the first cases he dealt with attracted widespread attention. The case involved a black person who was charged for assaulting a white man, and the court proceedings took place in B Court in the Johannesburg Magistrate's Court. *The Star* reported that once news spread that the defendant's attorney was black, members of the public rushed to the court, while lawyers and police officers stayed to watch Seme defending his client. *The Star* noted that Seme was 'well groomed' and spoke 'good English with a slight American accent', and that he conducted his case logically, thereby impressing those present in court. The newspaper also observed that it was the first time a black lawyer had appeared in a Johannesburg court, and alluded also to Mangena having appeared in a Fordsburg court.[10] The following year Seme was praised in the black press for successfully defending Mrs R.D. Bopela, a government employee who would otherwise have lost her job.[11]

As black lawyers in a racially segregated society, Seme, Mangena and other pioneering colleagues faced many challenges. One such involved the clash between Seme's status as an attorney and the racism of the society in which he lived. As Seme later described it, the incident occurred on the evening of 14 September 1911 when he was on a train to Volksrust, a town on the border of Natal and Transvaal, on legal business. He said that, like all solicitors, 'I of course travel first class'. When he requested the steward to bring bedding to his compartment, he waited for two hours in vain. He then decided to look for the steward in the dining car, where he met a rowdy group of young white men who were in a drunken state. When they saw Seme they jumped up and shouted: 'Kaffir in the first class! Kick him out, throw him out of the window!' The men then rushed at him with the clear intention of throwing him out of the moving train, knocking his hat from his head and hitting him in the process. Others joined in, at which point Seme shouted: 'You had better stop because I have a loaded revolver with me!' The mob's response was that Seme was lying because 'Kaffirs' were not allowed to carry revolvers. Once again, they rushed at him, whereupon, he wrote, he took his gun from his hip pocket and put it in a side pocket of his coat. At that point the men ran away. Two weeks after the incident, Seme received a notice from the Heidelberg Magistrate's Court informing him that he had been charged with pointing a revolver at a group of people, and for having behaved in a violent manner. When the matter was brought before the court, five young men testified against Seme. Nobody testified in his favour, and he was found guilty of the offence.[12]

Another incident involving Mangena further demonstrated that being a lawyer did not make a black man immune to racism. In fact, it seemed to invite it. Mangena was representing a young black man accused of having made indecent advances to a white woman. The man, whom newspapers described as a 'Zulu newsboy', was alleged to have made a 'click with his lips similar to kissing, and [to have] put out his hand to a young [white] lady as if to chuck her under the chin'. The woman complained that while the young man did not actually touch her, he came too close and the noise of his lips 'indicated a desire to kiss her'. The case came before the magistrate of the Germiston court. Upon hearing that the young black man had appointed Mangena to represent him, a group of white men is reported to have approached the young man's employer to ask him to persuade the young man to employ the services of a white attorney instead of Mangena. Consequently, the young black man was represented by two attorneys at the trial, and when the magistrate asked him to choose one, he opted for Mangena.

That is when trouble started. During cross-examination the white woman refused to answer Mangena. She is reported to have pointed to him and said, 'I refuse to answer questions put to me by that man.' The magistrate, Mr James Young, replied, 'Look here, you must answer the questions put to you by that man, or I shall commit you for contempt of court.' He then informed her: 'That Kaffir is an officer of this Court. He has been admitted by the Supreme Court to practise as a solicitor. You must understand that a black man has the same rights as a white man in this country.' The woman responded by asking: 'Is it absolutely necessary to answer?' To this, the magistrate replied: 'It is necessary to answer. You are only making a fool of yourself in taking up this attitude.'[13] Following this admonishment, the woman proceeded to answer the questions put to her by Mangena.

There would be many similar instances in which the first black lawyers would be forced to confront racial discrimination. However, that did not deter them from practising their profession. In the case of Seme, his reputation as an excellent lawyer brought him many high-profile clients. Especially noteworthy was his appointment by Dinuzulu ka Cetshwayo, who had been exiled to Middelburg in the eastern Transvaal and whom Seme represented in many engagements with the Botha government. After Dinuzulu's death in October 1913, Seme became the legal representative of his successor, Solomon ka Dinuzulu. However, by far the most prominent role that Seme played, and without a doubt the highlight of his legal career, was in his capacity as legal advisor to the Swazi nation, especially its royal family. So involved was Seme in its affairs that he became known as the Swazi nation's attorney.[14]

Seme and the Swazis

Seme's first contact with the Swazi royal family occurred soon after his return from England, around 1911. The person who introduced him was Richard W. Msimang, brother of H. Selby Msimang and son of Joel Msimang, founder of the Independent Methodist Church of South Africa. Originally from Swaziland, the Msimangs settled in Edendale in the Natal Midlands. They had strong connections with the Swazi royal family. Seme's connection with Richard Msimang was through their profession. After studying law at Queen's College, Taunton, in England, Richard Msimang returned to South Africa in 1912, and went on to play a prominent role in the SANNC, chairing the committee that drafted its 1919 constitution.

Seme's connection with Swaziland, and its royal family in particular, was extensive and deep. Hilda Kuper, biographer of King Sobhuza II, described Seme as 'an important influence in Swazi life', while it was Swazi historian J.S.M. Matsebula who first called him the '[Swazi] nation's attorney'.[15] On numerous occasions when communicating with white authorities, whether in Swaziland, South Africa or England, Sobhuza II described Seme as his and the nation's legal advisor. So close was Seme's relationship with the royal family that the latter funded the establishment of *Abantu-Batho* in 1912. It also helped that he had developed a close personal friendship with Prince Malunge, an influential Swazi royal who had forged a close relationship with the emergent black nationalist movement in South Africa and was a key supporter of the founding of the SANNC.

In order to understand the circumstances that drove the royal family to seek Seme's legal services, it is necessary to glance at the history of Swaziland, in particular the late nineteenth century. In 1932, Seme wrote of the Swazi nation's history in glowing terms, observing that the 'birth and growth of the Swazi Nation is a romance most worthy of the inspiration of great pens and writers'. In the same vein, Seme stated: 'the pages of such a history if it were written would shine like the starry heavens with immortal glory displaying as they must the portraits and wonderful adventures of noble men, of kings and queens whose lives, though unwritten, will never be forgotten, on these hills, in all ages to come'.[16] Seme may have had in mind a king such as Dlamini I, leader of the Embo-Nguni group that eventually settled in what is today known as Swaziland, or perhaps Mswati I, who is considered to be the founder of the Swazi nation. Like other tribes in southern Africa, the Swazis were greatly affected by the upheavals brought about by the rise of Shaka at the start of the nineteenth century. At the helm was Sobhuza I who had become Swazi king in 1815, the year before Shaka installed himself as king of the Zulus. Sobhuza was succeeded by his son, Mswati II, who, at the age of sixteen, became king in 1840. His quarter-century reign saw the area controlled by the Swazis significantly expand, 'spreading from Pongola in the south, north-westward through what is now Piet Retief to Lake Chrissie, and from thence to Machadodorp and the Crocodile River'.[17] For this reason, Mswati II has been described as the 'greatest of the Swazi fighting kings'.[18] The Swazi kingdom reached its zenith during Mswati II's reign, but its success was not to last.

When Mswati II died in 1868 he was succeeded by his son, Ludvonga II, whose reign lasted only four years, as he passed away in 1872. Ludvonga was succeeded by his half-brother, Mbandzeni, also known as Dlamini IV, who became king in 1875 after a protracted succession struggle. Mbandzeni's reign proved to be the most challenging in the history of Swaziland, and his legacy forged the relationship between Seme and the Swazi royal family.

This period in Swaziland's history, variously described as a tragedy and a catastrophe, was absent from Seme's enthusiastic description of the country.

The reign of Mbandzeni was marred by the granting of substantial land, mineral and monopoly concessions to whites, which almost robbed his subjects of their rights. To be sure, Mbandzeni did not invent the practice of giving away land in the form of concessions to white people. Historians have noted that it was Mswati II who first granted a huge tract of land in southeast Swaziland to Conrad Vermaak in the late 1860s. By the king's calculations he was establishing a defence against possible attacks from Zulus in the south.[19] It was during the reign of Mbandzeni, however, that the practice of granting concessions reached a level described as 'without parallel'.[20] The first group of white people to seek concessions was made up of farmers from the Transvaal who sought winter grazing for their livestock. Ignatius Maritz and Johan Ferreira from the district of Utrecht were two such farmers who in late 1877 were granted a concession of land by Mbandzeni; so large was it that they were able to subdivide the land into farms where about 400 people were able to settle. These farmers established their own small state on land that came to be known as Klein Vrijstaat.[21]

The discovery of gold in Barberton in 1882 drew the attention of British prospectors who then rushed to Swaziland to seek mineral concessions from Mbandzeni. As in the case of land and grazing concessions, Mbandzeni and his councillors allocated mineral concessions with alacrity. And the greater the number of land and mineral grants, the more fortune seekers arrived. In exchange for the grants, the king was promised miserly annual payments in cash or in kind – and sometimes the promises were not even honoured. In order to understand the scale and injustice of the concessions given by Mbandzeni, it is instructive to examine a few examples.

A particularly controversial concession was the one granted by Mbandzeni to John Thorburn in December 1888. The terms of the concession included the following:

Be it hereby made known that I, Umbandine, King and Paramount Chief of the Swazi Nation, acting with the full consent of my Council, do hereby grant, assign, and make over unto John Thorburn, his heirs, executors, administrators, and assigns the sole, full, free and exclusive right to prospect, mine, dig, search or otherwise explore for gold or other minerals or precious stones, on all such pieces, parcels, plots, or portions of ground or country in this my kingdom of Swaziland as have not up to the date hereof been granted, assigned, or apportioned as mineral Concessions or rights, and further, the sole, full, free and exclusive right of refusal of all such Concessions, mineral or otherwise, as may from time to time from the date hereof be abandoned or forfeited by present holders, the said John Thorburn, in each and every instance abiding by the conditions laid down by the working and rental of such Concession or Concessions, unless I, the said Umbandine, or my successors, agree to the modification of the same, and the said John Thorburn and his aforesaids, on discovering gold, or precious stones, or minerals of any description on or in any parcels or plots of ground or country which are by these presents made over to him or them, or which may from time to time, either by forfeiture, abandonment, or non-compliance with document or agreement, become property of the said John Thorburn, or his aforesaids, shall have sole, full, free and exclusive right to treat the same by machinery or otherwise, according to the usages of mining in all its branches, and for the sole and exclusive benefit of the said John Thorburn and his aforesaids, to whom shall belong the full and undivided profits thereof.

This concession was given to John Thorburn for the period of fifty years, renewable for a further fifty years. For his bounty Thorburn promised Mbandzeni the following: 'the said John Thorburn or his aforesaids shall yearly pay me or my successors in office the sum of one hundred pounds sterling for each and every Concession'. Furthermore, 'the said John Thorburn and his aforesaids hereby agree to pay to me or my successors in office a bonus of 3 000 pounds sterling on the completion of the erection of the first stamping machinery or battery on any of the mineral Concessions granted to him and aforesaids by virtue of this document'.[22]

In addition to the mineral concessions, Thorburn was granted the right to 'divert water races, dig and construct water races, build houses and workshops, and cut timber on each and every piece of ground on which he or his aforesaids may by virtue of these presents mine or dig for precious stones'. Thorburn or his 'aforesaids' were also granted mineral rights 'over each and every portion of this country which has not at the date and signing hereof been granted for mining purposes', as well as rights over 'all Concessions, whether mineral or otherwise, abandoned or forfeited by the original holders, their heirs, executors, administrators and assigns, of the said John Thorburn'. King Mbandzeni made a commitment that neither he nor his successors would grant mineral or other rights over and above those granted to Thorburn. Moreover, John Thorburn alone was permitted to dispose of those rights, as he pleased. Finally, the concession contained this clause: 'in making this grant or Concession I do not alienate any part of my dominion, but reserve to myself and successors the sovereignty of the country'. The agreement was signed at Embekelweni Kraal on 22 December 1888; the signatories were King Mbandzeni, Tekuba, Umjebeka, Jobbe and Helema (who signed with an X), and the witnesses were T.B. Rathbone and Allister M. Miller. This came to be known as the Unallotted Lands Concession.

In large measure, the Unallotted Lands Concession was typical, particularly with regard to its highly technical language. Indeed, it is unlikely that Mbandzeni and his councillors understood half of what they were committing themselves and the Swazi nation to. But in one respect the concession to Thorburn was different: it was broad and extensive, and he was effectively given a large part of Swaziland to mine, which later became a matter of contention. Another concession which would later be contested was the Private Revenue Concession, granted to John R. Harrington in July 1889. Mbandzeni granted Harrington the authority to collect all taxes, fees, rents and dues that were payable by other concessionaires. The first £12 000 collected annually had to be given to Mbandzeni, and the rest was due to Harrington. This concession was, however, expropriated in the early 1900s when the administration of Swaziland fell to the white authorities in South Africa. Expropriation meant that the money promised to Mbandzeni and his successors was no longer paid; as a result, the Swazis fiercely contested the termination of payment.

Several other concessions of various kinds were granted. For instance, through intermediaries the South African Republic acquired concessions for electricity and telegraphs, the construction of canals, railway buffets, land surveying, postal services, customs, and licences, as well as concessions to establish monopolies in certain sectors. Fred Eckersley, for instance, was granted sole and exclusive rights to erect stores, trading stations and hotels, while H.G. Darke and H. Henderson were granted rights to erect canteens. A concession was granted to G. Schwab to 'import any time he wants it in my Country all kinds of Goods from Delagoa Bay or anywhere else without paying for them any kind of Import Duty, or Transit Duty to Derby over the line'.[23] Schwab was to pay nothing for this concession. The

Mercantile Association of Swaziland, in contrast, was granted a concession to erect buildings for trading and farming in exchange for an annual fee of £20. There were some black people who also joined the scramble for Swazi concessions. John Gama, for instance, was granted a concession to supply goods or materials to Swaziland without paying taxes or duties, while Stephen Mini was granted the identical concession.[24] The granting of the same rights to different people, as in the case of Gama and Mini, was so widespread that a Concessions Court had to be established to resolve conflicting claims.

The extensive parcelling of Swaziland to private persons through the instrument of concessions formed the basis for its partitioning between 1907 and 1911. The partitioning began with a proclamation issued by Lord Selborne, British High Commissioner to South Africa at the time, who ordered that each concessionaire had to relinquish one-third of the land that had been granted for reallocation to the Swazis. The proclamation stipulated that the concessionaires would not be compensated for the portion they would lose. It further directed that the remainder of the land would be held in freehold title, which meant that two-thirds of any such land was effectively granted to concessionaires as their private property. All native Swazis who resided on such property were granted a five-year reprieve with the guarantee that during this period they would not be evicted or have to pay money for staying on the property. This proclamation came to be known as the Swaziland Concessions Partition Proclamation of 1907. In addition, various orders were issued stipulating that any land that did not belong to private parties was to be Crown Land, with the exception of the one-third that was set aside for native Swazis.

The 1907 proclamation was explained in detail in a notice issued by W.G. Bentinck, an official in Selborne's office, on behalf of the High Commissioner. Addressed principally to concessionaires, the notice dated 10 October repeats the main clauses contained in the proclamation: one-third of each concessionaire's land would be set aside for use by Swazis; affected concessionaires would not be compensated for their loss; native Swazis who lived on the remaining two-thirds of each concessionaire's land would be given five years' grace after which they either had to vacate the land or enter into some arrangement with the concessionaire to continue living on the property; land that remained after the partitioning between native Swazis and the concessionaires would be declared Crown Land; and finally, concessionaires who held mineral rights would not be affected by the partition, so they could continue mining even if the mineral deposits fell under native land.[25]

A special meeting of the 'Chief Regent and the Councillors of the Swazi Nation' was convened by the Deputy Resident Commissioner of Swaziland in Mbabane, also on 10 October 1907. The purpose of the meeting was to convey the decision of the High Commissioner on the partition of Swaziland. The Deputy Resident Commissioner repeated more or less the same points contained in the notice to the concessionaires. Here again, the terms of partition were not open to discussion, and even less so to negotiation. The difference between the communications lay in the tone, which was extremely condescending and patronising when native Swazis were being addressed. For instance, in explaining the decision not to partition the mineral rights, the Deputy Resident Commissioner said the following:

> The King [of England] does not wish that there should be any trouble or that you should put any difficulties in the path of any white man who wishes to work minerals, for you will see that every mine brings money into the country and is good for the general progress of your country, and that is a thing which everyone wants.

Furthermore, the Swazis were encouraged to accept the one-third proposal as the decision had come from the king after careful consideration. After all, the king of England, the statement read, was 'wise and can see into the future and he knows that his decision is best for you, his children, who cannot see into the future. This is why he has made it, because he cares for all his children, black as well as white.' The statement ended thus: 'It [the proclamation] is his final order, and every word of it must be obeyed'.[26]

In a public speech delivered in Mbabane on 14 May 1909, Lord Selborne, the primary architect of the partition of Swaziland, congratulated himself for having single-handedly conceived and implemented the partition. Contrary to the story sold to the Swazis that the order had come from the wise and caring king of England, Lord Selborne confessed that the idea had originated with him. He took full responsibility, saying: 'If on the whole the things have been badly managed blame me and me only, because I have really had absolute power during that period in Swaziland. I have had that opportunity because I commanded the confidence of the King and H.M. Government.' Selborne justified the partition on the basis that he considered it his duty to protect the interests of the 'weak' Swazis. Furthermore, he had come to the conclusion that the only way to protect the interests of his 'fellow-countrymen' (i.e. white people), and to ensure that they enjoyed the rights received through concessions, was through the 'policy of partition'.[27]

The deputation to England

The five-year grace period whereby Swazis could either become labour tenants on concessionaires' farms or vacate them lapsed in 1913. Left with a mere fraction of their original land, the Swazis faced an acute land shortage not only for settlement but also for sustaining their livelihood. It was at this moment that the royal family enlisted Seme's legal services, thereby becoming involved in the eventual formation of the ANC and the establishment of *Abantu-Batho*. In 1912 Seme drafted a petition for the Swazi Nation Council and Queen Regent Labotsibeni, which was submitted to the British High Commissioner to South Africa.[28] The following year the Swazis dispatched a deputation under the leadership of Prince Malunge, Labotsibeni's son, an uncle to Sobhuza II, and also Seme's close friend. In Barberton the deputation met with the new British High Commissioner, Lord Gladstone, and apprised him of the Swazi claims. It is more than probable that the petition drafted by Seme constituted the basis of their representations to Gladstone.

The Swazis pressed even harder for their claims after the end of the First World War when Seme's role became increasingly prominent. On 29 August 1921 Seme drew up a six-page petition that was signed by Queen Regent Labotsibeni at the Zombodze royal kraal on behalf of the Swazi chiefs and the council of the Swazi nation. The other signatories were Sobhuza II's mother, Lomawa, as well as Lomvazi Nkosi, Nogcogco Nkosi, Sigula Nkosi, Mandanda Mtetwa, Colo Nkambule, Msuduka Nkosi, Jokovu Nkosi and Josiah Vilakazi. The petition outlined the history of Swaziland, focusing on the relationship between the Swazi nation and whites, especially the English.[29] It argued that the independence of Swaziland had always been asserted and promised by various representatives of the British government. In this regard, the petition stated that 'the sovereignty of the King in and over his people and country should be definitely recognised'. The petition also made six specific demands: the Private Revenue Concession that had been taken over by the British-led Swaziland Administration should once again be put under the administration of the Swazi king;[30]

land that had been declared as Crown Land through the 1907 Swaziland proclamation should be returned to the king and the Swazi nation; there should be strict adherence to the terms and conditions stipulated by Mbandzeni when he had granted the concessions, and in cases where the concessions had lapsed, the land should revert to the Swazi nation; the administration of the Swazi National Fund should be vested in the Swazi king and the nation;[31] there should be recognition of the authority and jurisdiction of the Swazi king over all his subjects, those who lived inside the borders of Swaziland as well as those who lived outside;[32] and the king of Swaziland should have joint control with the British-led Swaziland Administration in the revenues and expenditure of Swaziland.

It would be close to five months before Prince Arthur Frederick, successor to Lord Buxton as the British High Commissioner to South Africa, replied to the petition. When he eventually did so, he summarily dismissed all the claims. He then went a step further. He chided the Swazis for referring to Sobhuza II as the 'king' of the Swazis in the petition. He argued that Sobhuza II was not a king but a 'Paramount Chief', and that the title *inkosi* by which Sobhuza – in his view – was addressed by the Swazis was not equivalent to the word king. He went on to declare: 'A Native Chief, like an official of the Government gains more dignity by using a title which is appropriate to his position than by using one which people might regard as high-sounding and pretentious.'[33] He warned the Swazis never again to use the title king.

This rejection by the High Commissioner and his insults directed at the Swazis and their king did not deter them from pressing on with their demands. Indeed, the year 1922 would witness an intensification of such demands. For two days, from 4 to 5 May, Sobhuza and his secretary, Benjamin Nxumalo, together with Seme, met with the Resident Commissioner in Mbabane to ask for permission to send a deputation of Swazis to meet with the British High Commissioner in person after his rejection the previous year. The Resident Commissioner seems to have expressed doubt that such a delegation would make any difference since the High Commissioner had already rejected their claims. On 30 May 1922 Seme wrote the Resident Commissioner a three-page letter in which he requested permission for the Swazis to send their deputation. Seme stated explicitly that he was acting on instruction of Sobhuza II and the Swazi nation, whom he described as his clients. He also made two points that would eventually dominate the discussion. Firstly, the Swazi deputation would have Dr Manfred Nathan, K.C., as its spokesperson and legal advisor at the meeting with the High Commissioner. And secondly, should it not be possible for the deputation to meet with the High Commissioner, or if the High Commissioner dismissed their claims as he had in December 1921, he (Seme) was instructed to seek permission for the Swazi deputation to go straight to England to state its case before the British government. The deputation, Seme stated, would consist of Sobhuza II, Benjamin Nxumalo, Prince Masumpe, and certain Swazi chiefs and councillors. In addition, Mr Ben Boshoff, a solicitor from Amersfoort in the eastern Transvaal, Dr Manfred Nathan, and Seme himself would accompany the deputation as legal advisors. Seme then reminded the Resident Commissioner that the 'non-European members of the deputation' would require passports. He concluded by stating that their request to either meet with the High Commissioner or alternatively sail to England was urgent 'in view of the possibility of a radical alteration in the affairs of Swaziland'. The latter of course referred to the strong possibility that Swaziland might be incorporated into the Union of South Africa – which the Swazis strongly opposed.[34]

Seme's letter was accompanied by another petition from the Swazi nation. There were two points of difference from previous petitions. Firstly, unlike the August 1921 petition, this one was signed by Sobhuza II and not the queen regent. Sobhuza had finally been installed as king. Significantly, he signed himself 'King and Paramount Chief in Council' in defiance of the High Commissioner's warning, though the addition of the title paramount chief may have been a placatory gesture.[35] The second difference, which was substantive, was the addition of four demands. The first was a request for the Swazi deputation to state its case to the High Commissioner in person. The second was an addition to an earlier demand about the King's Private Revenue: the Swazis demanded that money collected as part of the King's Private Revenue during the period November 1899 to February 1906 be paid back to the Swazis, as should all money taken by the British administration in Swaziland. The third addition was that concessions granted by Mbandzeni, but not confirmed by the court established to adjudicate on the concessions, had to be returned to their 'lawful owners, the King and Council of Swaziland'. Finally, the petitioners demanded that certain documents taken by the former South African Republic from Mr Shepstone, one-time advisor to Mbandzeni, which subsequently passed into the possession of the British-controlled Swaziland Administration, and from there to the archives in Pretoria, be returned to the Swazis.[36]

After the May meeting in Mbabane between the Resident Commissioner, Sobhuza II, Nxumalo and Seme, the Resident Commissioner dispatched a memorandum to the High Commissioner informing him about the Swazis' request to present their petition to him in person. In his reply dated 8 June 1922, the High Commissioner expressed willingness to meet with the deputation, but doubted whether any useful purpose would be served by such a meeting if the Swazis still insisted on going to England if not satisfied with his reply. The High Commissioner then addressed what had become a contentious matter: the role of the Swazi legal advisors. While stating that he had no problem with the Swazis seeking legal advice about any matter that concerned them, he objected to lawyers forming part of any delegation. He instructed the Resident Commissioner to 'explain to the Paramount Chief [Sobhuza II] that it is an invariable rule that, when a Native Chief is received by the High Commissioner, he should be accompanied only by his followers and a representative of the Government'.[37] He stated that he would not depart from the rule under any circumstances. The role of the legal advisors, including Seme, would become a hot potato as the saga deepened.

The formal reply to the Swazi petition only arrived on 20 June, via the Resident Commissioner. As expected, their demands were not accepted. That position was communicated verbally to Seme at a meeting on 7 July where the Resident Commissioner informed him that the High Commissioner could not be expected to give an answer any different from the one he had given the previous year. On 13 July Sobhuza II replied, rejecting their answer and proposing that the deputation be allowed to travel to England 'to petition His Majesty for redress'. He also repeated the request for passports that Seme had made in May. Finally, Sobhuza expressed the wish that there would be no objection to the deputation going to England.

With the High Commissioner rejecting their demands and the Swazis insisting on taking the matter further, it became clear that the only solution was to allow the Swazis to travel to England. Desiring an early departure, the Swazis pressed the British High Commission in South Africa for the passports that both Seme and Sobhuza II had requested. On 14 July 1922 Sobhuza wrote to the Swaziland Administration Government Secretary, Mr B. Nicholson, asking for a reply to the passport request. Nicholson duly informed Sobhuza that he could give no indication whether the passports would be granted or not; the High Commissioner first had to indicate whether the Swazi deputation would be allowed to travel to England in the first place. Suspicious of the pressure being exerted by the Swazis, Nicholson wrote to the Resident Commissioner in Mbabane, Mr Honey, saying that he suspected that Seme and Sobhuza II were attempting to send Benjamin Nxumalo and Prince Masumpe to England without the necessary permission being granted by the High Commissioner. His suspicions had been aroused, he wrote, by an encounter he had had with Sobhuza and Seme at the Resident Commissioner's office where Sobhuza had seemed very anxious to have passports for Nxumalo and Masumpe. He suspected that Sobhuza wanted these passports so that the men could sail with the advance party of Dr Nathan and Mr Boshoff, who were meant to leave for England on 28 July. These two lawyers were being sent ahead of the deputation in order to prepare for its visit; Seme was supposed to join them later, together with other members of the deputation.

Nicholson's suspicions proved baseless, however. Sobhuza indicated that his mother, Lomawa, would be installed as queen mother on 7 August, and he wanted to be back from England by that date. Seme had an additional reason though. He confidentially intimated to Nicholson that Dr Nathan, their lead legal advisor, might be appointed an acting judge, which would prevent him from representing the deputation in England.

While the Swazis were pressing for passports, the High Commissioner was occupied with getting approval for the deputation from the Secretary of State for the Colonies in England. The approval arrived in a telegram dated 17 August 1922, with the Secretary of State being none other than Winston Churchill. He expressed willingness to give permission but requested that General Smuts's views on the visit be sought. Smuts was Prime Minister of South Africa at the time, and the South African government had some interest in the matters raised in the petition, particularly the possibility of Swaziland being incorporated into South Africa. Churchill proposed that the Swazi deputation arrive after the reassembly of the British Parliament on 14 November 1922.[38] Then he wrote to the High Commissioner in South Africa informing him about a request for a meeting which he had received from Dr Nathan and Mr Boshoff, and seeking advice. The answer he received was apparently not supportive of the meeting, as Mr C.T. Davies, an official in Churchill's office, informed the two lawyers that a meeting with Churchill was not possible because the latter was only to meet with the Swazi deputation.

As things turned out, the Swazi deputation did not meet with Churchill when it eventually arrived in England in late December. Just two months before, in October, Prime Minister Lloyd George had resigned his position, with the result that other ministers, including Churchill, had also resigned. Sobhuza was informed of this development in an urgent telegram sent to him by Mr Honey. Sobhuza was advised to postpone the trip until a new government had been formed. The Swazis noted the delay but pressed ahead with arrangements. In fact, during that time there was a lot of correspondence between the Swazis and the Resident Commissioner's office about the funding of the trip. The Swazis decided to collect money from their subjects, but they apparently failed to collect the required amount. As a result they asked the Resident Commissioner's office in Mbabane to use the balance of the Land Fund to pay for the expenses of the trip. The fund had been established by Queen Regent Labotsibeni to buy land for settlement by Swazis after the partition of Swaziland; Prince Malunge, who had oversight of the fund, requested the Resident Commissioner's office to assist with its administration. When Sobhuza requested access to the fund, the Resident Commissioner refused, arguing that the Swazis should first declare the amount they had collected from their subjects, and show that there had not been any wasteful expenditure.[39] The decision infuriated Sobhuza, who conveyed the Swazi Nation Council's regret at the refusal to transfer the administration of the Land Fund to the Swazis to enable them to finance their trip to England.[40] Sobhuza contended that the Land Fund was not governed by any proclamation, and that it was a response to the Swazi Nation Council's request for voluntary contributions from Swazi subjects. It was incomprehensible to him that the British administration in Swaziland was now refusing to hand over the administration of the fund to the Swazis. After much haggling over the matter, and after Sobhuza accounted for the expenditure of money collected from his Swazi subjects, the Resident Commissioner eventually relented, allowing the Swazis to use the Land Fund to finance their trip.

The Swazi delegation was finally ready to sail to England. Their bookings with the Union-Castle Mail Steamship Company were done, and the departure date was 15 December 1922. The departure point was the city of Cape Town, South Africa, though it was decided to travel via Johannesburg and spend a few days there beforehand. The names of the members of the Swazi delegation had already been communicated by Sobhuza II in a letter to the Resident Commissioner dated 23 September 1922. They were: Sobhuza II, Chief Mandanda (chief *induna*), Chief Jabane (son of King Mbandzeni), Lozishina Hlope (member of the Swazi Nation Council), Ben

Nxumalo (member of the Swazi Nation Council and private secretary to Sobhuza II), Chief Ndabezimbi Fakudze (member of the Swazi Nation Council) and Pixley ka Isaka Seme (legal advisor to the Swazi Nation Council).[41] Dr Manfred Nathan and Mr Ben Boshoff were already in England as the advance party. As the departure date drew closer, the Swazis amended the list. The final list consisted of Sobhuza II, Chief Mandanda Mtsetfwa, Prince Msundvuka Dhlamini (who appears to have replaced Chief Jabane), Prince Jaha, Lozishina Hlope, Benjamin Nxumalo, Amos Zwane (who joined as Sobhuza's physician) and Seme.[42] There were two white officials who also went along: the Assistant Commissioner of Police, Major Gilson, and the Resident Commissioner, Mr Honey.

The deputation left Cape Town on 22 December, seven days later than initially communicated. By 10 January 1923 they had already arrived, and that same morning they had a brief meeting with the new Secretary of State for the Colonies, the Duke of Devonshire. The latter was accompanied by Dr W. Ormsby-Gore, Parliamentary Under-Secretary of State for the Colonies; Sir James Masterton Smith, Permanent Under-Secretary of State for the Colonies; Mr C.T. Davies, Assistant Under-Secretary of State for the Colonies; Mr J.F.N Green, Assistant Secretary; and Mr S.M.G Honey, Resident Commissioner of Swaziland. Major Gilson acted as interpreter for the Swazi deputation. From the records it appears that the legal advisors, including Seme, were not present. The discussion did not immediately dwell on the substantive matters contained in the Swazi petition. Sobhuza and the Duke of Devonshire exchanged pleasantries and the Swazi delegation handed over its petition.[43] The substance of the petition was only discussed twelve days later at a meeting with Ormsby-Gore at the Colonial Office. The legal advisors, Nathan and Seme, joined that meeting, though a third advisor, Mr Bernard Alexander, mentioned in the records, comes as a surprise.[44] Major Gilson again acted as interpreter. The meeting went through all the issues raised in the petition, with Ormsby-Gore leading the discussion and Nathan largely speaking on behalf of the Swazi delegation. During the course of the discussion Ormsby-Gore expressed surprise that the delegation had not raised the question of the transfer of Swaziland to South Africa. Nathan's reply was that he had gathered from a source in the South African government that the question of Swaziland's incorporation into South Africa was not an urgent matter, and consequently it was not urgent for the Swazis either, despite its inclusion in their petition. The meeting ended with Ormsby-Gore promising to relay issues raised to the

Secretary of State for the Colonies, who would in turn communicate a formal reply to the delegation.[45]

The Duke of Devonshire presented his reply at a meeting held on 31 January. The reply addressed each of the Swazi claims, which were all rejected. For instance, on the matter of the King's Private Revenue, the Duke stated that the decision taken by the British-controlled Swaziland Administration was satisfactory to him, and the matter was closed. On the issue of concessions, the duke argued that no good purpose could be served by acceding to the Swazi petition. On practically every point the Swazi claims were rejected. The deputation returned to Swaziland empty handed, and it was back to square one.

Aftermath

The trip to England was a huge disappointment for the Swazis. It did not help matters that when they returned there was much quibbling about expenses incurred on the trip. One expense was clothes shopping in London, and items bought included pants, boots, vests, ties, gloves, coats and suits. Some members of the deputation also bought alcohol, and all in all over £770 was spent.[46] While each member had made purchases, the focus of the dispute was the three items of clothing bought by Seme, a suit and two shirts. White officials in the Resident Commissioner's office in Mbabane as well as in the High Commissioner's office in Pretoria justified their focus on Seme on the basis that he was not a member of the deputation, but only its legal advisor, and was therefore liable for these expenses. Sobhuza acknowledged that Seme had indeed incurred the costs for the suit and two shirts and promised to talk to him about settling the account.[47]

Dr Manfred Nathan also called, demanding to be paid for the legal services he had provided to the deputation during the England trip. Nathan was so exasperated about the failure of the Swazis to pay him that he resorted to seeking assistance from the Resident Commissioner in Swaziland. In a letter dated 21 May 1924 Nathan stated that he was still owed over £967, of which £81 was for early consultations with Seme. He claimed that the Swazis had only paid him £100 since their return from England. He also informed the Resident Commissioner that Seme had recently written him a letter asking for a statement of balance due, which he had submitted. And Sobhuza II had also sent him a telegram promising that the account would be settled.[48] But nothing had come of those promises. This led Nathan to accuse Sobhuza of 'constant breaches of faith', which in his view indicated that he had no intention of paying him. His letter became even more acrimonious as he claimed that Sobhuza and Seme had on various occasions informed him that money to defray the expenses of the trip was being collected from the Swazi people. The failure to pay him showed that 'the money must have been misapplied'. Nathan requested the Resident Commissioner to call Sobhuza 'to account', adding, 'I venture to suggest further, that the Swazi people also have an interest in requiring Seme, as their attorney, to explain the manner in which their funds have been expended'. This was an apparent insinuation that Seme had either badly managed the funds or misappropriated them, though no evidence was put forward.[49]

The Resident Commissioner's reply to Nathan's request was unsympathetic. He said that the Swaziland Administration could not be expected to be sympathetic to his plight because it was unaware of what the Swazis owed him in the first place. In any event, the Resident Commissioner contended, Nathan should have insisted on some reliable guarantee that he would be paid before rendering his services to the Swazis. Furthermore, the Resident Commissioner rejected the allegation that Sobhuza II did not want to pay the fee, arguing instead that it was probably a question of means.[50] Despite his stated disinterest in assisting Nathan, the Resident Commissioner nevertheless decided to summon Sobhuza to his office to discuss Nathan's account. And so, on 15 April 1925, the Government Secretary wrote to Sobhuza II, requesting him to bring papers relating to the accounts of Mr Alexander Bros (probably Mr Ben Boshoff) and Dr Nathan.[51] It is unclear, however, whether Nathan's account was finally settled by the Swazis.

Sobhuza II v. Allister Miller and the Swaziland Corporation, Limited

After a meeting of Swazi chiefs to discuss the outcome of the deputation, it was decided that the Swazis should seek redress through the courts. The chiefs decided to focus their case on the Unallotted Lands Concession granted by Mbandzeni to John Thorburn, mainly because it contained a clause which stated that the concessionaire would respect all the prior rights of Mbandzeni's subjects. That concession and its guarantees were confirmed by the Swaziland Concessions Court in 1890. John Thorburn then sold the concession to the Swaziland Corporation Limited, and in 1908 Lord Selborne, British High Commissioner at the time, expropriated the rights contained in the concession, and his successor then compensated the corporation with the farm Dalriach. The corporation transferred part of the farm to Allister Miller, who then evicted some of the Swazis who lived there. The legal question the Swazis brought before court was whether Miller had acted wrongfully in evicting the Swazis who lived on that land, and whose ancestors had lived there for generations.[52]

When the matter was brought before a Special Court of Swaziland, Seme represented Sobhuza II and the Swazis, while Allister Miller was represented by Mr A. Mallin. The judge was Advocate S.T. Mourice, K.C., of South Africa, who was assisted by two officials of the Swaziland Administration.[53] The decision of the court was that the 1907 Land Partition Proclamation had nullified any rights to the land held by the Swazis, and that the British government had not exceeded its powers by compensating the Swazi Corporation Limited with the farm on which the Swazis were living.[54] So the Swazis lost the case, and their opponent, Allister Miller, was awarded costs.

The Swazis did not take the decision lying down. They decided to appeal to the Privy Council in London. Once again, it fell upon Seme to prepare the case and to enlist support from lawyers in Britain. In order to properly prepare for the appeal, Seme needed to be in London. And that was when the trouble started. His passport had expired and he needed it renewed by the South African authorities. Accordingly, on 25 June 1924 Seme wrote to the Secretary for Native Affairs informing him that he was the holder of passport number 46868/11 and was applying for its renewal. Instead of replying to Seme, the Secretary wrote to the Native Commissioner at Amersfoort seeking a recommendation regarding the renewal of the passport, and also seeking information about whether Seme would be able to maintain himself in London for the eighteen months if his passport were to be renewed and he was permitted to travel. It is unclear what the Native Commissioner's recommendation was, but the magistrate of the Wakkerstroom district in the eastern Transvaal where Seme's legal practice was located counselled against renewing Seme's passport. He claimed that Seme lived mostly in Swaziland and had no fixed address in South Africa. He further opined that Seme's financial position 'must be hopeless as he has to pay me approximately 750 pounds on behalf of certain natives at Daggakraal'. The magistrate suggested that Seme's renewal application was an attempt to run away from his debt.[55] The magistrate's letter struck a chord with the Secretary for Native Affairs, who then wrote to his colleague, the Secretary for the Interior, recommending that Seme's passport not be renewed in view of 'the information given by the Magistrate'.[56] On that basis, Seme's passport was not renewed and he was duly informed of the decision.[57]

In view of the fact that the rejection of Seme's application endangered the Swazi appeal against the judgment of the Swaziland Special Court, Sobhuza stepped forward and issued a guarantee that he would be personally responsible for Seme's upkeep while in London. This persuaded the South African government to renew Seme's passport in November 1924. Following this, Seme, together with Prince Jaha of Lundzi, sailed to England to prepare for the case.[58] In London Seme enlisted the services of E.F. Hunt, a respected lawyer, who in turn instructed A.C. Clauson, K.C., and Horace Douglas to lead the proceedings at the Privy Council. Somewhat surprisingly, the respondents, Allister Miller and the Swaziland Corporation Limited, were represented by the United Kingdom Attorney General Sir Douglas Hogg, K.C., and H.M. Giveen, both of whom had been instructed by the Treasury Solicitor. It is unclear how the British government came to be so involved in a matter that concerned private parties. What was clear, however, was that the Swazis were paying for their own legal costs while those of Allister Miller and the corporation were being paid by the British Treasury.

The case came before the Privy Council on Tuesday 2 March 1926 – earlier than the Swazi lawyers seem to have expected since their lead lawyer, A.C. Clauson, was unable to represent them and Horace Douglas led the argument on their behalf. Presiding over the proceedings was the Lord Chancellor, who was supported by Lords Haldane, Phillmore, Parmoor and Blanesburgh. When the judges inquired about Mr Clauson's whereabouts, Douglas explained that they only learnt of the date of the hearing the day before, and by then their lead lawyer had already committed himself to another case.[59] With several legal points being extensively canvassed and debated, the judges only delivered their judgment a month later, on 15 April. The decision was delivered by Viscount Haldane, with the full bench present. The court's decision was devastating to the Swazis. The final paragraph included the following: 'Their Lordships will humbly advise His Majesty that this appeal should be dismissed. As the question involved is concerned with constitutional issues and is of far-reaching public interest, they will advise, following precedents in other cases, that there should be no costs of the appeal.'

The judges dismissed the argument that the British government had no powers over Swaziland apart from those it held under 'the conventions and those which it acquired by the conquest of the South African Republic'. The court decided that the 1907 Partition Proclamation gave the High Commissioner power to acquire land and deal with it in the manner he deemed fit, including compensating the Swaziland Corporation Limited with a farm when its concession was expropriated. Furthermore, the court decided that the High Commissioner acted under powers derived from the Foreign Jurisdiction Act, which could not be 'questioned in a Court of law'. Finally, it decided that the 'Crown could not, excepting by statute, deprive itself of freedom to make Orders in Council, even when these were inconsistent with previous Orders'.[60]

The court's decision was relayed by the Resident Commissioner who called the Swazis into a meeting and read them the judgment. Afterwards he reportedly said that 'the laws of the King [of England] must be obeyed and cannot be questioned' and ended with the statement: 'The case has now been dealt with by the King's highest court from which there can be no appeal and that judgment is final.'[61] The Swazis had reached the end of the road. And for Seme, the decision was undoubtedly devastating as the Swazi case had become the main preoccupation of his life. He had hoped that there might be a chance of winning on appeal, but this was not to be. Nevertheless, this setback did not stop Seme from fighting alongside the Swazi nation on other battlefields.

Swazi tribes of the eastern Transvaal

One of Seme's major preoccupations was to secure land for Swazi tribes who lived in the eastern Transvaal. This had been a burning issue for the Swazis ever since the 1881 Pretoria Convention signed by the British government and the South African Republic. A key aspect was the delimitation of boundaries of the South African Republic, the Boer republic in the Transvaal. In defining the eastern side of that boundary the borders of what constituted Swaziland on its western side were also affected. After the delimitation was concluded, important royal kraals in areas such as Carolina, Barberton and Ermelo were incorporated into the Transvaal. Article 22 of the convention made provision for the establishment of a Native Location Commission whose mandate would be to reserve land for settlement by what the convention termed 'Native tribes'. According to the understanding of the Swazis, they were included among these tribes.[62]

When the 1913 Natives Land Act reserved certain areas for settlement by black people only, the Swazi royal family took up the matter of Swazis who had settled in the eastern Transvaal. In a letter addressed to the Resident Commissioner in 1918, Queen Regent Labotsibeni identified Voor-Slag, a strip of land running from Barberton in the north to the Pongola River, as an area for Swazi settlement.[63] Her entreaties to the South African government failed, with the authorities arguing that the area in question was for settlement by white people notwithstanding the fact that historically it was part of Swaziland.

Some fourteen years later, in 1932, the matter was taken up by Seme. He wrote and was also signatory to a petition on behalf of ten Swazi chiefs from the districts of Barberton, Carolina and Ermelo; according to the petition, these chiefs represented a population of about 60 000 Swazis. The petitioners were Chief Mhola Dhlamini, hereditary chief of Mjindini royal kraal, which then fell under Glentrope Farm; Chief Maguba Shongwe, hereditary chief of the Shongwe tribe in Barberton; Chieftess-Regent Monile Dhlamini, hereditary chief of Mekemeke royal kraal in Barberton; Chief Lugedhlane Ngomane, hereditary chief of Mjajane in Barberton; Chief Hoyi Ngomane, hereditary chief of Ngomane tribe in Barberton; Chief Maqekeza Ngomane, hereditary chief of the Ngomane section in Barberton; Chief Mbuduya Mahlalela, hereditary chief of Lomahasha in Barberton; Chief Myomo Ntiwane, regent of the Ndwandwe section in Barberton; Chief Maquba Dhlamini, hereditary chief of Embhuleni royal kraal in Carolina; and Chief Bashele Nhlapo, hereditary chief at Ermelo. The petitioners also invoked the 1881 Pretoria Convention. They contended that in fixing the boundary between the Transvaal and Swaziland, the convention had incorporated what were historically Swazi areas into the Transvaal, and failed in its promises to reserve land for them. They therefore demanded: 'it is now time that justice and equity be accorded to these Swazi tribes (your humble Petitioners) with reference to the creation of fair and suitable Native Areas for their occupation, due regard being had to the actual occupation of such tribes'. The petition was dated 25 March 1932, with Seme described thus: 'Attorney for Petitioners and President African National Congress'.[64]

Though nothing substantive resulted from the petition, Seme was not discouraged. In July 1936 he took the matter up with Sobhuza and wrote that he wished to pay him a visit to discuss how it might be handled. What seems to have encouraged Seme was the 1936 Native Trust and Land Act, which promised to set aside more land for black settlement. Mentioning that the South African government was having land surveyed, Seme informed Sobhuza: 'We are coming in for a big slice in the Barberton District but it appears that we are not getting our claim recognised in Carolina and Ermelo.' The time was right, he said, to remind the Minister of Native Affairs of the land claim by the Swazi chiefs from the eastern Transvaal. He recommended, furthermore, that an application be made for the establishment of a Native Council for the Swazi chiefs in the eastern Transvaal in terms of the Native Affairs Act of 1920. Though wishing to make that application on their behalf, Seme told Sobhuza that he first wanted to discuss the matter with him.[65]

At first glance Seme's request for permission to meet with Sobhuza seems strange, given the close relationship that existed between the two men. Yet Seme, who had a home in Swaziland at the time and met with Sobhuza fairly regularly, had good reason for writing this formal letter. Prior to the letter, Sobhuza had been summoned to a meeting with the Resident Commissioner in Mbabane on 6 July 1936. The Commissioner complained that Seme had visited the Pigg's Peak area, met with chiefs there, and returned to the Transvaal with Induna Peme. The Commissioner was concerned that the reason for Seme's visit had not been explained to him. Sobhuza expressed regret that Seme had not notified the white authorities about his visit, and went on to explain that Seme was meeting the chiefs in connection with the petition of the Swazis in the eastern Transvaal. Sobhuza also explained that Induna Peme was his representative whom he had appointed to accompany Seme when meeting the chiefs, as dictated by protocol. He then promised to ensure that the white authorities and everyone concerned would be informed whenever Seme planned to meet with the chiefs.[66]

Clearly, Seme's latest letter to Sobhuza II had been written to placate the Resident Commissioner's office. This is evidenced by a reply to Seme from A.G. Marwick, the Resident Commissioner in Mbabane at the time, who in a letter dated 16 July 1936 acknowledged receiving a copy of Seme's letter to Sobhuza in which Seme sought permission to visit Sobhuza. Interestingly, instead of Sobhuza himself giving permission to Seme to meet with him, it was Marwick who had 'much pleasure in giving you [Seme] permission to come'. In addition, he asked Seme to call round at his office en route to his meeting with Sobhuza.[67]

A petition on behalf of the eastern Transvaal chiefs was eventually submitted to Marwick on 3 September 1936. Though it was substantially similar to the 1932 petition, it differed in certain respects. The first notable difference was that the covering letter addressed to the Resident Commissioner was on the ANC's letterhead, from the 'President's General's Office, 221 Joubert Street, VOLKSRUST' (Seme was then president of the ANC). This letter contained a startling statement by Seme: '[It was] the desire of the Paramount Chief Sobhuza, II [*sic*] that I should always supply Your Office with a copy of all my communication with the Union Government, with reference to above matter.' This suggests one of two things: either the white authorities in Swaziland were suspicious of Seme's motives, or they wished to be informed in the event of inquiries from Pretoria. Whatever the case, there is no actual evidence of any such demand being made of the Swazi authorities or their legal representatives.

There was also a difference of tone in the 1936 petition, which was far more deferential, if not obsequious.[68] It went so far as to praise the Minister of Native Affairs for 'excellent services', expressing the wish that these 'may long be enjoyed by this country and our Native people over whom Your Honour rules today'. While the chiefs had based their claims in the 1932 petition on the history of Swaziland and how the Swazi areas had been incorporated into the Transvaal in 1881, they changed tack in 1936. This is especially evident in their statement that they 'gratefully accept the declared policy of the Union Government which is envisaged in the recent Native legislation' – namely, the Native Representation Act of 1936 and the Native Trust and Land Act of 1936. They went on to express their support, and praised 'the establishment of the Native Representative Council for the Union and the Local Native Councils under the Native Affairs Act No. 23 of 1920'.[69]

Significantly, these very laws were under fierce attack by most black leaders in South Africa. The Native Representative Act of 1936 in particular was reviled because it disenfranchised black people in the Cape Province. The Native Councils established by the Native Affairs Act of 1923 had also been opposed by significant sections of the ANC when the law was passed. It was extraordinary therefore for a sitting ANC president to openly support and praise laws to which the organisation he led was strongly opposed. It cannot even be argued that the views contained in the petition were not those of Seme himself, but rather of the petitioners. Seme had signed the petition in his capacity as president general of the ANC, and not as the petitioners' attorney: he had been struck off the roll in September 1932, and was no longer practising as an attorney.

The petitioners based their motivation for land on the Native Trust and

Land Act in particular. In point number 6 of the petition they stated the following:

> That Your Petitioners humbly pray herein that Your Honour may be pleased to meet Your Petitioners personally in order to receive their gratitude for the provisions of land already made for them under the First Schedule of the Native Trust and Land Act of 1936, and during such a Conference to properly consider together the status of the three Royal Kraals, on the eastern Transvaal, being as they are the inalienable property of the Paramount Chiefs of Swaziland and its followers the original tribes and subjects of the late Republic of the Transvaal.

Point number 10 stated:

> That Your Petitioners humbly pray that Your Honour may be pleased to establish one General Native Council for the Swazis, in the Transvaal so as to include all the Swazi tribes residing on the Transvaal-Swaziland borders in the Union, namely Your Petitioners and the Swazi Chiefs and tribes in the Districts of Ermelo and Piet Retief. The said General Swazi Native Council to be under the Chairmanship of a senior officer of the Department [of Native Affairs] appointed by the Minister or any other law.[70]

The petition was signed by the same chiefs who had signed the 1932 petition; Seme also attached his signature, though of course this time he did not add 'attorney'. The obsequious tone of the petition and its support for the reviled laws did not win the petitioners the land they sought. But the failure to elicit a positive response did not discourage the Swazis from taking up the issue again in the late 1930s. In 1939 Sobhuza was still writing letters and petitions, pleading the same case.[71] And as he had done for decades, Seme was right there, supporting the Swazi cause.

* * *

The history of Swaziland in the first half of the twentieth century is closely linked with Seme's labours on behalf of the Swazi nation. It is therefore unsurprising that he was popularly known as the Swazi nation's attorney. Indeed, his involvement and dedication to Swazi causes balance his more pedestrian record as ANC president. In 1932 Seme wrote that the history of the country, its customs and its people was a romance that should inspire great pens; it was a romance that certainly seems to have lured Seme to dedicate himself to Swaziland's greatest cause, the return of the land it had lost in the late 1800s. He felt keenly the injustice of that loss, so much so that he wrote to Alain Locke about the Swazi struggle for land, contending that this struggle was about the freedom of the African people. It was probably his greatest disappointment that he did not live to see Swaziland gain its independence.

Seme's involvement in Swaziland went beyond politics, however. He developed a deep friendship with the royal family, with Prince Malunge in particular, and from his relationship with Mbandzeni's daughter, Princess Lozinja, a son was born. In 1921 Seme assisted Sobhuza with the purchase of six stands in Sophiatown, Johannesburg, and helped him to buy a house that had formerly belonged to Solomon ka Dinuzulu.[72] So the relationship between Seme and Swaziland ran deep. In a sense, he was more than just their attorney; he was one of them.

5

Zulu royals

Seme's burgeoning legal career took him also to the house of Senzanga-khona, the Zulu royal family, in whose affairs he soon became involved. Unlike John Langalibalele Dube, who had a much longer history of championing the cause of the Zulu royals, Seme only developed a relationship with the family after his return from his studies overseas. The relationship quickly blossomed, and soon his influence was profound and far reaching. As with the Swazis, the challenges faced by the house of Senzangakhona were daunting. At stake was its continued relevance in the life of the nation that Shaka ka Senzangakhona had forged when he rose to power in the early nineteenth century. For over six decades from the founding of the Zulu kingdom, the royal family had been at the centre of every major event and decision in the life of the Zulu nation. The defeat of the Zulu army at the Battle of Ulundi in July 1879, which was followed by the division of the kingdom into thirteen chiefdoms that in turn led to a devastating civil war, had transformed the kingdom that had humbled the powerful English army at the Battle of Isandlwana: the once mighty Zulu kingdom was a shadow of its former self.[1]

While Seme's initial involvement in the affairs of the Zulu royal house concerned Dinuzulu ka Cetshwayo, a figure who had come to symbolise the fall of the kingdom while at the same time becoming a rallying point for a resurgent Zulu nationalism, his areas of interest soon broadened to concerns over the status and fate of the Zulu nation as a whole. Seme was, in fact, a latecomer in championing Dinuzulu's cause. The persecution of Dinuzulu by the Natal colonial authorities over the Bhambatha Rebellion – commonly known as *impi yamakhanda* – had so angered the black educated class that it had developed into a major political cause.[2] Dinuzulu was involved in neither the planning nor the execution of *impi yamakhanda*, yet on 9 December 1907 he was arrested by Natal colonial authorities who accused him of complicity. He was charged with twenty-three counts of treason.[3] On 3 March 1909 he was found guilty on four counts; these included allowing Bhambatha and Mangathi, the leaders of the rebellion, to stay at his home, as well as harbouring Bhambatha's wife and children at his oSuthu royal kraal. Despite evidence that he himself had paid the poll tax and encouraged others to do the same,[4] Dinuzulu was found guilty and sentenced to four years' imprisonment, as well as being fined a further £100 or twelve months' imprisonment; following this, he was sent to Newcastle prison.

Dinuzulu's conviction, sentence and imprisonment greatly distressed black people across the length and breadth of what became the Union of South Africa in 1910. Most affected, of course, were black people in KwaZulu and Natal, the vast majority of whom regarded him as their king even though the Natal colonial authorities had reduced his status to that of a mere chief. Leading a chorus of protests against the persecution of Dinuzulu was John Langalibalele Dube, who used the pages of his newspaper, *Ilanga lase Natal*, to chronicle the injustices meted out by the authorities against Dinuzulu. So concerned was Dube about Dinuzulu's fate that he organised a petition on behalf of the Zulus; it pleaded Dinuzulu's innocence and requested clemency from the Governor of Natal.[5] For his relentless championing, Dube has been referred to as Dinuzulu's *imbongi* or praise singer.[6] While Dube was waging a campaign on behalf of Dinuzulu through *Ilanga lase Natal*, Alfred Mangena was fighting the same battle through the courts in London, where he was a law student at the time.

When Seme took up the cudgels on Dinuzulu's behalf around 1912, Dinuzulu had already been released and was living in Middelburg in the eastern Transvaal. He had been released on the recommendation of the Natal colonial authorities who wanted him removed from Natal and Zululand where he still enjoyed a strong following and his incarceration was a source of discontent. With the Union of South Africa imminent, the Natal authorities had proposed that Dinuzulu be moved to the Transvaal, away from Zululand and Natal, in exchange for the remission of the remainder of his sentence as well as an annual state payment of £100 for his livelihood and that of family and followers who lived with him in the Transvaal. On 31 May 1910, Prime Minister General Louis Botha approved the recommendation and Dinuzulu is reported to have acceded. So, in 1911 Dinuzulu moved to Rietfontein, a farm approximately thirteen kilometres from Middelburg. He was accompanied by several of his wives and children, as well as his *Ndunankulu* (chief counsellor or advisor), Mankulumana ka Somaphunga Nxumalo of the Ndwandwe.[7] It was while he was living at Rietfontein that concerns about Dinuzulu's health were first raised, concerns that would eventually draw Pixley Seme to the Zulu king.

Dinuzulu's health

For at least two years before Seme arrived on the scene, Dinuzulu's health had been deteriorating. When he took a turn for the worse towards the end of 1911, Dinuzulu sought approval from the Department of Native Affairs to allow him to visit Dr Snyman, a physician from Kroonstad in the Orange Free State. It took more than fifteen months for the department to reply. In November 1912 Dinuzulu became ill again and consulted several doctors in Middelburg.

One of the doctors who became involved was Johannesburg-based Dr Godfrey, who, at Seme's suggestion, visited Dinuzulu in Middelburg on 17 November 1912. In his 'Report as to Chief Dinuzulu's Health', Dr Godfrey stated that Dinuzulu was suffering from 'great bodily pain' and that he had 'no hesitation in coming to the conclusion that the Chief was and is suffering from a Constitutional disease, commonly known as "Rheumatic Gout" (osteo-aethritis [sic])'. The Middelburg district surgeon who examined Dinuzulu on 13 October 1913 diagnosed him as suffering from kidney failure, which led to 'urenic poisoning and delirium which may culminate in coma and *exhaustion*'.[8] Whether the district surgeon's diagnosis reflected an additional condition to what Godfrey had diagnosed almost a year earlier is difficult to judge. In any event, Godfrey's opinion in November 1912 was that the use of medication to relieve Dinuzulu's pain was 'utterly useless', as his patient's condition continued to deteriorate.

Dr Godfrey suggested an alternative course of treatment. He proposed that Dinuzulu be given a course of 'MINERAL WATER TREATMENT', which in his view was beneficial for people suffering from gout and rheumatism. Dinuzulu should be treated at 'some Mineral spring', such as Carlsbad in Germany.[9] The treatment, at £4 per consultation, required financial resources that the patient did not have, and so Dr Godfrey requested Seme to assist him in his attempts to relieve Dinuzulu's suffering.[10]

Dr Godfrey's report was sent to Seme on 19 November 1912.[11] The same report was also published in two Johannesburg-based newspapers, the *Sunday Post* and the *Transvaal Leader*. It is noteworthy that in the several letters that Seme and Godfrey subsequently wrote to government authorities regarding Dinuzulu's health, both mentioned the publication of the report.

The motivation for publication was probably to force the government's hand in permitting Dinuzulu to receive treatment in Germany – the report itself was eventually sent to the Governor General in March the following year.

In the meantime, Seme sprang into action. On 19 December 1912 – a month after he received Dr Godfrey's report – Seme wrote to Prime Minister Botha. He began by saying that Botha may 'have heard of ex-Chief Dinuzulu's illness which has been giving his relatives and friends a good deal of anxiety'. Seme went on to state that he was writing in his capacity as Dinuzulu's legal advisor. He also explained that, acting on Dinuzulu's instructions, he had sent Dr Godfrey to Middelburg to examine him. Furthermore, once Dr Godfrey had compiled the medical report, Seme had passed it on to Dinuzulu's relatives and friends, who desired government approval for the recommended treatment. The family would not trouble the government with the financing of the trip – instead, it would 'find the money immediately', which, in all likelihood, would be raised from Dinuzulu's former subjects in Zululand. However, what the family *was* asking, Seme made clear, was that government not put obstacles in the way of attempts to implement Dr Godfrey's recommendation.[12]

Other than a formal acknowledgement by Botha's private secretary, Dr W.E. Bok, dated 21 December 1912, there was no reply to the letter or its contents.[13] Two months later Seme wrote another letter to the Prime Minister. He complained that it had been eight full weeks since he had written the first letter, and still there was no reply. He informed Botha that Dinuzulu's family and friends had waited patiently for a reply, loyal and sympathetic with regard to the ministerial crisis he faced – a likely reference to the resignation of justice minister General J.B.M. Hertzog from government. But now the family had decided on another course of action, instructing Seme to take up the matter of Dinuzulu's health with the Governor General, Lord Gladstone. The family had also requested Seme to express its gratitude to the Prime Minister for 'all his past favours to the ex-Chief and themselves'.[14] Sensing that the letter might annoy Botha, Seme was quick to explain that the family's decision had been motivated by the urgency of Dinuzulu's health situation and the anxiety it was causing them. Seme also apologised for his 'importunity' in writing the letter, adding that he was acting on instruction from the family.[15]

Seme's second letter to Botha was merely a courtesy, however. On the very same day, he dispatched a letter to the Governor General reporting on

Dinuzulu's failing health and informing the Governor General about his attempts to enlist the government's support via the Prime Minister. Seme told the Governor General that Dinuzulu's trip to Carlsbad could no longer be postponed without risking further deterioration of his health. He pleaded with the Governor General to get assurance from the government that it would not stand in the way of the family's plans to send Dinuzulu to Carlsbad, and gave the assurance that Dinuzulu's friends and family held the government in high regard.[16] In his reply the Governor General made no commitments and merely informed Seme that the matter had been referred to the Minister of Native Affairs. What the Governor General did not mention was that he had written to the Prime Minister to tell him about Seme's letter; it is noteworthy that he made no request to take any action, however.[17] For almost three weeks Botha made no reply, either to Seme's letter or to that of the Governor General.

Botha's silence appears to have infuriated Godfrey, who wrote a passionate and strongly worded appeal to the Governor General on behalf of his patient, Dinuzulu. He stated that his appeal was directed at the Governor General's humanity and Christianity. He accused the Department of Native Affairs of being unconcerned about Dinuzulu's suffering, and charged that the government seemed not to care because Dinuzulu was 'only a kaffir'. This indifference was confirmed by the fifteen-month wait Dinuzulu had had to endure before any response was forthcoming to his request to visit Dr Snyman in Kroonstad. Godfrey suggested that the delay was long enough to guarantee that 'the poor fellow' was 'dead, buried and his body turned to that which we all must eventually, i.e. dust'. In Godfrey's opinion the treatment meted out to Dinuzulu was not deserved even by 'vilest criminal or a prisoner', and the manner in which the entire affair had been handled was 'too painful'. It was a shame that Dinuzulu's treatment was 'perpetrated under the glorious British flag which we are told is an emblem of liberty, freedom, and justice'. Demonstrating his faith in English values, Godfrey stated that England would not condone the manner in which Dinuzulu was being treated by the South African government, and appealed to the Governor General to assist him in preventing the Native Affairs department from standing in the way of Dinuzulu receiving the medical assistance he required.[18] The Governor General simply acknowledged Godfrey's letter and informed Botha's office about it without pressing for any action to be taken in assisting Dinuzulu.

Despite the Governor General's inaction, Seme and Godfrey nevertheless reported to him on all their dealings with the government. When Dinuzulu was eventually permitted to consult Dr Snyman in Kroonstad, Seme dispatched a telegram to the Governor General informing him of the government's approval; so too when Dinuzulu was examined by Snyman. He lodged a complaint that Dinuzulu had been refused permission to travel home via Johannesburg so as to meet Dr Godfrey, and pleaded with the Governor General to persuade the government to grant him the necessary permission.[19] As before, however, the Governor General simply acknowledged the telegram via his private secretary, informing Seme that the matter had been 'referred to His Excellency's responsible advisers', i.e. the South African government.[20]

After a long delay, Botha replied to the Governor General's letters on 20 March 1913. He acknowledged that Dinuzulu had sought government approval to visit Dr Snyman in Kroonstad, and while he conceded that it was 'some time before the request was acceded to', approval had eventually been granted in February. As for the request to visit Carlsbad, Botha stated that Dinuzulu had not made the request for permission; instead, Seme had made representations (as if Seme had not made those representations on behalf of Dinuzulu). Regarding the request to visit Johannesburg en route from Kroonstad – a request that had been strongly made by Godfrey as well as Seme, and which was refused by the Native Affairs department – Botha stated that his government would give permission for Dinuzulu to be in Johannesburg for three days to see Godfrey for a medical check-up; the government was also making arrangements for Dinuzulu's accommodation and stay in the city with the purpose of avoiding the attention of crowds who might gather to see him.[21]

There was a further flurry of correspondence, with Godfrey writing to the Governor General, and the latter forwarding his letters to Botha's office. The correspondence failed to achieve its goal, however, and at no point did the Governor General show his hand as to whether or not he supported the pleas of Seme and Dr Godfrey. That changed on 2 April 1913 when, in a report to Lewis Harcourt, MP and Secretary of State for the Colonies, the Governor General claimed to have heard that Dinuzulu's suffering was 'largely due to excessive drinking and lack of exercise'.[22] While he did not reveal the source of the information, he seemed to believe the allegation. This was despite the fact that at least two physicians, Dr Godfrey and Dr Snyman, had diagnosed Dinuzulu as suffering from rheumatic arthritis and sclerosis. The Governor General also appeared to credit Botha's opinion that should Dinuzulu apply for permission himself, rather than 'others purporting to act in his interests', the government would not turn down his application.[23] The white authorities in South Africa seemed determined not only to dismiss Seme's role as legal advisor, but also to drive a wedge between him and the royal family.

Although the government eventually approved Dinuzulu's request to travel to Carlsbad,[24] in the end, Dinuzulu did not go to Carlsbad, and he died a few months later, in October. Seme's attempts to assist had clearly failed. However, if the government believed that the setback of Dinuzulu's death would discourage Seme from becoming involved in the affairs of the house of Senzangakhona, it was mistaken.

The death of Dinuzulu

The news of Dinuzulu's death on Saturday morning, 18 October 1913, reached Zululand via various sources. One was the Department of Native Affairs in Pretoria, which sent a telegram at 11:48 that very day informing the Natal Chief Native Commissioner that Dinuzulu had died, and requesting him to 'please convey information with suitable message of sympathy to [the Zulu Royal] Household about his death'. The telegram stated that there was likely to be a request by the royal house for Dinuzulu to be buried in Zululand rather than in Middelburg where he had died, with the Native Affairs department expressing no objection to such a request.[25] That same day the message was duly conveyed to the offices of various magistrates in Zululand, the first being those of Vryheid and Nongoma; it was also sent to the District Native Commissioner for Zululand who was based in Eshowe.[26] Most Zululand chiefs – among them Zombode, Nqodi, Muzimubi, Moya and Mchitheki – claimed to have heard the news of the death from Dinuzulu's first cousin, Mnyayiza ka Ndabuko. This got Mnyayiza into serious trouble with the white authorities who were annoyed that he had informed the chiefs without their authorisation. The magistrate of the Nkandla division went so far as to propose that Mnyayiza be called to Pietermaritzburg to explain his action. This was, however, turned down by the Natal Chief Native Commissioner, who said that although he did not agree with Mnyayiza's action, the latter had not broken any law and therefore no steps could be taken against him.[27]

What spread the news of Dinuzulu's death to every corner of Zululand and Natal was a report in *Ilanga lase Natal*. The headline was neutral and simple: '*UDinuzulu Aseko*' (Dinuzulu is no more). But the emotion it unleashed was immediate and powerful. The report stated that the whole of Zululand was in mourning; even though Dinuzulu had died in exile, his followers had always harboured the hope that the government would one day return him to the land of his forefathers, Zululand. The article provided a history of the collapse of the kingdom, and accused Zibhebhu ka Maphitha of conniving with the white authorities in Natal to bring about its destruction. It also decried the fact that Dinuzulu had been blamed for the Bhambatha Rebellion instead of being thanked for saving lives by not taking up arms against those who had imposed the poll tax in the first place.

According to the report, Dinuzulu had been extremely ill in the weeks leading up to his death, and although he had suffered for many years from arthritis and rheumatism, the illness that had led to his demise was *umkhuhlane* (a fever). He had, moreover, begun to lose his mind, and was in great pain from sores in his throat. So ill was Dinuzulu that two doctors had been sent to attend to him. Observing that their medication was not effective, the family had sent for an *inyanga* (traditional healer) from Johannesburg. The newspaper claimed that a few days before his death Dinuzulu had invited Reverend R. Twala to pray for him. It was Twala who had informed *Ilanga lase Natal* that Dinuzulu had become a Christian, and had allegedly developed the habit of asking his children to gather before him to sing his favourite hymn, '*Wazithwala izono zami uJesu*' ('Jesus suffered and died for my sins').[28]

The *Ilanga* report was by John Dube, who also wrote a moving obituary on 31 October 1913. In language both rich and evocative, Dube described the death of Dinuzulu as a great misfortune for the Zulu nation which would forever be poorer for his loss ('*soze sife sigxaza amanzi njengengcuba*'). He then launched into Dinuzulu's *izibongo*,[29] singing his praises:

> *UDlothovu akabhekeki ufana nemisebe yelanga*
> *Umavela ajahe ofana neBhunu lako Pewula*
> *Usifuba singungu, babili bathathu abatsheli bantu*
> *Ithole elimpungampunga lako Msweli loke liwaphule amadoda*
> *Ubhensa bahlabe amanxeba amabili.*

> [The shining Dlothovu who cannot be looked at, like sunrays
> He who gives chase like Paul [Kruger's] Boers
> He who keeps confidences and never reveals secrets

The grey-coloured heifer of Msweli whose strength breaks men
He who bends his back to take two stab wounds.][30]

...

Umasheshe afike njengezulu ukuya kwaNdunu
Ohlasele yedwa njengohlanya
Amadevu ayingoqe ngokugoqa inyoni emhlophe
Usinakanaka sinjengezincwadi zabelungu, bona abathi beziloba babe
  bezinakaza
Umpondo zamila enjeni kazi enkomeni lapha zesabani ...

[He who arrives at Ndunu at lightning speed
He who attacks alone like a madman
He whose curling moustache entraps the white bird
He who brings chaos, like the white men's books that spread confusion
  as they are written
Horns that grow on the head of a dog rather than a cow ...][31]

By the time Dube's obituary was published, Dinuzulu had already been buried. Much had happened between his passing on the morning of 18 October and his burial in the afternoon of 27 October. Dinuzulu's wish that he be buried among his ancestors at Nobamba in the Babanango district of Zululand had been granted by authorities.[32] And so, two days after his death, Dinuzulu's coffin was transported by train from Middelburg through Witbank, where Seme joined it, and on to Glencoe, where the coffin was transferred to a train bound for Vryheid. Accompanying the coffin were Dinuzulu's *Ndunankulu*, Mankulumana ka Somaphunga Nxumalo, as well as Harriette Colenso, Reverend Twala, and other members of Dinuzulu's family, including the wives who had been with him in exile. Harriette Colenso was a friend of the Zulu royal house, having followed in the footsteps of her father, John William Colenso, the Anglican Bishop of Natal, in championing the causes of the Zulu royals, especially those of Dinuzulu.

Dinuzulu's death and the activities surrounding his burial were an extremely sensitive issue for the white authorities in Natal and their agents in Zululand. Despite his long absence, Dinuzulu still had a huge following in Zululand as well as Natal. The Natal authorities feared that his death might be blamed on government, and that this might in turn lead to a revolt. So the authorities both in Natal and Pretoria adopted a deliberate strategy of avoiding any confrontation with Dinuzulu's supporters by providing them with support in the burial preparations. The first step of course was to grant Dinuzulu's wish to be buried among his ancestors at Nobamba in Babanango, and subsequently the authorities covered expenses for transporting his coffin from Middelburg to Vryheid.

The authorities' apprehension on the one hand, and their strategy of offering support on the other, were both in evidence when the funeral party reached Vryheid. The magistrate for the Vryheid division dispatched a telegram to his assistant in Babanango, instructing him to provide two ox-wagons to the funeral party for the last leg of the trip to Nobamba. He also advised the assistant magistrate that he should make it his duty 'to meet them [the funeral party] and keep in touch with Mankulumana and Miss Colenso'. He further instructed that, while a large crowd was undesirable, no person should be prohibited from attending the funeral. He stated that 'reliable' men were required to accompany the funeral party in order to report 'proceedings for information of Government' and to report 'any special or unusual circumstances direct to the Chief Native Commissioner and myself [i.e. the Vryheid magistrate] by wire'.[33] The assistant magistrate complied, and in addition provided ten bags of mealies and a bull for slaughter for the more than 6000 mourners in Nobamba.[34]

The funeral took place in the afternoon of Monday 27 October 1913. It was an emotional affair. *Ilanga* reported that, following Christian rites, a funeral service was conducted by Reverend R. Twala, with an address by John Dube. Other Christian leaders who spoke at the funeral were Reverend Makanya from Durban and Reverend Mndaweni from Babanango. Afterwards, traditional Zulu burial rites were presided over by Mankulumana, Dinuzulu's *Ndunankulu*. Among the rituals performed was sending a group of men to climb down into the grave to receive Dinuzulu's body. Those chosen by Mankulumana to perform that important task were asked to wash their bodies before entering the grave. *Ilanga* gave the men's names as Ngazana ka Hlohloyi, Colwana ka Chakijana, Mankenke ka Mkhosana and Mfihlo ka Mhlambi. The report stated that one of the four men was extremely afraid of being killed after performing the task of receiving Dinuzulu (as was claimed to occur in the burial of a king); so afraid was the man that he trembled inside the grave and exhaled a loud sigh of relief when he climbed out. A man named Ndongeni ka Nkoteni was selected to stand guard over Dinuzulu's grave, bearing the weapon of the late chief.

Dinuzulu's thirty-four wives also participated in the funeral service, and thousands of mourners sang the song 'Cetshwayo ka Mpande':

Uzitulele akaqali muntu okaNdaba
Izwe lonke lonke loku uzitulele
Sidedele siminye abafo
Aho – aho – sidedele abafo.[35]

[The one who holds his peace, provoking no one, son of Ndaba
Even when the whole world begs you to act, you remain peaceful
Allow us to deal with these enemies
Aho – aho to deal with them.][36]

After the funeral rites had been performed, Mankulumana took to the stage to speak about Dinuzulu, the man he had served loyally. Together with Dinuzulu, he had been charged and imprisoned over the Bhambatha Rebellion. When Dinuzulu was banished to Middelburg, Mankulumana was also sent there. He was present at Dinuzulu's deathbed, and was chief organiser of his funeral. What Mankulumana said in his speech would, however, become a source of controversy, as it was subject to different interpretations. The reason for his speaking at the funeral in the first place was in response to the assistant magistrate of Babanango, who had sent the government's message of condolence. In a report addressed to the Natal Chief Native Commissioner regarding proceedings at the funeral, the assistant magistrate claimed that Mankulumana had responded thus to the government's message:

I thank you for the condolence of the Government, and I am grateful that you who are the Magistrate of this district are present. It is you [i.e. 'the Government'] who killed the one we have now buried. You killed his father, and killed him. We did not invade your country but you invaded ours. I fought for the dead man's father; we were beaten. You took our King away, but the Queen sent him back to us, and we were happy. The one whom we now mourn did no wrong. There is no bone which will not decay. What we ask now is, as you have killed the father, to take care of the children. We wish to always have a kraal here to take care of this grave, and we ask you to secure this land so that there may always be a kraal here.[37]

The assistant magistrate now claimed that Mankulumana had ended his funeral speech with the statement: '*a ne na konzo*'. There was much debate in the Department of Native Affairs as to whether Mankulumana's speech was incendiary or not, and what he actually meant by the phrase '*a ne na konzo*' and the word 'kill'. Part of the confusion may be attributed to the translation from isiZulu, and the incorrect spelling of the key phrase '*a ne na konzo*', the correct spelling of which is '*aninankonzo*' (you have no mercy/humanity/compassion). The assistant magistrate's interpretation was contradicted by a *Mercury* report, which found the speech to be conciliatory, and it was this version that was favoured by the Natal Chief Native Commissioner.[38]

Another controversial incident at the funeral involved the selection of Dinuzulu's heir and presumably his successor as chief of oSuthu – and king of the Zulu nation (a position abolished by the white authorities). In the view of the authorities, a united Zulu kingdom had been destroyed and the kingship abolished, but to the majority of Zulus the house of Senzangakhona was still the royal house; Dinuzulu had been their king, and his heir would succeed him as king of all the Zulus. Consequently, the stakes were high regarding the choice of heir. Before the funeral, *Ilanga* reported that Mankulumana had conveyed a message that he would announce Dinuzulu's chosen heir at the funeral.[39] When the time came, Mankulumana revealed Dinuzulu's preference: David Nyawana would be his heir. This was corroborated by Lokothwayo Xulu (also known as Mlokothwa or Hlohla), one of Dinuzulu's closest aides, who claimed that Dinuzulu had confided in him about David Nyawana becoming his heir. Lokothwayo was supported by other aides, including Ndabankulu ka Lukwazi, Zidunge ka Ntshingwayo and Mvingana ka Marolo. On the basis of this information, David was declared Dinuzulu's heir and successor. But he lasted in this position for less than a day. The very next day Solomon Nkayitshana, who was also Dinuzulu's son and a contender for the throne, gave Harriette Colenso a document which he claimed had been written by his late father, nominating him as his successor. It appears that Harriette Colenso was the only person who saw the document and its contents. Convinced by Solomon's claim to the throne, she seems also to have persuaded Seme to support Solomon, though Seme's role in the succession dispute between Solomon and his half-brother David was murky.[40]

The rival claims for heirship caused confusion and dissent among remaining mourners and influential figures in particular. What seems to have encouraged Solomon, and given him an advantage over his rival, was David's apparent unpopularity among the Zulu people – he was allegedly 'a boy of violent temper, and he strikes the people'.[41] Many people were therefore upset at Mankulumana and Lokothwayo's nomination of David. Upon showing the document to Colenso, Solomon was chosen as Dinuzulu's successor and was greeted with the royal salute, '*Bayede!*'

Ilanga reported on the positive sentiments expressed at Nobamba when Solomon was chosen. Its headline, accompanied by a photograph of young Solomon sitting on a chair, announced: '*Use Bekiwe uZulu*'; Solomon was the new king of the Zulus chosen by Dinuzulu and the Zulu nation. In the accompanying report, *Ilanga* stated that one only had to look at the photograph to see that Solomon was the son of a king. It wished him well in his position and repeated the salute '*Bayede!*'[42] It was one thing for the likes of Dube, Seme, Colenso and the Zulu nation to recognise Solomon as Dinuzulu's successor and therefore as a chief or king. But the critical question was whether the white authorities, especially those in Natal, would accord him recognition. And what steps did he need to take, if any, to gain that recognition? The answer to that question would occupy him and his closest advisors for several years.

Solomon and the struggle for recognition

The immediate preoccupation of the authorities, particularly those in Natal, was not Solomon and his selection as Dinuzulu's heir. Their main concern was possible unrest that might erupt in Zululand in reaction to Dinuzulu's death. Anxious that Dinuzulu's followers might blame them for the death, they went to extraordinary lengths to gauge the mood of Zulus in its aftermath. The Natal Chief Native Commissioner dispatched letters to several magistrates in Zululand and parts of Natal requesting reports showing 'what the Natives are saying and doing in connection with Dinuzulu's death'. He also inquired whether the situation was quiet, and requested them to report on anything found to be out of the ordinary.[43]

The reports from the various magistrates were a mixed bag: if the authorities harboured any hope that the Zulus did not support the house of Senzangakhona and its claim to leadership of the Zulu nation, the reports would have been disappointing. The magistrate of Vryheid reported that the rank and file of the native population, as he described the mourners at Dinuzulu's funeral, were in great sympathy and quite supportive of the Zulu royal house. In news that would have discomfited his superiors in

Pietermaritzburg, the Vryheid magistrate similarly reported that 'Dinu-zulu's death is almost universally attributed by Natives to his enforced exile by Government who are blamed for his death as is evidenced by MANKULUMANA'S [sic] bitter speech at the funeral ceremony', though there was no related unrest in his division.[44] On a more encouraging note, the Nongoma magistrate reported that, while most people had initially believed that white people were responsible for Dinuzulu's death, upon lis-tening to Mankulumana, Lokothwayo and Ndabankulu, they had changed their views; instead, some believed he had died from a bowel illness which resulted in him bleeding from his mouth, while others believed that he had contracted a fatal venereal disease from a certain girl. The magistrate also reported that there was an expectation in Nongoma that Solomon would occupy the position of chief.[45] The report of the Mahlabathini acting magistrate echoed the Nongoma report in that the people in Mahlabathini expected Solomon to be appointed to his father's position as chief. They were of the view that if the white authorities were to recognise Solomon as his father's successor, he would need to develop a close relationship with the government. The Mahlabathini acting magistrate then ventured to propose that if Solomon were to be appointed as Dinuzulu's successor, he should be placed under the supervision of three government officials.[46]

Apparently unsatisfied with the reports from the magistrates, the Natal Chief Native Commissioner dispatched 'political messengers' throughout Zululand to gather intelligence about the mood of black people regarding Dinuzulu's death. The leading messenger was Nongejeni Zuma, son of Chief Mnyakanya Zuma of the amaNxamalala in Nkandla.[47] Nongejeni Zuma was assisted by Socwatsha Ngcobo. The report compiled from intel-ligence gathered in Vryheid and Zululand was detailed and extensive. It also included information on what had transpired at Dinuzulu's funeral. The two messengers reported that most chiefs and izinduna were alarmed at the manner in which Solomon had been selected as successor, with some arguing strongly that the selection had not been handled correctly.

In the eyes of the white authorities, the most disturbing aspect of the reports would have been information relating to Solomon, who had been selected as successor to Dinuzulu. The problem of course was that Dinuzulu had been stripped of all his titles by the time he died in October 1913. His position as chief of oSuthu, to which he had been appointed upon his return from exile in St Helena, had also been taken from him following his arrest and conviction over the Bhambatha Rebellion. The oSuthu area, over which he had ruled, was subsequently divided among four chiefs: Mpikanina ka Ziwedu ka Mpande, Muzimubi ka Mnyamana, Mchitheki ka Zibhebhu and Moya ka Mgojana – though the latter was not in fact a chief at the time of Dinuzulu's ousting. Were the white authorities to recognise Solomon as successor to his late father's title as chief of oSuthu, it would have meant taking back the areas allocated to the four loyalist chiefs. The authorities were therefore reluctant to have Solomon reclaim the oSuthu chieftainship.[48]

Their greatest fear, however, was Solomon becoming a rallying point for the revival of the Zulu royal house and the idea of a united Zulu nation. To counter this, the authorities sought to restrict Solomon's movements and his interactions with important constituencies in Zululand. What followed was an intricate game, with Solomon trying to project himself as a Zulu king while working surreptitiously to gain the support of important chiefs on the one hand, and the white authorities taking every step to thwart his ambitions and undermine him in the eyes of the Zulu nation on the other. The Natal authorities were especially concerned that, in his attempts to become king, Solomon would enlist the support of educated people such as Seme. This fear was expressed on various occasions. For instance, in a letter to the Secretary for Native Affairs, the Chief Native Commissioner claimed that it was 'not unreasonable to suppose and to assume that such educated and enlightened natives as Mr John Dube and Mr P. ka I Seme are labouring quietly and diplomatically amongst the Zulu speaking people with the sole object of achieving a complete reunion of the Zulu Nation and thereby a resuscitation and revival of the Zulu Royal House and power'.[49]

The suspicions of the white authorities in Natal were not far-fetched. Seme in particular was actively involved in supporting Solomon. Just a few weeks after Dinuzulu's burial, Seme wrote to Prime Minister Botha's private secretary, Dr Bok, informing him that he would be acting as Solomon's legal advisor, as he had for his father. Seme also informed Bok that Solomon was in Middelburg visiting the farm where his father had died. He reported that Dinuzulu's estate 'both at Middleburg [sic] and in Zululand, was hopelessly embarrassed owing to several debts which the said estate is obliged to meet'. He then asked that a request be made to Botha to allow Solomon to spend five days on the Reef (Johannesburg) on a fundraising mission, and to visit other areas in the eastern Transvaal on his way back to Zululand, also to raise funds.[50] Botha turned down the request. Seme then took it upon himself to visit certain parts of Zululand to raise funds on behalf of Solomon. In December 1913, for instance, he and Mnyayiza ka Ndabuko ka Mpande visited the Piet Retief area that fell under Chief Tunzi ka Ndengezi of the Yende people, to raise money for Solomon's upkeep.[51] Though they were only able to raise about £20, their visit raised the suspicions and ire of the Natal authorities. Upon learning of the two men's visit to Tunzi ka Ndengezi, the authorities sent two police constables, Mpiyonke Xulu and Kleinbooi Madonsela, to observe and report on the activities of Seme and Mnyayiza. Furthermore, Mnyayiza was called to meet with the Chief Native Commissioner in Pietermaritzburg to explain what he and Seme were up to at Chief Tunzi's kraal.

The meeting, held in February 1914, was attended by the Commissioner himself, accompanied by Situnzi Zuma, who is described in the minutes as 'Induna of the Chief Native Commissioner's Office', and Socwatsha Ngcobo, the 'messenger of the office' (i.e. the Chief Native Commissioner's officer). Accompanying Mnyayiza were Nkomo Ndebele, Manzana Msimango and Lokothwayo 'Hlohla' Xulu, a former aide to Dinuzulu. The meeting is significant for the threatening tone adopted by the Chief Native Commissioner, as well as for his view of Seme. The Commissioner began by giving his version of the history of the Zulu kingdom:

> You know that Tshaka reigned before the European occupation, and he was killed by Natives. Dingana fought the White House and was killed by strangers. Mpande, who was under Government's protection died a natural death. Cetshwayo fought with the Government and died on the hills. Dinuzulu also disregarded the Government's orders, and he died elsewhere.

The Chief Native Commissioner then made it clear what route Solomon should follow. 'I want to know what you are doing with this boy, taking him all over the place. It is well that he should be left and taught to respect the Government's authority,' he began, before requesting Mnyayiza and other Zulus to

> induce the boy, Solomon, to respect Government's authority, to look to the Government in every way, to ask Government for anything he requires, and, should he have any complaint, to make it to the Government. But it is wrong to parade him about the country as you

have been doing. I wish to make it quite clear to you that Dinuzulu's son must not be led in the wrong direction as it appears he is being led.

The correct path to be followed, said the Chief Native Commissioner, was the one followed by Mpande. This message was echoed by Situnzi Zuma,[52] who urged Mnyayiza to guide Solomon, who in any case knew the right path since he had been 'brought up amongst the Europeans'. He added that if Solomon followed the white man's laws he would grow up a loyal subject. Perhaps as a demonstration of his loyalty to his employer, the Chief Native Commissioner, Situnzi reminded Mnyayiza and his party that '[p]eople can only hope to prosper by obeying the Government's commands and being loyal to it ... Times are different now to when Tshaka reigned' – a sentiment shared by his companion, Socwatsha Ngcobo.

But the Commissioner had another agenda, and he proceeded to counsel Mnyayiza against associating with Seme:

> You people know what lawyers are. This man Seme is a Natal man. I know his father, who lives at Richmond. Lawyers want money only. That is all they are after, and nothing else. They will end by leaving you in the lurch. Of what were you afraid? Why did you not come to the Government instead of to lawyers and travelling all over the country with them? It was competent for you to come to the Government and set forth fully your aspirations and desires. But this going about the country with lawyers I cannot understand.[53]

Laden with innuendo, the Commissioner's claim also contained falsehoods. Seme's parents had died while he was a youngster, well before he left to study in the United States. By calling Seme a 'Natal man', and stating that his father came from Richmond, an area where many educated black people lived, the Commissioner was trying to drive a wedge between Seme and prominent members of the royal family such as Mnyayiza. This would not be the first time – or indeed the last – that white authorities would try to detach the Zulu royals, and Solomon in particular, from educated black people such as Seme.

Seeming to have a special dislike for Seme, the authorities could not countenance his involvement in royal affairs. They used every opportunity to drive him away from the royals. One example that demonstrated their determination to marginalise him involved a meeting in December 1913 between the Secretary for Native Affairs and Mankulumana ka Somaphunga, former *Ndunankulu* to Dinuzulu and Solomon's chief advisor and guardian. The meeting took place a few weeks after Seme's letter to Prime Minister Botha in which he claimed to have been Dinuzulu's legal advisor and to be writing on behalf of Solomon. Seme's professed status seems to have greatly annoyed the white authorities. So when Mankulumana visited Pretoria to meet with Botha and the Secretary for Native Affairs, the authorities did not pass up the opportunity to question Seme's standing. Mankulumana was pointedly asked whether he was aware of the contents of Seme's letter to Prime Minister Botha. Seeking to cast doubt on Seme's credibility, the Secretary for Native Affairs questioned Mankulumana, asking whether he had 'ever received any statement showing exactly how the moneys [*sic*] already collected have been expended?'[54] The money referred to had been collected from Zulus in Johannesburg, Natal and Zululand for Dinuzulu's medical travel expenses to Carlsbad. Although the trip did not material-ise, some money had been collected and Seme was a prominent member of the committee responsible for raising funds. The Secretary was strongly insinuating that Seme had used the monies collected for his own benefit.

As if this was not enough, the Secretary said he wanted to know whether Seme's requests for Solomon to visit the Reef and Zululand for fundraising purposes had been sanctioned by the Zulu royals. He also wanted to know whether Mankulumana had advised Solomon to seek Seme's assistance. These pointed questions put Mankulumana on the spot. It was quite clear that the authorities were unhappy about Seme's involvement. And it was also apparent what response they were hoping for. Mankulumana replied that although he had not in fact sought Seme's assistance and that Seme had instead come to him, Seme had not concealed his intention to write to Botha requesting permission for Solomon to undertake a fundraising trip. Mankulumana admitted that Seme had been Dinuzulu's friend ever since assisting him during his illness. What Mankulumana did dispute – however dubiously – was that Seme had been Dinuzulu's solicitor: 'He is not our solicitor as Dinuzulu had no case requiring a solicitor'.[55] He went on to say that Harriette Colenso might be considered Dinuzulu's advisor since she had assisted him during his legal troubles. Though Mankulumana claimed not to know Seme well, he insisted that Seme was Dinuzulu's friend.

On the matter of funds collected on Dinuzulu's behalf, Mankulumana admitted that both he and Seme had been involved in raising money in Johannesburg. However, he claimed that this money had since disappeared, and he suspected that Seme was keen on the fundraising venture in order to make up for its loss. Furthermore, Mankulumana alleged, Seme was afraid that Solomon might ask for this money so as to pay Dinuzulu's debts, and Seme was anxious that he would not be in a position to give the money to Solomon. Mankulumana then reported that he had asked Solomon to talk to Harriette Colenso about the money that was supposedly in Seme's possession, and he voiced his suspicion that Seme feared he might be caught out.

Mankulumana's claims about Seme's involvement in the disappearance of the money were obviously damaging to Seme. It is difficult to judge whether they were true or false, though it seems inconceivable that Mankulumana would lie about such an important matter. Considering Seme's reputation regarding money matters, it seems feasible that he used the Carlsbad money for his own benefit. Mankulumana's allegations did not, however, discourage Seme from getting involved in other affairs relating to the Zulu royals. One matter in which he seems to have successfully exerted his influence concerned the education of Solomon and David. The proposal to send them to a college, preferably Lovedale in the Cape, had initially been made by the Bishop of the Anglican Church in Zululand. In a letter addressed to the Zululand District Native Commissioner, the bishop reported that he had visited Nkonjeni in the Mahlabathini district where he had learnt of some mischief involving Solomon and David. He told the District Native Commissioner that the two brothers were 'going on very badly, seducing girls, getting drunk, and doing nothing but loafing about'.[56] He expressed his fear that they would end up as criminals and decried their 'pernicious influence' in Zululand. To remedy the situation, he suggested that they be sent to a college for education.

The bishop's proposal received enthusiastic support from the Natal authorities. The Chief Native Commissioner to whom the matter had been referred expressed his support for the suggestion. His preference, however, was not Lovedale; he suggested that they be sent instead to a missionary school at KwaMagwaza outside Melmoth. Further support was forthcoming from influential people such as Mankulumana. There was one objection, however, and it came from a surprising source: Seme. *Ilanga lase Natal* reported that Seme opposed the education of Solomon and David, and questioned the government's motives in wanting to educate the two princes. He claimed that no 'King of the Bantu people' educated by white authorities had fared well afterwards. Seme gave the example of Lobengula (Mzilikazi's son and successor as king of the Ndebele), alleging that four of his five children taken by the government to be educated had not survived. The last remaining child, he said, 'asked the Government to let him return [home], as he had learned sufficient. The Government refused, saying it was still acting on his behalf, and he also died with his mother.'[57] Seme's objections were widely circulated within government circles in Natal and Pretoria. The government was sufficiently concerned and irritated by Seme's allegations regarding Lobengula's sons that the Secretary for Native Affairs, Edward Dower, decided to write to Harriette Colenso to refute Seme's claims and to request her to use her influence in Zulu society to quash the allegations.[58] And yet Seme's objections seem to have received support in influential circles in Zululand, as Dower subsequently informed the Natal Chief Native Commissioner that it had become clear that the Zulu people were opposed to the education of Dinuzulu's sons. He also suggested that the two brothers were opposed to going to school because they preferred 'to remain as they are, native-like'.[59] Though Dube was opposed to Seme's view on the matter, going so far as to congratulate Prime Minister Botha for what he described as his intention to educate Solomon, Seme's view prevailed and neither Solomon nor David attended college as intended by the government.[60]

The other matter in which Seme involved himself concerned Dinuzulu's *ihlambo* ceremony. The *ihlambo* is a ceremony undertaken some time after the death of a king. According to Zulu tradition, the purpose of the ceremony is to cleanse the nation of the darkness cast by the death of a king. As Seme explained it, the ceremony also provides the Zulu nation with an opportunity 'of paying its last respects to the dead and to enable the close relation of the late Chief to take part in Public Service'.[61] The ceremony includes various activities, one of which is the participation of Zulu regiments in a hunting expedition. However, the congregation of a large crowd of Zulu regiments so soon after Dinuzulu's death unnerved the authorities, making them resistant to the event taking place. They seemed concerned that Solomon would use the event to press his claim to the kingship, and that the assembled *amabutho* might cause trouble over Dinuzulu's death.

It was in this context that Seme entered the fray on behalf of Solomon. He wrote a letter to the Prime Minister in which he claimed that he had been instructed by Solomon to request the government's approval for the Zulus to attend the *ihlambo* ceremony. Seme informed Botha that it was important that the *ihlambo* take place before the start of the ploughing season, i.e. before Christmas that year (1914). The reply was swift and went straight to the point, with Seme being informed that the Prime Minister had responded directly to Solomon, and not to Seme.[62] There was no further explanation, though the slight was clearly intended to communicate an important message to Seme that the government did not recognise his standing in matters concerning Solomon and the Zulu royals. The explanation for the snub came a little later in a letter from the Secretary for Native Affairs to the Natal Chief Native Commissioner. The Secretary asked the Commissioner to inform Solomon that the government had received a letter from Seme, who claimed to be acting on behalf of Solomon. The Secretary wanted a message to be passed to Solomon that the government did not 'recognise Seme in any matter as between Solomon and the Government'. If Solomon wished to communicate any message to the government, he would have to do so via the magistrate of his district, who was the local representative of the government.

If Seme needed any proof that the government was determined to drive a wedge between him and the Zulu royals, this letter sufficed. From then on, Solomon would write directly to the government, using the prescribed channels. In some instances, Seme wrote the letters pretending to be Solomon. One such example is a letter in Seme's distinctive handwriting, signed by Solomon, and addressed to the magistrate of Babanango, in November 1914, regarding Rietfontein, where Dinuzulu lived during his period of exile.

Solomon's attempts to distance himself from Seme were no guarantee, however, that he would be recognised as Dinuzulu's heir. Indeed, certain influential sections of the Natal administration remained sceptical of giving him an official position. And the magistrates from the Nongoma and Ndwandwe jurisdictions, two areas over which Dinuzulu ruled as oSuthu chief, were vehemently opposed to having him recognised as a chief at all. These two areas, it must be added, were jurisdictions where the white authorities had imposed chiefs loyal to the white government. A letter from the Ndwandwe magistrate to the Natal Chief Native Commissioner demonstrated the deep opposition to Solomon. The magistrate reported that the arrival in his district of Dinuzulu's two sons had caused excitement among people who, he said, expected Solomon to be appointed as their chief. If that were to happen, he argued, it would undermine the authority of those chiefs who had remained loyal to the white authorities during the Bhambatha Rebellion.[63] This view was shared by the Chief Native Commissioner, who also observed that Solomon was gaining support among the people in Zululand and argued similarly that unless this support was curtailed Solomon would undermine the authority of those chiefs who were loyal to the government.[64]

It took the government three full years to recognise Solomon as Dinuzulu's heir and chief of oSuthu. Though this was a long-awaited fulfilment of Solomon's ambition, the terms of his appointment were humiliating. They were also a reminder of how the once-mighty Zulu kingdom had fallen since its glory days under its founder, Shaka ka Senzangakhona. The white government summoned Solomon to the Union Buildings to meet the Prime Minister, where he was to learn his fate. Botha began the meeting by informing Solomon that he had been Dinuzulu's 'great friend', and by claiming that he was 'one of the men who made him King'. Seemingly not satisfied with such an important achievement regarding the descendant of Senzangakhona and the son of Cetshwayo, the warrior who had defeated the British army at Isandlwana, Botha made an even bolder claim. He informed Solomon that he himself had always looked after the Zulu nation. In fact, Botha continued, he was a believer in the Zulu nation. Perhaps as a demonstration of this, Botha informed Solomon that he had always had Zulus as workers on his farms.

In the apparent belief that he had succeeded in establishing his bona fides, Botha turned to the reason for summoning Solomon to the Union Buildings. He informed the heir of Dinuzulu that he had decided to appoint him chief of oSuthu. Botha then outlined his expectations. He informed Solomon that if he wanted to keep the position he had just been offered he would have to be loyal to the government. He would also have to understand that his area of responsibility was limited: he could not claim to be anything more than a chief of oSuthu, and he could definitely not claim to be king of the Zulus. Furthermore, he was to live in peace with the descendants of his father's enemies, especially the descendants of Zibhebhu and Kambi. He should also respect and take instructions from officialdom, from the district magistrate right up to senior officials at the Native Affairs department. Crucially, he was not to raise or mobilise any regiment or *amabutho*. If Solomon needed work to be done by men under his charge, he should not recruit younger ones. Instead, he should mobilise older men who would go about doing their work quietly. In a reference to Seme, Botha told Solomon that he did 'not recognise any intermediaries between you and myself. You have not been brought here through the inter mediation of any attorney, but at the instance of my own officers.' Botha advised Solomon to use government officials rather than Seme if he wished to communicate anything to him.

Further to this, the Prime Minister offered Solomon an annual allowance of £300 for his services as a chief. However, he cautioned that this would be cancelled in the event of Solomon failing to follow his instructions and those of other government officials. Moreover, the position to which he had been appointed would be revoked if he did not follow the instructions of government.

Botha then made a request relating to the First World War: Solomon should mobilise 4 000 Zulus to assist with dock work. He reminded Solomon that his father and uncle Ndabuko had mobilised between 30 000 and 50 000 men to fight Zibhebhu at the Battle of Tshaneni. Then, expressing disbelief that Zulus had not volunteered to assist the British Empire in the war effort, he suggested that Solomon's first task as chief should be to mobilise the requisite number of men.

Solomon's reply to Botha's terms was one of full acceptance. He declared that he had been labouring under a burden, presumably a reference to the government's not recognising him as chief. Now Botha had lifted that burden from him, he said. Describing himself as Botha's 'child', Solomon assured Botha that he would do everything in his power to fulfil Botha's wishes.[65] His uncle, Mnyayiza ka Ndabuko, also expressed appreciation to Botha for making Solomon a chief, and thanked him profusely for the allowance of £300. Such was the state of the once mighty Zulu kingdom.

Rietfontein

Shortly after Dinuzulu's death the question arose as to what to do with members of his family who had joined him at the farm Rietfontein in Middelburg. Solomon was of the view that the Zulu royal house, especially Dinuzulu's children, should be granted continued use of the farm. In a letter written by Seme on behalf of Solomon, the latter stated that Rietfontein held a spiritual significance for the family and also for the Zulu nation since it was the place where Dinuzulu had died. He stated further that his family had always understood that Rietfontein had been granted for his father's permanent use, which meant that it could be used by the family even after his father's death.[66] Some months before Solomon's letter of November 1914, Harriette Colenso had also made representations to the government on behalf of the Zulu royal family regarding Rietfontein. She had proposed that Dinuzulu's children who remained at the farm after his burial be allowed to live there for at least another two years.

The government was, however, adamant that Dinuzulu's children should leave Rietfontein. In fact, it decided to subdivide the farm and sell the plots for white settlement. It was at that point that Seme once again intervened on behalf of Solomon and the Zulu royal house. He wrote several letters to the government pleading for the farm not to be sold to white people. One of the letters, addressed to the Governor General, he described as a 'very serious appeal of the Zulu people' regarding Rietfontein. Seme claimed that he had been asked by a meeting of 'the representatives of the Zulus' to write the letter to the Governor General requesting him to consent to their purchase of Rietfontein on behalf of the Zulu nation. He informed the Governor General that Zulu tradition made the farm sacred and inviolable owing to the fact that Dinuzulu had spent his last days there.[67] That same day, Seme wrote another letter to the Minister of Native Affairs regarding the same matter. He stated that the 'Zulu Local Committee' had met to discuss the government's intention to remove Dinuzulu's children from the farm Rietfontein, and that the committee regretted the intention to convert the farm for white settlement. He stated that his committee, the Zulu Local Committee, wished to purchase the farm on behalf of the Zulu nation because of its significance for the nation, and pleaded with the Minister of Native Affairs to accede to his request so that Solomon could be relieved of his distress at the plan to evict his family.[68]

Seme did not explain who the members of the Zulu Local Committee were or how the committee had been established. Though the letters he wrote on behalf of the committee or of the Zulu representatives bore the letterhead of his law practice, Seme made no claim to be writing in his professional capacity as an attorney. Interestingly, Seme invoked his Zulu identity in his interactions with the Zulu royal house or when his target audience was Zulu – a fact that was at odds with the professed Pan-Africanism of the speech he had given at Columbia University some years before. In any event, his appeals to the government regarding Rietfontein fell on deaf ears, and Dinuzulu's family were evicted from the farm.

Zulu involvement in the First World War

Prime Minister Botha's request for involvement of the Zulus in the First World War on the side of the British generated heated debate in Zululand

and Natal. Most of the debate was conducted on the pages of *Ilanga lase Natal* and *Abantu-Batho*. As expected in a matter of such importance, Seme vigorously participated in the debate, with his views on the matter attracting much attention and also generating controversy. On 17 November 1917, in an article that appeared first in *Abantu-Batho* and later in *Ilanga lase Natal*, Seme put forward three reasons for participation in the war.

First, the outbreak of the war was a blessing to the Zulus because it afforded them an opportunity to develop a relationship with King George V, the British monarch at the time, and also with the white government in South Africa. He argued that relations between the Zulu nation and the British had been strained ever since the Anglo-Zulu War of 1879, which had resulted in the death of several British soldiers at the Battle of Isandlwana in January that year. The British monarch's request for the assistance of the Zulus was a demonstration that they were held in high esteem by white people both in England and in South Africa. If they agreed to participate, this would give the Zulu nation a good name and help to bring about reconciliation between them and the British. Seme went on to argue that the British would be very pleased to see Zulus arriving to assist them after they had killed so many of their compatriots at Isandlwana.

Second, participation in the war would enhance Solomon's stature in the eyes of white people and make the authorities more willing to trust him. In Seme's view, the difficulties endured by the Zulu kingdom since the reign of Cetshwayo were largely caused by an absence of trust between Zulu monarchs[69] and the white authorities. That trust deficit was exploited by certain chiefs and counsellors to the monarchs, who curried favour with the authorities at the expense of the kings, especially Cetshwayo and his successor Dinuzulu. Seme claimed that some of the chiefs owed their position to the fact that they had sold out the Zulu kings and the nation to white people:

Sifa kangaka nje sibulawa izinja lezi esezatola ubukosi kubelungu ngenxa yokuba kuyizona ezakonza ngenkosi yazo – ngoba zihlelinje kutlwa yizona ezazi imikondo ezingayikombisa abelungu.

[We are dying today because we have been sold out by these dogs to white people, who in exchange for their positions as chiefs have sold out their king to the white people. They always look out for ways in which they can betray us to white people.]

Seme warned Solomon that by not pledging allegiance and openly showing support to the white authorities, he would suffer the same fate as his father, Dinuzulu, and his grandfather, Cetshwayo, had suffered. The two Zulu kings, Seme claimed, had been betrayed by their chief advisors. And in the case of Cetshwayo, the king had also been betrayed by his own *izinduna* and chiefs, who had sold him out to the white people. He singled out Mnyamana ka Ngqengelele, Cetshwayo's *Ndunankulu*, as one of the traitors:

Ngisho njalo yena uNdunankulu uMnyamana. Yena uqobo watumela amaNgisi lapo inkosi yake icashe kona, baze bayibamba. Ngitsho yena uZibebu ka Mapita yena owayenikelwe umuzi omkulu ka Jama ka Ndaba!—nakuya etabata lomuzi wenkosi eya kokonza ngawo esilungwini! Futi esebulala ngawo inkosi yake.

[I mean *Ndunankulu* Mnyamana, who showed the British the spot where Cetshwayo was hiding which resulted to his capture. Zibebu ka Mapita was given Jama ka Ndaba's large kraal to look after and he used it to betray and destroy his king.]

Seme also saw traitors in the ranks of educated black people. One such grouping he warned Solomon against was the leadership of the ANC at the time, whom he accused of not caring about matters that concerned the chiefs. Of the ANC leadership he said:

Awubheke nangu uKongolose opetwe izihlakanipi! Akuko 'ndaba okekul-inganiswe nokulinganiswa kuzo ukuti lezike zifanele amakosi ohlanga. Kusobala ukuti ilowo nalowo utanda ukuziveza embusweni – abanandaba namakosi.

[Look at the Congress, which is led by clever people. There is nothing that the Congress discusses that concerns matters of interest to traditional leaders. It is clear that what each and every person in Congress cares about is to be liked by the white authorities. They do not care about chiefs.]

Seme urged Solomon to follow in the footsteps of his great-grandfather Mpande, who pledged allegiance to the white authorities and was rewarded with their protection. Of Mpande he said:

Kuhle ke wena ulingise uMpande uzinikele ngamandhla onke ongaba nawo ezandhleni nasemsebenzini yonke yombuso – kakulukulu ku Joji Wobuhlanu. Futi wenze loko ngesibindi esigcweleyo ngoba amaJalimane asoze afike kulelizwe – ingani eNgilandi kuseduze kangaka nje akalingi nokulinga ukuwelisa amabuto awo kona?

[It would be good for you to pledge support to the white authorities as Mpande did, especially to George V. You should work courageously for the white authorities – is there any possibility that the Germans will cross the oceans to fight you if they are unable even to cross to England to fight the British army?]

Finally, Seme argued that the Zulus should participate in the war effort because other nations had already committed themselves. Seme was concerned that if the Zulus refused they would lose the respect and high regard of other nations. Moreover, the English might bear a grudge for the Zulus' refusal of wartime assistance, and the historic leadership role of the Zulus might be taken over by other ethnic groups:

Futi ubuholi bama Zulu ezizweni ezinsundu bunganikwa Abesutu noma amaSwazi. Futi mina ngiyabona ukuti impela sekutanda ukuba njalo; ngani? Ngenxa yezici engizibeke encwadini le engasenhla. Ngize ngikulume? Ingani naku sesidhlulwa Amakula lapa eNatal! Wona ngenxa yokusenza kwawo ezimobeni naku namhla avulelwe lapo singangeni kona tina.[70]

[Leadership that the Zulu nation provides to other black groups would be taken over by the Sothos and Swazis if we do not participate in the war. Already it looks like they have taken over. We are being overtaken by the coolies in Natal, who because of their work in the sugarcane fields have been allowed to go to places that we are prohibited from visiting.]

Seme advised Solomon to go to the top of the Suthu and Nobamba mountains, and to summon all the Zulus to gather before him and instruct the best among them to go overseas to assist George V. He advised Solomon to send a regiment of about 3 000 men, which would be led by *izinduna* and a priest. Solomon should insist that he be given the right to choose a captain who would command the Zulu regiment. Seme warned Solomon not to accept just any white commander, but instead to choose 'trusted' white men such as Zithulele (Colonel Royston), who was well known in Zululand and Natal for recruiting black labour to work on the gold mines in Johannesburg.

It is understandable that Seme's article caused controversy. In his passionate advocacy for Zulu participation in the war on the side of the British, he also attacked several respected leaders in Zulu society. The accusations he levelled at Mnyamana and Zibhebhu were scathing, to say nothing of broadsides delivered to the leadership of the ANC. The attack on the ANC signalled the breakdown in his relationship with its leadership, John Dube in particular, whose resignation as president general was the result of constant attacks in the pages of *Abantu-Batho*.

Some *Ilanga* readers were deeply offended by Seme's insulting description of Solomon's trusted advisors as dogs who could not be trusted, and his accusation that ANC leaders did not care about the chiefs. One correspondent, Gundane Zulu, warned Solomon against Seme. He questioned Seme's standing in addressing Solomon directly through the columns of newspapers without going through advisors such as Mankulumana. He also questioned Seme about his relationship with Dinuzulu:

> *Uti umntwana [Solomon] alahle bonke abantu alalele wena usuke wenzani loku nako noDinuzulu ufela oBhalule njalo uwena ummeli wake. Sake sezwa nini ukuba kwaqoqwa malini yake efuna ukuya eJalimani. Wake wasenekela nini ngalezo zika Dinuzulu ofanele ukweluleka uSolomon. Bakitshwa yini oMiss Colenso pansi koMntwana sitshele lezo kuqala. Uzalwa uSinono nabanye ozibonga ngabo, pezu kwetu uti tina siyizinja. Bake benzani labo bazali bako ozibonga ngabo, babusa sipi isizwe? Uwena oyinja uqobo uti emakosini amaningi omdabu izinja.*[71]

[You say Solomon should not listen to anyone but you, but what did you do for Dinuzulu as his lawyer, since he died at Bhalule [Middelburg]? What did you do with the money you collected so that he could go for treatment in Germany? Who chased away Miss Colenso from Dinuzulu? You say your fathers are Sinono and others, but what did they do? Did they rule any nation? You call us dogs, but the real dog is you who accuse us of not caring about our traditional leaders.]

It is unclear whether Solomon read Seme's article, and if he did, what he made of it and the debate it generated. However, the meeting Seme advised him to call did not take place, and nor did 3 000 Zulu recruits sail for England. It is important to note that the 3 000 Zulu recruits would have served as part of the South African Native Labour Contingent. They were not intended to fight as combatants in the war.

Rather oddly, a few months before the article's publication, Seme had written to Solomon discouraging Zulu participation in the war effort. He recalled that Solomon had informed him of the unwillingness of the Zulus to take part in the war, and expressed understanding of this position by saying, '*lempi iyesabeka kakulu*' (this war is very frightening). In the same letter, Seme stated that volunteers faced the prospect of not returning from the war; he expressed concern that newspapers were not reporting the facts, which in his view suggested that the British were losing. He therefore found it difficult to advise that a regiment be sent overseas if the situation did not look promising. In view of this letter, Seme's later stance is surprising and seemingly inexplicable.

The letter to Solomon is noteworthy for another reason also. It reveals the extent of Seme's fallout with Dube, which appears to have been sparked by a power struggle over the leadership of the ANC. Seme explained to Solomon that he had not communicated with him for a while because he had had to deal with Dube, whom he accused of undermining his interests while he was away in Zululand:

Awu impela umfanyana kaDube ngafica esekwele phezu kwendhlu yami, kodwa pela ngasengi fikile mina Mbabala yenduna egwebigijima. Ngafika ngabadiliza pansi. Naye uDube wase baleka eqonda eNatal. Sengi mmangalele manje ngoba kute ngenxa yokushisa kwenhliziyo yake, futi engazi ukuti ngiyeza wase etumela epepeni lake indaba yokuti sengidhliwe. Ngi mumangalele ke. Uzozikomba lezompahla engidhliwe zona.

[I found the Dube boy undermining me everywhere here in Johannesburg. I brought him down to earth. He ran away back to Natal. I have also sued him for a claim he made in his newspaper that my property has been attached or confiscated by the authorities. He will have to show which property of mine has been attached or confiscated.]

What is clear from the letter is that the fallout was partly due to competition between the two men relating to influence over the Zulu royal house. Seme claimed that Dube and his unnamed associates were jealous that he had Solomon's ear, and that he frequently visited Solomon. He added that Dube and his associates refused his invitations to visit the royal house because there was no money to be gained, and he claimed that his detractors accused him of standing in their way of benefiting materially from the royal house.

Seme's claims were bizarre, to say the least. Dube had a much older relationship with the Zulu royal house. Also, he had played a leading role in championing Dinuzulu's cause while he was being persecuted by the Natal authorities. Largely because of that, Dube was chosen to be a speaker at Dinuzulu's funeral, an honour that was not extended to Seme. As for Seme's accusations about material motives, Solomon in fact accused Seme of owing him money. In any case, there was not much money to be had as the Zulu royal house was at the time experiencing financial distress and was dependent on financial support from the state. The only explanation for Seme's claims is that he was trying to curry favour with Solomon at the expense of his rival and nemesis, John Dube.

Other claims he made in the letter suggest that Seme was trying to demonstrate his loyalty to Solomon by accusing others of harbouring ill will against him. For instance, he suggested that there was a plot by sections of the Zulu nation, especially those from the Nhlazatshe district, to sow discord between Solomon and his half-brother, David. He cautioned Solomon to look out for himself as the white authorities would never miss the opportunity to use his enemies inside the Zulu royal house to divide the Zulu nation, in the same way that the Natal colonial administration had tried to use Solomon's uncle, Manzolwandle ka Cetshwayo, to sow divisions in the Zulu nation.[72]

Solomon rejected Seme's claims and handed the letter over to the authorities in his own bid to demonstrate his allegiance to the white government. Here too it appears that Seme's claims had no merit, and were rather attempts to curry favour with Solomon.

* * *

Seme's involvement in the affairs of the Zulu royal family is the least understood of his public roles. And yet his involvement was deep and far-reaching. He attended not only to the private concerns of the Zulu royals, but also to their public responsibilities. Indeed, so deeply embedded was he in the affairs and intrigues of the royal family that he married Phikisile, Dinuzulu's eldest daughter and Solomon's half-sister, in the 1920s. Soon afterwards, in the 1930s, Seme went through a difficult period after being struck off the roll of attorneys. He left the Transvaal and went to live with Princess Phikisile in Mahhashini, at one of the royal homesteads in the Nongoma district, where the royal family looked after him. The confusing and inconsistent relationship he had with Solomon was, thus, not the sum total of Seme's connection with the royals.

It was Seme's involvement in matters that concerned the broader Zulu nation that is especially interesting. Here Seme asserted an identity that was narrow and exclusive, going so far as to pose as a representative of the Zulu nation as a whole and a guardian of its interests against other groupings which, he strongly implied, were outside the orbit of Zuluness. Whenever he assumed this narrow identity, Seme the Zulu was at odds with Seme the African nationalist.

6

Daggakraal

The year 1912 was probably the busiest and most exciting in Seme's life. Not only had his dream of black political unity come to fruition through the formation of the South African Native National Congress, but he had also established *Abantu-Batho*, a newspaper that would report on black affairs. His reputation as a lawyer was spreading far and wide, as evidenced by his increasingly close relations with the royal families of Swaziland and Zululand. However, one of his boldest initiatives was the formation of the Native Farmers Association of South Africa Limited, a company he single-handedly formed in early 1912 and registered in Natal. The purpose of the company was to purchase land from white people and resell it to black people.

The establishment of the Native Farmers Association and its subsequent purchase of several farms in the eastern Transvaal was arguably his boldest move, more significant perhaps than the formation of the ANC. Seme founded the company at a time when white public opinion against the purchase of land by black people was becoming increasingly vocal and hostile. Voices in Parliament and in cabinet, led by General Hertzog, argued strongly that a law be passed prohibiting black people from purchasing land from white people.[1] Part of that opposition came from the Transvaal, driven mainly by Seme's scheme to buy land from white farmers for black settlement. It was extremely courageous of Seme to form a company whose primary purpose was the purchase of land in the face of increasingly virulent opposition. The 1912 purchase of land by his company probably precipitated the decision by government to submit the Natives Land Bill to Parliament without notice when Parliament opened in January 1913.[2]

The Native Farmers Association was a company founded, owned and managed by black people. The shareholders were all black, as were the directors. At its founding, the Native Farmers Association is estimated to have had fifty to sixty shareholders. The issue of shareholding would later prove controversial, though the main dispute was whether people who contributed money to the company were buying shares or buying land. Be that as it may, Seme held a controlling stake in the company, which perhaps explains why he was the founding chairman of the board of directors, with his associate Ezra Nkosi as company secretary. Other board members were Nsula Mazibuko, Andries Hlongwane and Mbosho Shabalala, who was later replaced by Absalom Nkosi.[3] The list of directors supplied by the company to *Abantu-Batho* was much longer; in addition to the names mentioned above were Samuel Sibeko, Marsh Seme (Pixley Seme's eldest brother), Mfisha Ngwenya, Diamond Dlamini, Jonas Seboko, Lucas Mazibuko and Alexander Dlamini.[4]

In anticipation of the establishment of the company, Seme bought three farms in the Wakkerstroom district of the Transvaal from Willem Cornelius Gouws. In the deed of sale, Seme is described as purchasing the farms in his capacity as a trustee, agent and attorney of a company yet to be formed. The farms that he bought were certain portions of the farm Daggakraal, certain portions of the farm Driefontein, and certain portions of the farm Driepan, all of which belonged to Gouws and were located in the Wakkerstroom district. The land area Seme bought totalled just over 4 857 hectares, and at £3 per hectare it cost slightly more than £14 000. Seme was expected to pay £200 upon execution of the sale, with the £14 000 to be paid through a first mortgage bond at an interest rate of 4.5 per cent per annum. The bond was to be fully repaid by 1927 as from 12 April 1912, the date of signing by Gouws and Seme. Clause 6 of the deed of sale stipulated that the purchaser, Seme, would take over the sheep and cattle on the farms. The sheep numbered approximately 2 000, and there were 150 cattle. Clause 7 of the deed stipulated that Seme, as the purchaser, would take over everything on the farms, including agricultural implements and household furniture. For all this, it was agreed that Seme would pay £1 000.

Soon after buying the three farms, Seme established the Native Farmers Association of South Africa Limited to which he ceded his rights and obligations. The company started selling plots of land to black people for settlement. Soon, this purchase and reselling of farms to black people for settlement caused uproar in the Wakkerstroom district. Protest meetings were organised by white farmers and petitions were sent to the government to intervene. Farmers who met at one such meeting expressed the view that 'it would be highly injurious to the farming interests in the country if natives or syndicates of natives were allowed to hold ground in their own names'. They argued that, while at the time there were few cases of black people purchasing land, 'an organised start has been made by natives to acquire ground and in view of the enormous revenue derived by natives on the mines in the Transvaal it would require only a very simple system of cooperation among the natives prompted by educated natives in the country to enable them to acquire a large number of farms every year'. Complaints at the meeting were specifically directed at the purchase of the farm Daggakraal by Seme's company, which was allegedly bought 'at a high figure much to the consternation of the adjoining farmers who contemplate difficulties and realise the depreciation in value of their own properties owing to the proximity of a native location of this nature'. The white farmers then resolved that it was 'highly undesirable and inimical to the interests of the White Population of South Africa that natives or syndicates of natives should acquire farms in the Union'. They pleaded with the government to 'introduce legislation prohibiting the sale of farms to natives or syndicates of natives and prohibiting the holding of farms by natives in their own names'.[5]

Part of the reason for this hostility towards the Native Farmers Association is revealed in a letter from the district assistant magistrate to the Secretary for Native Affairs, stating that the feeling of white farmers was strongly against black people purchasing white farms. However, the main reason for the hostility was that farmers in the district, some of whom relied on black sharecroppers, were afraid that they would lose labour if their black labourers started buying land that they could cultivate for their own benefit.[6] Indeed, it was these very sharecroppers who were being targeted by Seme's company to purchase the land plots.

The Minister of Native Affairs to whom the farmers' resolution had been directed was none other than General Hertzog. In a letter to the farmers dated 3 September 1912, Hertzog's private secretary informed them that the minister 'sympathises with the farmers in this matter, which is receiving serious attention'.[7] The attention referred to in the letter was the attempt by the Native Affairs department under the leadership of Hertzog to invoke provisions of the 1895 Squatters Law, which prohibited squatting on white farms by black people without their being granted a permit to do so. The Squatters Law also limited to a maximum of five the number of black households that were allowed to live on white farms as squatters. Armed with this law, the Native Affairs department sent a circular to the Native Farmers Association instructing it to comply with the law by effectively removing black families from the farms it owned because those families were contravening the Squatters Law. In his reply, Seme pointed out that most farmers in the Wakkerstroom district employed a lot of black people who were squatters on their farms. He charged that those white farmers were contravening the law. He also pointed out that when his company bought Daggakraal and the two other farms from Willem Gouws, they 'found on the land more native squatters than they [sic] are at the present time'. Seme wished to be informed whether the government intended to enforce the law since most farmers were contravening it.[8]

Seme then took matters a step further. In his capacity as a farm owner and director of the company, he started exercising prerogatives that had hitherto been the preserve of white employers: he issued permits for employees at the farms in Wakkerstroom to travel to Johannesburg to perform certain tasks for him. Black employees were required by law to be issued passes by employers who instructed them to do work in a particular place. Thus, Seme complied with the law. The Native Affairs department was very displeased by his actions and prevented the employees from travelling to Johannesburg. Seme issued a letter of demand to the department, claiming hundreds of pounds for the loss of service. In a letter addressed to Mr Bell, a pass officer at Volksrust, Seme demanded payment and threatened that 'legal proceedings will be instituted against you without any further notice' if the money was not paid by the date stipulated.[9]

The matter was taken so seriously that it was referred to the Secretary for Native Affairs in Pretoria, who described Seme's demands and threats as 'remarkable'. He advised the Volksrust office to wait and see whether Seme would follow his threats with a summons, and in the event of this occurring they should inform the Department of Justice, which would defend the Native Affairs department against Seme.[10] Seme does not appear to have pressed on with his threats, and the matter died down. But the battle lines had been drawn over Seme's company and its purchasing of land in the eastern Transvaal.

The only option the government appeared to have for dealing with Seme's company was enforcing the Squatters Law. There was a flurry of correspondence about whether the law was applicable to the circumstances surrounding the Native Farmers Association. The problem for the government was that most white farmers in the Transvaal, and the Wakkerstroom district in particular, were in contravention of the law, as Seme had pointed out. This point was emphasised by the Volksrust Sub-Native Commissioner who in a letter to the Secretary for Native Affairs revealed that the provisions of the Squatters Law had not been enforced. The Sub-Native

Commissioner warned the Secretary for Native Affairs that the enforce-
ment of the law would have 'a far reaching effect'.[11] He did not explain
what he meant by this, but it is clear that he was drawing attention to the
many white farmers who would be found to be in contravention of the law
were it to be enforced. It was, however, the legal opinion obtained from
state law advisors at the Department of Justice that completely closed off
the avenue of using the Squatters Law to force Seme and his associates to
abandon their project of buying farms for the settlement of black people.
In a lengthy opinion, the legal advisors argued that when the Squatters
Law was enacted it was not envisaged that a black-owned company would
own land. The prohibition of ownership of land by black people meant
individuals, not corporations. On that basis, the ownership of land by the
Native Farmers Association could not be considered unlawful. The legal
opinion was a blow to the government, and calls for new legislation that
would make it utterly unlawful for black people to buy, sell or own land in
certain areas became louder. Those calls would be answered with the passing of the Natives Land Bill, which became law in June 1913. However, for
Seme and company, the failure by the government to enforce the Squatters
Law gave them the space to move full-steam ahead with their operation.

The Native Farmers Association of Africa
Eluding the clutches of the Squatters Law proved to be a temporary
reprieve. The Native Farmers Association soon faced another, altogether
different problem: it ran into financial difficulties. Initially financed by
the African Guarantee and Indemnity Company, an institution owned
by I.W. Schlesinger,[12] the association, however, failed to meet its financial obligations, in particular the repayment of the £14 000 bond. It then
approached another of Schlesinger's companies, the Colonial Bank and
Trust Company, which found the Native Farmers Association to be in dire
financial straits with bookkeeping arrangements of the 'crudest form'.[13]

Nevertheless, the Colonial Bank and Trust Company agreed to rescue
Seme's company under certain conditions. The first was that Seme's company be abandoned, and that a new one be formed and registered in the
Transvaal rather than Natal. Secondly, the secretary of the company, as well
as its auditors, had to be white people ('Europeans'). Thirdly, the control
of the company had to be vested in 'Founders' Shares', a condition that
would later prove to be the subject of much debate. All of the founders'
shares were to be given to the Colonial Bank and Trust Company. Fourth,

Seme's company had to transfer all its assets and liabilities to the new company for and 'in consideration of 5,000 Ordinary Shares in the new Company'.[14] The Colonial Bank and Trust Company had to receive 4975 ordinary shares as financial support for the new venture, and it would guarantee £15000 as the working capital of the new company. Seme's old company directors were made directors of the new company. However, the majority holder of the founders' shares had the right to appoint and dismiss company directors. If Seme and his fellow black directors agreed to subscribe to the working capital, Schlesinger's bank would give Seme half of the 4975 ordinary shares to which it was entitled; furthermore, the bank would sell to Seme the majority of the founders' shares, thereby giving him control of the company.

Seme agreed to the terms, a step which was followed by the liquidation of the old company and the transfer of its assets to the new company. The agreement was signed on 7 September 1912. Signing Seme's old company away were Absalom Nkosi and Alexander Dhlamini in their respective capacities as director and secretary. The Colonial Bank and Trust Company was represented by William Bullock and Lewis Gordon, respectively director and secretary of the bank. The new company was represented (somewhat ironically, perhaps even cynically) by Andries Hlongwane, a director of Seme's company that was about to be liquidated. The new company was registered under the Transvaal Companies Act in October 1912, a few weeks after the signing of the agreement to liquidate the old company. It was named the Native Farmers Association of Africa Limited. The only change in the name was the removal of the word 'South'.

The new company was registered on 25 October 1912 and it was capitalised with £25000, divided into 24975 ordinary shares and 25 founders' shares, with each share valued at £1. The Colonial Bank and Trust Company owned all 25 founders' shares and 4975 ordinary shares. The black farmers who had had shares in the old company were given 5000 shares in exchange for liquidating their company and transferring its assets to the new company. Seme was given 14994 ordinary shares, while the six directors of the old company were given one share each. This shareholding arrangement was short-lived, however. Two months later, on 20 December, another 45000 ordinary shares were issued to the African Guarantee and Indemnity Company, the company controlled by Schlesinger and his white associates that had originally financed the Native Farmers Association of South Africa. That increased the number of shares held by the Native Farmers Association of Africa from the original 25 000 shares to 70 000 shares. The reason given for increasing shareholding by 45 000 ordinary shares was that the company needed to buy certain stands in Orange Grove Township in Johannesburg. Part of the agreement signed on 12 December was that the majority of the founders' shares would be transferred to Seme, which resulted in him holding 13 of the 25 shares, with eight being controlled by the Colonial Bank and Trust Company and the remaining four by its white directors.

The signing of the agreement that resulted in the liquidation of the old company and the formation of a new one had not, however, enjoyed universal support. A section of the black population in Daggakraal seemed unhappy, if not so much with the terms of the agreement, most decidedly with the implementation thereof. One source of conflict was the repayment of the bond that the old company had taken out when purchasing the three farms from Gouws. The secretary of the Daggakraal Natives Association, an organisation of residents who had bought plots from the company, recorded that the source of the disagreement was liability for a debt owed to Willem Gouws. Some Daggakraal residents understood the agreement to mean that 'the new Company would pay off Mr Gouws' bond; make a survey of the farms into 10 morgen plots and enable every native who paid his instalment in full to get valid transfer of his plot without further delay'.[15] However, their understanding of the agreement was not shared by the company, despite numerous deputations to Schlesinger imploring him to implement the terms of the agreement. When the new company was formed, the understanding of the residents was that they would not be held responsible for the outstanding debt.

The Daggakraal Natives Association was also concerned about the level of power and control wielded by black people in the new company. The secretary of the association contended that the new company was formed 'by manipulation of share capital' and alleged that it was Schlesinger who had in fact formed the new company. He argued that 'the old native Company has passed entirely into the hands and control of the Colonial Banking & Trust Company of Africa Limited. The original native shareholders are in such a hopeless minority that they need never even to be consulted'. This arrangement was, according to the secretary, 'the mother of all dissatisfaction among natives of Daggakraal'.[16]

The issue of control was not an idle one. When the Natives Land Bill was signed into law in June 1913 it stipulated that a company could only be considered to be owned by black people if they had a controlling interest in that company. The question that faced the Native Farmers Association was whether black people did in fact have a controlling interest in it. The answer proved contentious, for the vast majority of its ordinary shares were owned by white people through the Colonial Bank and Trust Company and the African Guarantee and Indemnity Company. In addition, the Native Farmers Association had bought property from a white woman, Mrs Potgieter from Wakkerstroom, and the bond was held by the African Life Insurance Company Limited, yet another company controlled by Schlesinger. So the question was to what extent could a company where the majority shareholders were overwhelmingly white people be considered to be black owned?

The argument advanced by the company was that although the majority of ordinary shares were owned by white people through the Colonial Bank and Trust Company and the African Guarantee and Indemnity Company, Seme in fact controlled the company since he owned the majority of the founders' shares. According to clause 77 of the company's articles of association, the holder of a majority of founders' shares was entitled to certain prerogatives, such as the appointment of company directors. Since Seme did hold the majority of the founders' shares the company argued that it was compliant with section 10 of the Natives Land Act which required black people to have a controlling interest in a company for it to be considered black owned or controlled.

In support of its argument, the company pointed to the composition of its board of directors, which numbered five: Seme, Mazibuko, Shabalala, Nkosi and Hlongwane. However, four of the five black directors had alternate directors (the exception was Seme), who were all white. The alternate directors were Schlesinger, Bullock, Burton and Atterbury. Company records showed that the alternate directors on several occasions exercised powers of directors, which, although allowed by the company's articles of association, raised serious questions as to who really controlled the company. Was it the black directors or their white alternates?

Close scrutiny of the company shareholding only succeeded in raising more questions than answers. Suspicions were especially aroused by the manner in which Seme had acquired the founders' shares and the close to 15 000 ordinary shares he held in the company. The agreement that Seme's old company had reached with Schlesinger's Colonial Bank was that the shares of the new company would be issued at £1 per share. That was the price paid by the Colonial Bank when it acquired its shares. The same amount was paid by the African Guarantee and Indemnity Company. However, Seme did not pay £15 000 for his 15 000 ordinary shares. He only paid £1 500, which translated to two shillings per share. Furthermore, the £1 500 that had bought the 15 000 shares was not paid by Seme himself. He was loaned the money by the Colonial Bank. It was on the basis of his holding of these 15 000 shares that Seme was given the 13 founders' shares, which he did not pay for either.

Given those arrangements, the question arose as to whether Seme did in fact control the company, or whether he was being used by its real owners to evade section 10 of the Natives Land Act. It would be a few years before the government decided to institute an investigation into the affairs of the company, and whether it was compliant with section 10 of the Natives Land Act. However, the circumstances that led to that investigation began much earlier in the company's life. Soon after its establishment, the new company bought two farms in addition to Daggakraal, Driepan and Driefontein, the three farms originally bought by the old company. The two new farms were 'Potgieter's portion of Daggakraal farm', or Daggakraal II as it eventually became known, and Vlakplaats. The two farms combined totalled 2 282 morgen, and they cost the company £11 000, an amount that the company secured in a bond from the African Life Insurance Company Limited, the directors of which were Schlesinger and Bullock.

On 15 January 1913 the Native Farmers Association sold the two new farms to Chief Maitse Popo Moloi from Harrismith in the Orange Free State. According to the deed of sale, Moloi would pay for the farm in instalments: on 15 February 1913 he would pay the company £2 000, to be followed by a payment of £3 700 on 15 July 1913, with the balance to be paid in ten annual instalments of £2 850 each, making a total of £34 200. Included in the agreement was a condition that if Moloi defaulted on any payment the whole sale would be void, with money already paid being forfeited.[17] Moloi and the Native Farmers Association further agreed that the company would immediately survey the two farms into ten-morgen lots, apparently to enable Moloi to distribute the lots to his followers who had contributed to the purchase price of the two farms. Their contributions to the purchase price were, however, not recognised in the sale agreement because Moloi was named as the sole purchaser. That omission notwithstanding, 200 of Moloi's subjects moved to the two farms upon the completion of purchase. They also continued contributing to the purchase price, until an amount of £7 058 had been paid.

However, on 23 April 1915 Chief Moloi informed the company that he was unable to continue payment of the instalments, and appealed to be released from further liability. In a blow to many residents who had sold their livestock and other belongings to help pay for the farms, Chief Moloi offered to forfeit all the money already paid and to give it up to the company 'as liquidated damages for my failure to carry out my agreement'.[18] On 23 May 1915 Chief Moloi entered into an agreement with Seme, Burton and Hobbs, who represented the Native Farmers Association, in which he agreed to forfeit all the money he and his associates had already paid. He also agreed that he, Moloi, had 'no claim for any consideration' from the company.[19]

The company informed the farm residents that the sale had been cancelled, and offered to sell the ten-morgen plots to individual residents for £100 each. An amount of £10 had to be paid as an initial instalment in order to secure a plot. All those who had contributed to Moloi's scheme had forfeited their money; they therefore needed to buy plots as individuals, as per the company's new offer.

The cancellation of the sale was devastating to many farm residents. Almost all of them had made enormous sacrifices in order to contribute towards the purchase of the two farms. The despair the residents felt was captured in the affidavits they wrote in the aftermath of the purchase cancellation by Moloi. They all told of the huge sums they had paid towards the purchase of the farms, only to be told that their money had been lost. Zacharia Lakage stated that he had sold his cattle and horses in order to buy the land. He said he had paid a total of £303 to Moloi's nephew, Jonas Moloi. After selling his cattle and horses and paying the money, Lakage said, 'Moloi now states that the money has been lost and that we have to start afresh ... we now have to buy a plot of 10 morgen in extent at a yearly payment of 12 pounds 10 shillings for 12 years'.[20]

Resident after resident told a tale of devastation and despair at the turn of events. They had come to Daggakraal, they said, because Jonas Moloi, who had met Seme in the middle of 1912, informed them that Seme was looking for about fifty men to join him in a company he had established to buy land for black people. Seme met them that year and told them about two farms they might buy if they could get enough men together to purchase the farms. The men then sold their livestock and paid Seme the requisite amount. For the greater part of the negotiating process with Seme and the financing of the scheme, Chief Moloi was not involved. When, some time later, Moloi did become involved, this ultimately led to him signing the deed of sale.

Seme agreed with the residents that, long before he got to know Chief Moloi, he had been dealing with individual residents with whom he had discussed the purchase of the two farms and also the financing. However, he contended that their individual claims to the land could not be recognised because the company had signed the deed of sale with Chief Moloi. In his view, Chief Moloi was the sole purchaser of the two farms. Therefore, Moloi's failure to pay the instalments meant that each person who had contributed towards the purchase had forfeited his contribution.

Seme's argument then took another interesting turn. Even though he had been dealing with the residents for a while, long before he came to know Moloi, Seme chose to describe them as Moloi's followers: 'I never told the followers that they would get plots for the money paid by them. The followers told me that everything they had belonged to the Chief.' Seme then added: 'The Company was never notified that money was paid on behalf of individuals, the contract was with the Chief.' He went further, saying, 'I know that an individual member of a tribe has no right to land, there is no individual tenure'.[21]

According to Seme, since ownership of the land is vested in the chief, all land belongs to him, and the residents had paid the money so that the farms could be bought for the chief. This contention was, however, fiercely contested by the farm residents. Jonas Moloi, for instance, stated that they were buying the farms for themselves: 'We signed the agreement that we were buying the farm, I did not sign as a witness'. He gave a clear account of the sale agreement: 'Daggakraal was not bought in the name of the Chief, it was bought in the name of 23 or 24 men [and] I was one of the men. An agreement was drawn up at the Office [the company's office], it was read to us by Mr Schlesinger ... Maitse [Chief Moloi] can read but very little English, I interpreted the document'. Furthermore, he had assisted in the collection of the necessary funds: 'I collected monies but not on behalf of Maitze. I never paid monies on his behalf.' He had been given receipts from the company, he said, but this was for money paid on behalf of the residents, and not Moloi.

At a moment when the farm residents were still reeling from the cancellation of the sale agreement and the company's order that they should pay again for the plots or face eviction, the Native Farmers Association delivered another blow: it began to sell the plots of those who were unable to pay to other black people who wanted to buy land. While this added to the despair, it also resulted in contestation over ownership of the plots. This soon evolved into a tribal conflict between the Zulus on the one hand and a group called the Basotho on the other.

One case of contestation over the ownership of land ended up in the Transvaal Supreme Court. The company had allocated a plot of land that originally belonged to Molapisi Sehlako, one of the men from Harrismith, to Tyes Dhlamini while Sehlako was away in the Free State. Upon his return, Sehlako found Dhlamini on his land and conflict ensued. Dhlamini insisted that the plot belonged to him and took the matter to the Magistrate's Court in Wakkerstroom, where he was represented by Seme. Though Dhlamini won the case, it was followed by an appeal at the Transvaal Supreme Court where it was heard by Judge President De Villiers, Justice Wessels and Justice Curlewis. The judges handed down a scathing decision which found that the manner in which the company had treated Sehlako constituted 'palpable injustice'. Judge President De Villiers also commented on the cancellation of the contract of purchase that Chief Moloi and the company had entered into. He expressed doubt that the cancellation was genuine and stated that the money of the farm residents had been 'recklessly sacrificed' by the chief in collaboration with his cousin Jonas and the company. The government was advised to investigate the affairs of the Native Farmers Association as there was a likelihood that black residents had been defrauded of their money while purchasing the land.

De Villiers proposed that a commission of inquiry be appointed to investigate 'how a company, in which Europeans held more than half of the shares, can ostensibly be controlled by one native who unfortunately is at present a solicitor of the Court, holding thirteen founders' shares'. The 'native' in question was of course Seme. Suspecting that Seme was simply being used as a front by white businessmen at the expense of black people, De Villiers stated that the 'whole matter cries out for investigation'.

Justice Curlewis pointed to the fact that the company had bought the two farms for £11 000 and a few weeks later sold them at a huge profit to Chief Moloi and other black buyers from Harrismith for more than £34 000. It was, moreover, extraordinary that Chief Moloi would cancel a sale after over £7 000 had already been paid. This suggested that the company was set up as an attempt to 'evade the law prohibiting the sale of land by white persons to natives in certain areas'.[22] Judge Curlewis expressed support for Judge President De Villiers's call for the government to investigate the company.

The judges' suspicion that the company did not actually belong to Seme and other black people was in fact held by many in government, particularly in the Native Affairs department. A few years before, the Secretary for Native Affairs at the time, Edward Dower, had said he had little doubt that the company was 'initiated for the exploitation of the Natives – launched as it was under the aegis of (a) the Colonial Bank and Trust Company, Ltd., and (b) the African Guarantee & Indemnity Company, Ltd'. It did not help matters that the purchase price of the two farms seemed exorbitant to observers both in government and without. One outside observer who was outraged at the purchase price of the farms was Reverend W. Francis Hill of the Community of the Resurrection at Rosettenville in Johannesburg, who had visited Daggakraal in January 1916. He was horrified that the farm residents were being overcharged for a piece of land which in his estimation was worth £1 or £2 a morgen instead of the £10 to £12 charged by the company. Writing that the whole scheme appeared to be 'a huge fraud', he urged the Native Affairs department to take action.[23]

Reverend Hill's letter bolstered the existing view in government that drastic steps needed to be taken against the Native Farmers Association. In November 1916, for instance, Dower wrote directly to the Attorney General informing him that his department was of the view that the company be prosecuted for contravening section 10 of the Natives Land Act. He went on to reveal that the company was 'vividly before my mind when suggesting that in the Native Affairs Administration Bill purchases by Native companies should be regarded as communal'.[24] The Attorney General took up the investigation into the Native Farmers Association in late 1916. His initial view was that the Native Farmers Association was not a native company as defined in the Natives Land Act of 1913, and he noted that black people could hardly be said to hold a controlling interest in the company.

Sensing that it was about to get into serious trouble, the Native Farmers Association decided to remove all alternate directors who were white. It appointed John Dube as a director to join Seme and the other existing black directors. Furthermore, the company, through its lawyers, Bowman and Gilfillan, wrote to the Secretary for Native Affairs expressing anxiety about the investigation by the Attorney General and offering its full cooperation. It requested a meeting with the Native Affairs department to give its side of the story in order to avoid the Attorney General receiving information 'only from the side of the natives'.[25]

The company's lobbying seems to have been effective as the Attorney General decided not to press charges despite the finding that it was not a black-owned company and was therefore in contravention of the Natives Land Act. The Attorney General duly informed the Native Affairs department that he had reached an agreement with the company lawyers, and that he would overlook the previous transactions conducted by the company on condition that it ceased to sell land to black people. If the company agreed and complied with the conditions set by the Attorney General, it would not be prosecuted.

The decision by the Attorney General must surely have come as a relief to the company. However, the Supreme Court decision which effectively accused the Native Farmers Association of running a scheme to defraud black people and called for it to be investigated spurred its real owners, Schlesinger and his associates, into action. Their move would have very bad consequences for Seme.

Ousted

The aftermath of the Supreme Court case was difficult for Seme and other black directors of the Native Farmers Association. Various parties were slowly tightening the noose around the company's neck. The government was considering a commission of inquiry to investigate its affairs. Creditors were knocking at the door demanding repayment of loans. And farm residents, emboldened by the court's decision, were pushing for reparations. In their quest for justice, the residents enlisted the services of Cyril Kershaw Barry, an attorney in the Wakkerstroom district. In one of the letters Barry wrote to the secretary of the Native Farmers Association on behalf of his clients, he demanded that the company give them land in return for the money each of them had paid. If the company failed to guarantee that it would transfer the land to his clients within a specified period, the money each one had paid would have to be refunded. Barry threatened that if the company failed to meet the conditions he would institute legal proceedings without further notice.[26]

White shareholders gradually began to extricate themselves from the company. Upon government inquiries being initiated, Schlesinger, through his lawyers Bowman and Gilfillan, distanced himself from the company. He claimed that he 'was quite in the dark as to what is taking place' in the company. He blamed Seme for the mess the Native Farmers Association had become and claimed that other black directors of the company were being influenced by Seme, a state of affairs that he characterised as 'undesirable'.[27]

For Seme, that was just the start of things. By the following year (1919) the white directors' hostility to Seme and other black directors had worsened considerably. The former company secretary, Mr Hobbs, who had resigned his position after the Attorney General's findings, wrote to Schlesinger accusing Seme of embezzling over £1000 paid to him by Chief Moloi as an instalment for the two farms Moloi had bought on behalf of black people from Harrismith. Hobbs suggested that that amount was just the tip of the iceberg. In an appeal to the majority shareholder, Schlesinger, Hobbs argued that the company could only be saved if Seme was removed as chairman. He also proposed that the company be liquidated.[28] Schlesinger wasted no time, and the very next day, on 4 March 1919, he wrote to the Acting Under-Secretary for Native Affairs echoing Hobbs's view:

> I fully realize that it is absolutely useless to attempt anything in this connection unless the management of the Company is placed out of the reach of Seme and his native Directors. At the moment Seme by virtue of his shareholdings has full control of the Native Farmers' Association, but as Seme owes a considerable sum of money to this Company and moreover, has all his shares pledged with us, we are in a position to call upon him to pay up his indebtedness at once failing which, his shareholdings will be sold to cover the advances made to him from time to time.

The truth had finally come out. Here was a confession from Schlesinger that their long-held position that the Native Farmers Association was – on the basis of Seme's majority holding of the founders' shares – black controlled, was in fact a fiction. When Schlesinger and his white associates decided that they no longer needed Seme, they conveniently remembered that the shares they had effectively given him free of charge were a sham, and that he owed them 'a considerable sum of money' that they could call up – knowing full well that he did not have enough money to settle the debt.

Schlesinger took it a step further. On behalf of the company, he put forward six proposals to the government:

- that they foreclose on Seme and take over his shares in the company;
- that they register the shares taken from Seme in the name of the Colonial Bank and Trust Company Limited;
- that immediately after taking the abovementioned steps, they call a general meeting of the Native Farmers Association where they should remove Seme and other black directors;
- that in place of Seme and the others, white directors be appointed;
- that the company name be changed to reflect its true character as a white company; and
- that apart from the plots already allocated to black people, and in compliance with the Natives Land Act, the company no longer sell any land to black people.

But Schlesinger's offer to the Native Affairs department had a sting in the tail. He stated that the six proposals would be implemented on condition that the department gave him written assurance that all previous sales to black people by the company would be 'recognized as sales made by a native to a native'.[29] The department agreed to Schlesinger's proposals as well as his condition, and requested him to reimburse those who had lost money through the cancellation of the sale agreement.

Following this acceptance, Schlesinger and his white associates dispatched a letter to Seme and other black shareholders requesting them to convene an extraordinary general meeting of the company. Five resolutions were put forward for consideration at the meeting: the resignation of Seme and other directors, failing which they would be removed from office; the removal of Seme as the majority holder of the founders' shares and the transfer of those shares to the Colonial Bank and Trust Company whose chairman was Schlesinger; the nomination of Schlesinger, Atterbury and Bullock as directors of the company to be voted on at the meeting; the nomination of Burton for appointment as director of the company representing holders of ordinary shares; and finally, changing the company's registered office from Daggakraal to the Realty Trust Buildings in Johannesburg, where Schlesinger's other companies were based.

The proposed resolutions were accompanied by letters addressed to each of the black company directors. One of the directors, Reuben Dhlamini, was informed that the Colonial Bank and Trust Company had taken over all the founders' shares and intended to exercise the powers given by article 77 of the company's Articles of Association (i.e. the power to appoint company directors). In exercising that power, Schlesinger and founders' shares representatives were requesting Dhlamini to resign his directorship, failing which steps would be taken to remove him from office. The letter was signed by Schlesinger, Bullock and the bank's secretary, Gibb.[30]

This exercise of company power successfully ousted Seme and his black associates from the Native Farmers Association. When things became difficult, the white people with whom Seme had collaborated to evade the law abandoned him. And the black people who had been the victims of his duplicitous alliance with Schlesinger were once again left to fend for themselves. Seme's dream of building a black company that would buy land throughout South Africa was in ruins.

The removal of black directors was not the end of the company's woes. On the contrary, they deepened. The primary problem facing Schlesinger and his associates was how to address the aftermath of the Supreme Court judgment. The court had unequivocally stated that the cancellation of the sale agreement by Chief Moloi and the company's acceptance thereof was sufficiently suspicious to warrant an investigation. Moreover, after the cancellation the company had taken a decision to sell farm plots to individuals who had not been party to the original purchase. This meant that two groups were claimants to the same land: those who had originally bought plots under the Moloi scheme, and those who bought the plots after the company decided to sell these already allocated plots to outsiders following Moloi's cancellation of the agreement.

In an attempt to address this conundrum, Schlesinger, in his new capacity as the managing director of the Native Farmers Association, negotiated a deal with the Chief Moloi group whereby they would be allowed to stay on the farms they had originally bought on condition that they accepted they still owed the company about £15 000 to be paid over a period of fifteen years at an interest rate of 7 per cent. Individuals who had contributed towards the purchase of the two farms would be allocated plots commensurate with their individual contributions. A critical element of the agreement was that the company would evict all individuals who were not party to the agreement.

The farm residents were put under tremendous pressure by the company as well as their attorney, Mr Kleyn, to sign the agreement. At a meeting held with the residents on 4 June 1920 in Daggakraal, three residents in particular, Zacharia Lakage, Elia Matona and Hermanus Tshabalala, expressed serious concerns about the agreement and were reluctant to sign. Kleyn then threatened them with withdrawal, saying that he was only prepared to represent those who signed the agreement. Faced with this threat, the three men duly signed. Their concerns included the failure by the company to give an undertaking that if the residents signed the agreement they would keep the plots they already occupied. Another concern was the repayment terms.[31] The farm residents had failed to pay their attorney's fee, which amounted to just over £1000. So, to expect them to pay an annual amount in excess of £2000 for the next fifteen years was extremely unrealistic. As things turned out, the residents failed to meet the terms of the agreement and the matter dragged on. Unfortunately for Schlesinger and his associates, this time there was no Seme to blame for the mess.

The Native Farmers Association had committed to remove all residents on the two farms who were not signatories to the agreement with Moloi and his followers. But the problem with the company's commitment was that it had sold plots on to various other people after cancellation of the sale agreement with Moloi in May 1916. Most of the individuals to whom the plots were sold were from Wakkerstroom and other neighbouring districts. They later came to be known as Zulus even though they included individuals drawn from other ethnic groups, such as Swazis. These Zulus had continued to pay their instalments, though the payments were made not to the company but rather to Ben Boshoff, an attorney from Amersfoort. Accordingly, they continued to erect houses on the same farms that were occupied by Moloi's followers. By making the commitment to Moloi's people to evict individuals who were not party to the agreement, the company was effectively committing to evict these Zulus. The seeds of conflict between a group that came to be known as the Basotho on one side and the Zulus on the other were planted by the company. The group referred to as Basotho were the people who had come with Moloi from Harrismith.

The Basotho–Zulu divide would dog the company for many years and make it almost impossible to settle the land issue at Daggakraal and Vlakplaats. The magistrate and the Native Commissioner of Wakkerstroom, Mr L. Ham, accused the company of negligence or lacking foresight in its handling of the matter. He further blamed it for what he called the misunderstanding and friction between the Zulus and the Basotho. He was especially critical of Schlesinger's decision to enter into an agreement with Chief Moloi and his followers which excluded the group that came to be referred to as the Zulus. As a result of that decision, the 'Basutos will require the Company to give them quiet and undisturbed possession [of the land] while the Zulus will have every right to resent ejection'.[32]

The magistrate's proposal for a solution to the conundrum was to convince the two sides, Zulus and Basotho, to find common ground which would allow for some measure of coexistence. Several meetings were organised by the company and representatives of the government with each of the two groups; the meetings were held separately, as stakeholders tried to broker a compromise. One such meeting took place on 19 August 1920 at Daggakraal. It was attended by the district magistrate, as well as Ben Boshoff, an attorney who styled himself a defender of black people's interests in the Wakkerstroom district, and a Mr Beck. Also present were several black residents who had paid considerable sums of money towards the purchase of the farms. Boshoff tried to explain the costs and benefits of accepting the agreement with Chief Moloi and his followers, which would have resulted in the ejection of the Zulus. At that point Seme showed up, and all the black people present stood up and left. Leaving Boshoff and his associates on their own, they followed Seme out and held a separate meeting. When they returned, they insisted on an amendment to the company's agreement with Moloi, proposing a change to the terms of payment of the outstanding debt to the company.

Seme's participation indicates that he was still involved in the affairs of Daggakraal and the other farms even though the company had fired him. In fact his continued involvement in the affairs of Daggakraal became a source of huge concern and irritation for the company as well as the government. It did not help matters that the farm residents continued to demonstrate their trust in Seme despite his involvement in the mess that had developed. When he promised to assist them in their efforts to get the company to transfer ownership of the land, each resident willingly handed over the fee he demanded. The payments were confirmed in affidavits from Mtumzeli Budulwayo and Andries Malevu: Seme had called residents to a meeting at Vlakplaats where he requested each person present to pay £1 to enable him to go to Pretoria to get their title deeds. Seme asked the residents to commit to paying him an additional £4 on his return from Pretoria if he succeeded in bringing them the title deeds. Malevu and Budulwayo claimed to have paid Seme the £1 he had asked, but no title deeds were forthcoming.

Information that Seme was collecting money from the farm residents prompted the secretary of the Native Farmers Association, J.W. Maxfield, to write to the Secretary for Native Affairs to state the company's view on Seme's activities. Maxfield stated that Seme had no authority to collect money from the farm residents on behalf of the company. He informed the Secretary for Native Affairs that the company had previously warned Seme that he should stop pretending he was still acting for them.

In addition to this, Seme was involved in another controversy involving money. Sometime in 1920 Stephen Moloi had given an amount of £170 to Seme to deposit on his behalf and in his own name at the bank in Amersfoort. When Seme brought proof of deposit it showed he had only deposited £140 of the amount given. There was no explanation for the discrepancy; instead, Seme deposited the outstanding £30 at a later stage. The next year, when Moloi asked Seme to withdraw the £170, Seme told him to wait a while because 'the money is not up yet'. Moloi waited until 1922 and Seme had still not brought him the money. Again Moloi asked Seme for the money, but Seme did not hand it over to him. Moloi then decided to report the matter to the district magistrate. When he saw Seme again and demanded his money, Seme complained that the matter had been reported to the magistrate and told Moloi that he had decided not to hand him the money but rather to give it to the magistrate.[33] Seme admitted that he owed Moloi the money and stated that he was 'ready to hand over to you the monies with me'.[34] However, he failed to do so on the due date. When asked by the South African Police at Amersfoort why he had not paid Stephen Moloi, Seme said he had used the money on behalf of King Sobhuza II of Swaziland. He promised the police that he would pay Moloi as soon as he received an amount of £1 000 from Sobhuza, which he expected soon.[35] Seme gave the magistrate, Mr Ham, the same assurance, explaining that he would then pay Moloi and other people to whom he apparently owed money.[36] Ham seemed to find Seme's claim that Sobhuza owed him such a large sum amusing and he called for Seme and the Daggakraal attorney, Ben Boshoff, to be investigated.

Government investigations revealed the existence of two other companies in which Seme was involved: the Native Landowners Association of Africa Limited and the Native Farmers' Union of South Africa Limited. Both were registered in Natal, under Natal laws, though their headquarters were located at Seme's office in Johannesburg. As with the Native Farmers Association, the main purpose of these companies was the acquisition of land by black people. The aim of the Native Landowners Association was to 'educate the native mind as to the importance of acquiring interests in land, the advantage of individual tenure over and above communal or tribal tenure so-called'. It also advocated for the 'establishment of permanent native settlements, small holdings and other forms of settlement'. The company would employ judicial and parliamentary means to ensure that black people secured 'the fullest, free and unfettered rights' to own land anywhere in South Africa. Pixley ka Isaka Seme and Alfred Mangena were named as permanent directors and trustees of the company, with each having the power to appoint a successor. Their legal firm would be the company's solicitor for a period of at least five years. The first secretary general would be Saul Msane – ANC secretary general from 1917 to 1919 – who would draw an annual salary of £96.[37]

Seme was the driving force behind the Native Farmers' Union of South Africa, which was similar to the Native Farmers Association. Registered in Natal and established primarily to buy specific farms, it appointed black directors, but behind them were Schlesinger and his Colonial Bank and Trust Company, which provided the necessary funding. The provisional black shareholders were Seme, Charles Nkabinde, Isaac Nxumalo, Elias Gule, Baleni Luvuno, Jamba Hlatywako, Naphtali Gule, Zebulon Msizazne and Diamond Khubheka. Seme was designated company manager, while a white lawyer from Dundee in Natal, James W. Godfrey, was named company solicitor, with Simon Gule as secretary. As in the case of the Native Farmers Association and Daggakraal, the Native Farmers' Union intended to buy three farms from Earnest Conforth of Dundee. The scheme fell apart, however, when Seme and his associates failed to pay the amount due for the farm.[38]

The affairs of the Native Landowners Association and the Native Farmers' Union were a subject of intense government scrutiny in the early 1920s at a time when Seme himself was being investigated. As far as Seme was concerned, nothing incriminating came of this. What did emerge, however, was that the companies' affairs were being run by the lawyer James Godfrey. Godfrey's association with Seme is unclear. The secretary of the Native Landowners Association, Mr H.V. Msane (possibly a relative of Saul Msane, who had died in November 1919), confessed to the Johannesburg Director of Native Affairs that he was entirely ignorant concerning company affairs. He said he was appointed to the position for no other reason than he was 'in Seme's office at the time the association was started'.[39] He also revealed that Seme had sent him to Dundee to recruit black people there to be company shareholders, and to explain how it would operate. From the time of that visit, it appeared that Godfrey was running the company affairs without Msane's knowledge. One thing Msane did seem to know was that the company owed money to one or two white farmers for land it had purchased, a situation not dissimilar to Daggakraal and other farms in the eastern Transvaal. But still, the government had nothing criminal that it could pin on Seme.

The State v. Seme

Seme's luck ran out in 1927 when he was charged and convicted for stealing £100 from Ndhlozi Manana, a black resident of the Wakkerstroom district. Justice Barry of the Supreme Court sentenced Seme to one year of hard labour, which was suspended when Seme agreed to pay a fine of £184 before 31 May 1927. However, the event that led to this conviction had taken place fourteen years before, at the beginning of 1913. Ndhlozi Manana, a squatter on a farm at Twyfelfontein in Wakkerstroom, decided to buy a plot of land from the Native Farmers Association in 1913. To assist him with the purchase of the plot, Manana gave £100 to Aaron Mota, a relative who had already bought his own plot from the company and was quite active in its affairs. Together with Mota he went to Daggakraal where he met Seme, who was at the time chairman and managing director of the Native Farmers Association. Mota then handed Seme the £100 from Manana, informing him that the money was for the purchase of a plot of land at Daggakraal. Seme issued a receipt that read 'Received from Aaron Mota of Daggakraal the sum of 100 sgt. For safe custody and to be used at my discretion to buy land for Ndhlozi Manana.'

However, Manana never received the plot of land. Several years later he asked Seme about the plot, and Seme's reply was that Manana should go to the resident magistrate to ask for the land. His reason was that he was no longer in charge of the company and was therefore unable to account for the money paid by Manana for the purchase of the land. When Manana was cross-examined during the trial, he reported the following: 'He [Seme] said he had no ground, that the Europeans were holding the ground.' The Europeans to which Seme was referring were Schlesinger and his associates who had taken over the company.

The photograph was taken and published by the *New York Times* a few days after Seme won the Curtis Medal at Columbia University in April 1906

Seme at his graduation ceremony at Columbia University, June 1906

In this photograph of the graduating class of 1906 at Columbia, Seme is seated towards the left (he is the only black person)

THE

COLUMBIA MONTHLY

VOL. III   APRIL, 1906   No. 6

THE REGENERATION OF AFRICA

BY P. KÀ ISAKA SEME

Curtis Medals Orations, First Prize, April 5, 1906

ADIES AND GENTLEMEN: I have chosen to speak to you on this occasion upon "The Regeneration of Africa." I am an African, and I set my pride in my race over against a hostile public opinion. Men have tried to compare races on the basis of some equality. In all the works of nature, equality, if by it we mean identity, is an impossible dream! Search the universe! You will find no two units alike. The scientists tell us there are no two cells, no two atoms, identical. Nature has bestowed upon each a peculiar individuality, an exclusive patent—from the great giants of the forest to the tenderest blade. Catch in your hand, if you please, the gentle flakes of snow. Each is a perfect gem, a new creation; it shines in its own glory—a work of art different from all of its aërial companions. Man, the crowning achievement of nature, defies analysis. He is a mystery through all ages and for all time. The races of mankind are composed of free and unique individuals. An attempt to compare them on the basis of equality can never

be finally satisfactory. Each is himself. My thesis stands on this truth; time has proved it. In all races, genius is like a spark, which, concealed in the bosom of a flint, bursts forth at the summoning stroke. It may arise anywhere and in any race.

I would ask you not to compare Africa to Europe or to any other continent. I make this request not from any fear that such comparison might bring humiliation upon Africa. The reason I have stated,—a common standard is impossible! Come with me to the ancient capital of Egypt, Thebes, the city of one hundred gates. The grandeur of its venerable ruins and the gigantic proportions of its architecture reduce to insignificance the boasted monuments of other nations. The pyramids of Egypt are structures to which the world presents nothing comparable. The mighty monuments seem to look with disdain on every other work of human art and to vie with nature herself. All the glory of Egypt belongs to Africa and her people. These monuments are the indestructible memorials of their great and original genius. It is not

An excerpt of the award-winning speech that Seme delivered for a student debate contest at Columbia University in April 1906. The speech won him the Curtis Medal in gold, and his achievement was widely reported by newspapers in the United States and other parts of world, including his homeland, South Africa

Seme riding a horse while a student at Oxford University, 1908

Seme (standing third from left) in 1908 at an event of the Cosmopolitan Club, an organisation he co-founded at Oxford University. Standing in the right-hand corner is his African-American friend Alain LeRoy Locke

Seme (right) standing beside Dinuzulu ka Cetshwayo, the dethroned and exiled Zulu king at the time. On the left is one of Dinuzulu's medical doctors, Dr Godfrey. This photograph was likely taken in 1912 or 1913 when Seme and Godfrey worked closely to assist Dinuzulu to get treatment overseas for his ill health

The South African Native National Congress delegation to England, June 1914. Left to right: Thomas Mapike, Rev. Walter Rubusana, Rev. John Dube, Saul Msane and Sol Plaatje

A portrait of Seme as a lawyer. Seme's legal work included representing black people in cases of land dispossession and providing legal advice to chiefs in their engagements with white government authorities

The SANNC delegation to London in 1919, led by Sol Plaatje. Left to right: Richard Selope Thema, Sol Plaatje, Josiah T. Gumede, Rev. Henry R. Ngcayiya and Levi T. Mvabaza

Seme (lying down), with the Swazi queen mother Labotsibeni behind him. Seme became very close to the Swazi royal house after his legal efforts to help the Swazis reclaim land that they lost to white land concessionaires. He came to be known as the Swazi nation's attorney

Seme (wearing a light suit) and King Sobhuza II (seated) with the Swazi delegation to England to protest against the partition of Swaziland, December 1922

The Swazi delegation to England in December 1922. Seme is seated on the extreme right, and Sobhuza II is seated in the middle. Standing at the right is Sol Plaatje, who was in England at the time on other business

Seme in middle age. The date of this photograph is unknown, although it is likely to have been in the 1930s when he was president general of the ANC

PictureNet

Umteteleli wa Bantu

Seme as the president general of the ANC, 1934

Seme's tombstone at Newclare Cemetery in Johannesburg. The tombstone was erected in September 1985 by the Inkatha yeNkululeko yeSizwe (known today as the Inkatha Freedom Party)

The problem for Seme was that Mota had asked him on several occasions about Manana's plot of land, before Schlesinger took over the company. According to Mota's evidence at the trial, Seme had always replied that the company, i.e. the Native Farmers Association, would sort things out with Manana's plot of land. But that never happened.

Seme's version of what took place differed from that of both Manana and Mota. He claimed that Manana had said he was paying the £100 in order to join the company, and that he, Seme, could use the money at his own discretion. He conceded that Manana had made it clear that what he wanted was a plot of land. He also conceded that Manana did not get the land and was not issued shares in the company in view of his payment. Seme contended that Manana was partly to blame for not receiving the piece of land for which he had paid: 'It is Manana's fault. He has been responsible to some extent, but more so his headman who did not come and attend meetings.' According to Seme, Manana should have attended meetings of purchasers which were called by the company. His failure to do so resulted in Seme forgetting about him as well as the fact that he had paid the sum of money for purchase of a plot. He also blamed Manana for having paid the money and then disappearing for many years without inquiring about his plot. With regard to the shares, he would have given them to Manana had he asked for them: 'The shares belonged to me to distribute. Manana did not come for them.' And when Manana did eventually ask for his money, Seme claimed that 'the company was already a European company'.[40] This was a revealing admission: when the company was investigated by the state regarding its compliance with provisions of the Natives Land Act, Seme's argument and that of the company was always that it was a black company and therefore compliant with the law. During the trial he changed tack, however, by claiming that it became a European company when Schlesinger got involved in late 1912 and the old company was liquidated.

When it became clear to Seme that his defence of blaming Manana and everyone other than himself for the disappearance of Manana's money was not working, he put up a different defence. He pleaded that he was inexperienced in handling a big operation such as running a company. That was the reason he had approached Schlesinger for assistance. The mistakes he made at the time needed to be understood in the context of an inexperienced person lacking the necessary support to run a company. He conceded that he may have been negligent in the manner he handled the Manana matter, but he had no criminal intent in not using the money for its intended purpose. He pleaded with the court to take this into consideration and 'impose a fine or a suspended sentence, realising the great difficulties which I single-handed had to cope with'.[41]

Justice Barry remained unconvinced by Seme's defence, however, and stated: 'the only conclusion that I can come to is that under these circumstances this 100 pounds has been misappropriated by the accused'. Seme was then sentenced to one year's imprisonment, suspended if he agreed to refund Manana his money plus interest of £84 before the end of May 1927, to which he agreed.

What had begun as a noble initiative by Seme ended in ignominy when he was convicted and sentenced for theft. This turn of events would have been an especially painful blow to Seme considering the pride he took in his status and position as a solicitor, and therefore an officer of the court. However, it was not surprising that things turned out this way. He had gained something of a reputation for playing fast and loose with the hard-earned cash of black people who came to him in the hopes of buying land – people who wished to escape the fate of being squatters on white-owned farms and the prospect of eviction when the Natives Land Act came into effect. Seme's alliance with Schlesinger, and the manner in which they dealt with Chief Moloi and his followers, only served to demonstrate the extent to which he was prepared to sacrifice the interests of black people for his own benefit.

Nevertheless, Seme's defence regarding the heavy responsibility of running a company in which hundreds of people had an interest should not be altogether discounted. It is indeed plausible that his intention was not to steal Manana's money, as he argued at the trial. Taking into account evidence showing that the books of the company were in a mess, it is possible to imagine a situation where an amount of £100 might be used for purposes other than originally intended.

Although Seme's financial affairs were not scrutinised during his trial, it should be noted that he had chronic financial problems. He was in and out of court defending himself against creditors. At one point in 1916 the Alliance Bank, which had financed his family home in Sophiatown, Johannesburg, took him to court when he failed to repay the loan, and subsequently put the house up for auction.[42] However, Seme appears to have come up with payment, as the auction advertisements were withdrawn. Ben Boshoff, his legal associate, claimed that Seme tried to sell his home as well as other Sophiatown properties to a group of black farm residents in Daggakraal; the sales did not materialise, however.[43] In order to understand why and how Seme experienced continual financial difficulties, it is useful to turn to the observations of his one-time secretary, Selby Msimang: 'He lived beyond his means and his general behaviour was that. It was almost as if he was showing out [sic] that he was an educated person. The standard of living and his deportment generally had become second nature to him as a result of his contact with Oxford.' Msimang described Seme as 'a wonderful spendthrift'. He also claimed that there would be months when he was not paid for his secretarial services unless Msimang himself 'had made provision ... early in the month' in order to ensure that he would get paid at the end of the month.[44] While Seme was not found guilty of misappropriating funds owing to his financial difficulties, his lifestyle and the manner in which he managed his finances nevertheless provide insights into the many controversies in which he became entangled – which all had a common source: money.

* * *

Seme's involvement in the Native Farmers Association, with its bold initiative of buying farms for black settlement, is among his outstanding legacies. Daggakraal, the farm he bought in April 1912 from Willem Cornelius Gouws, still stands as a testament to the breadth of Seme's vision. It is also a tribute to the many generations who made enormous sacrifices defending what Seme and his associates had set in motion in 1912. Sadly, as with many of Seme's initiatives, the Native Farmers Association eventually tarnished his reputation. Indeed, later allegations of misappropriation of black people's funds had their origin in the company – allegations that would continue to dog Seme.

It would, however, be too easy to dismiss Seme's achievement in starting the Native Farmers Association on the basis of his conduct. To appreciate the significance of his initiative, it should be recalled that just a few months after Seme's land purchases the Natives Land Act was passed, making it unlawful for black people to purchase or sell land in areas such as Wakkerstroom, which were considered white. Indeed, if not the actual reason for the passing of the Natives Land Act in 1913, the purchase of Daggakraal and other farms by Seme and his associates may well have accelerated it. Such was the full significance of Seme's land initiative.

7

Betrayed trust

Information about Seme's private life is scant, and the little that has been written is often incorrect. Far more is known about his public life, where he gained a reputation for his authoritarian leadership style and for being somewhat arrogant. And yet those who knew Seme in private always remarked about his sense of humour and cheerful disposition. Ten years after his death in 1951, Professor Z.K. Matthews, who had known Seme well, described him thus: 'As an individual he was of a cheerful disposition with a keen sense of humour. He was always immaculately dressed and his manners showed that he was a man who had absorbed the best in both African and Western culture.' Matthews noted too that Seme was widely read and also popular among those who knew him.[1]

The sense of humour is evident in letters Seme wrote to his African-American friend, Alain Locke. Perhaps more than any other person outside Seme's immediate family, Locke was a constant presence in his life and something of a kindred spirit. Their friendship and correspondence continued after Seme's return to South Africa. There is an ease and informality in the manner Seme communicated with his friend which is absent from his communications with others. Writing to Locke in early 1911, Seme thanked him for settling the debts he had left behind in England and informed him that he had decided to return to South Africa without saying his goodbyes because it dawned on him that he 'could not play the Duke with only an income of two guineas a week'; he needed to come back home and earn an honest living, he said.[2] He also updated his friend about developments in his life in South Africa. He informed him, for instance, that his career as a lawyer had taken off splendidly; ever humorous, he mentioned that his only problem was the fact that his clients were farmers, which meant that they paid his fees 'in ducks and pigs'.[3]

Other letters to Locke reflect Seme's increasing involvement in efforts aimed at uplifting the lives of black people in South Africa. In one letter sent in January 1912, soon after the founding of the SANNC, Seme told Locke that South Africa was steadily awakening. He wished that Locke were in South Africa so that he could assist in addressing problems facing black people and participate in 'organising and directing Native Journalism along National Lines'.[4] Seme told Locke that there was a lot of money to be made from the black journalism enterprise in South Africa; indeed, Seme himself was in the process of setting up *Abantu-Batho*, which was launched a few months later. Seme tried to entice his friend to come and work for his newspaper by telling him that he could take vacations in Victoria Falls, the Garden of Eden and 'many other enchanted spots of this great continent'.[5] But his entreaties were in vain, and Locke did not come to South Africa.

The next year, in January 1913, Seme mentioned to Locke that he might soon get married. He said there were 'very strange proposals in mid-air just now', although he did not elaborate – and he did not divulge the name of the woman he intended to marry.[6] In all their correspondence up until then there had not been much talk about relationships or marriage, but now Seme expressed the wish that his friend might find a partner soon so that they could be married at the same time. As things turned out, whatever wedding plans there may have been never did materialise. It would take Seme another three years before he got married. His choice of a wife was Frances Mabel Maude Xiniwe from King William's Town in the Cape Province.

Betrayal

There is no information as to how Seme came to meet his future wife. It is, however, not surprising that he decided to marry Frances Xiniwe, for he was a man of good taste and acutely aware of social status. The Xiniwes were a family of extraordinary achievement and culture, attributes that would have attracted Seme to them and drawn him to Frances. Frances's parents, Paul and Eleanor Xiniwe, were a celebrated couple not only in the Cape Province, but also in black society further afield. Paul Xiniwe came from humble beginnings, and for several years before going to Lovedale College he worked on the railways as a timekeeper, and later as a telegraph operator. He then decided to train as a teacher, and after completing his studies he taught for many years in schools in the Eastern Cape, in Port Elizabeth in particular. He then decided to abandon teaching and became a merchant, opening stores, and also buying properties in East London, King William's Town and Port Elizabeth. His reputation spread after opening the Temperance Hotel in King William's Town, a popular spot for black travellers.[7]

Paul Xiniwe's wife, Eleanor, came from a prominent family in Middle-drift, the Ndwanyas. Her brother was Daniel Ndwanya, who had trained as a teacher at the Healdtown Institution and later became a law agent with a flourishing and famous practice. Daniel was also a member of the deputation that went to England in 1909 to protest against the proposed colour bar in South Africa. Eleanor, who had been educated at Middledrift, was distinguished in her own right, and when her husband died she took over the family businesses and expanded them. Her son-in-law, T.D. Mweli Skota, would later claim that her achievements were equal to those of her husband, and describe her as the first African woman 'to control success-fully such vast business interests'.[8]

A striking beauty, Eleanor was also a woman of refined taste. A photo-graph published in *The Guardian* shows her together with her husband and other members of the African Choir that toured England and North America in the early 1890s.[9] The Xiniwes' gifts were passed on to their five children, who became talented musicians. Frances became an accom-plished pianist, while her sister Mercy was a good singer. In addition to their musical talent, the sons were gifted sportsmen, with the eldest, Bertram Buxton, becoming a well-known cricketer. B.B. Xiniwe, as Bertram was popularly known, was elected as a member of the Native Representative Council (NRC) in 1937 and became leader of the ANC in the Cape in the 1940s.[10]

Frances's family pedigree would have been attractive to a man such as Seme. The fact that she was an accomplished pianist was undoubtedly a further draw for Seme, who had developed an interest in the piano as a student at Oxford. But Seme was not the only one interested in the Xiniwe sisters. Ben Tyamzashe, known for his talent as a composer, married Mercy. In addition to being a musician, Frances was also a teacher, having been trained at Lovedale. Though the circumstances of their meeting are unknown, it would not have been difficult for Seme to meet Frances, given the prominence of her family. There were very few educated black women at the time, and the fact that Frances was a teacher at the well-known Lyndhurst Road Public School in Kimberley would have drawn the atten-tion of a man seeking a mate, as Seme was.

The couple were married on 11 May 1916. Their marriage certificate describes Seme as a thirty-six-year-old male, while Frances is reported to be only twenty-two years of age. The wedding took place at Sacred Heart Church in King William's Town. Frances's eldest brother, Bertram, signed as a witness together with Seme's friend, William Zungu. The marriage certificate gives Sophiatown, Johannesburg, as Seme's place of residence, while Frances's address is her hometown, King William's Town. After they were married, Frances joined her husband in Sophiatown, and not long afterwards their son Quinton was born. The marriage was, however, soon rocked by scandal. In October 1916, a mere five months after their wedding, Seme discovered his wife in an adulterous relationship with an unnamed man. Seme stated in court papers that he did not know the identity of the man and it appears as if Frances was also not willing to divulge this information. Seme was understandably upset and angered, and from Frances's letters it appears that he had stopped speaking to her. Her only communication was through letters, which she used to express profuse apologies for what she had done. In one letter she begged Seme for forgiveness, pleading, 'Pixley dearest don't harden your heart ... I am sorry for what I have done. This is really from the bottom of my heart, darling. Do come dearest my heart is breaking within me'.[11] But Seme remained unmoved by his wife's pleas for forgiveness, and filed for divorce. He asked the court to dissolve the marriage by reason of his wife's adultery, and demanded custody of their son and forfeiture of all benefits of the marriage by his wife.[12] He also requested that Frances be liable for the legal costs of the divorce proceedings. Frances did not file answering papers and instead wrote Seme another letter asking for forgiveness. Clearly alarmed at her husband's action, she wrote: 'I know dearest one that I must have wronged you indeed very much to have taken such steps against me ... Indeed dearest I am short of words you will pardon me'.[13] It appears that Seme finally relented and agreed to meet Frances, as she expressed gratitude but also begged him not to be too angry. It is not known whether the meeting took place, but if so it did not change Seme's mind, and he went ahead with the divorce proceedings. The date for the hearing was 3 May 1917, and on the appointed day Seme arrived with his legal representatives, though neither his wife nor her representatives were anywhere to be seen. The hearing proceeded despite her absence, and having heard the evidence the court dissolved the marriage with costs and declared Frances Seme to have forfeited all the benefits derived from the marriage by antenuptial contract, including custody of their son, who was given to Seme.[14] Their marriage was over almost a year to the day of their wedding.

The Semes left behind nothing that sheds light on their marriage or the reasons behind its collapse. All we are left with is the court record, which reveals that adultery was committed and that Seme had filed for divorce because of it. The reason for his wife's adultery can only be guessed at since the state of their marriage prior to that is unknown. Whatever the case, it should be noted that a year before their marriage, Seme had fathered a son, Zwangendaba George Seme, with Princess Lozinja of the Swazi royal house. There are conflicting claims about the nature of Seme's relationship with the princess, which may have been solemnised by traditional rites, though there is no evidence to support this claim which Zwangendaba himself has disputed. Seme's daughter, Helen Mamama Seme, suggests that her father named his son Zwangendaba because the first news he had of his birth was from others. All this suggests that Seme's relationship with Zwangendaba's mother was not very close – possibly as a result of Seme's lengthy absences while establishing his practice in Johannesburg.

Yet Seme's relationship with Princess Lozinja and the birth of Zwangendaba may provide clues as to the complexities of his marriage to Frances. It may even be possible that their relationship was in trouble before the actual wedding took place. In any event, the divorce did not signify the end of the road for either Seme or his former wife, who in 1920 married T.D. Mweli Skota. As editor of *The African Yearly Register*, with its brief biographies of eminent black men and women of the day, Skota's fame soon spread. He was also known for his involvement in the leadership of the ANC, becoming its secretary general in 1923 and again in the late 1920s and early 1930s during Seme's presidency. He was also a sub-editor of *Abantu-Batho* in its early years, though his own newspaper, the *African Shield*, soon folded. Skota's marriage to Seme's former wife seems to have had no adverse effect on the two men's relationship.[15] Skota's marriage to Frances ended when she died at a young age in 1933.

It would take Seme almost a decade before committing to another marriage, though in the interim he led an interesting personal life. After meeting Anna Sibeko from Daggakraal, Seme had a son named Dumakude, though the couple did not get married. Seme's only surviving child, Helen Seme, has claimed that her father had another child, a daughter, with another woman from Daggakraal. While the name of the woman is unknown, the daughter was called Dalida, presumably after Seme's sister. These numerous relationships have led Helen Seme to describe her father as *isoka*, a man loved by women. When Seme finally decided to marry again, he chose another princess.

Princesses

Seme's next choice was the most dazzling jewel in the crown of the house of Senzangakhona: Dinuzulu's eldest child and Solomon's half-sister, Princess Phikisinkosi Harriet. He seems to have followed a similar path to the one that had led him to Princess Lozinja of the Swazi royal house. Seme had started out as a legal advisor to the Swazi royals, and this soon developed into close friendships with some of its key people, including Prince Malunge. He was also close to Queen Labotsibeni and King Sobhuza II. From there, he became involved in a relationship with Princess Lozinja, which resulted in the birth of Zwangendaba. In the case of the Zulu royal house, he similarly began as legal advisor to the king, Dinuzulu, before becoming a trusted advisor to the family. Admitted to its inner sanctum, Seme was able to keep company with the princesses, including Phikisinkosi (Phikisile).

Given his keen knowledge of history, Seme would have been aware of the significance of marrying Dinuzulu's first daughter. Princess Phikisile's conception and birth had occurred in extraordinary circumstances. Dinuzulu was about to be exiled to the island of St Helena, and the royal house was concerned that he would depart, perhaps never to return, without leaving an heir. He was therefore encouraged to impregnate a woman in whom he had shown some interest, the daughter of Dloko Ndwandwe, one of the prominent *mnumzane*, whose homestead was situated on the other side of the Isikhwebezi River in northern Zululand. The hope of the royals was that the offspring would be a boy, who would then become heir to the Zulu throne. In defiance of the royal wishes, the child turned out to be a girl. She was named Phikisinkosi – 'She who defied the king'.[16]

It was the woman who dared defy a king whom Seme married in 1926. There is no information about their courtship, but it has been suggested that, unlike the marriages of Solomon's other sisters whose purpose was the building of alliances in Zululand, Seme's marriage to Phikisile was not arranged. Soon, the couple was blessed with two boys and a girl. The first-born was a boy named Silosentaba Godfrey. Silosentaba (*isilo sentaba* or 'king of the mountains') was a reference to his mother, who would have been king had she been born male. The second child was another boy, Pilidi Douglas, with the youngest being a girl, Mamama Helen. According to Helen, another daughter was born after her, but she died as a child.

Helen Seme recalls that her father was concerned that her children were growing up in the urban surroundings of Sophiatown, and wanted to send them to his Daggakraal farm. He had involved her brothers in farming chores, and taught them how to milk cows. They used to squirt the milk directly into their mouths and spray it onto each other's faces, which would then be white from the milk.[17] Helen remembers Seme as a doting father who loved his children. This loving family environment changed, however, when Seme was struck off the roll of attorneys. The family went through a period of enormous hardship, with Seme losing his properties. He was forced to leave Johannesburg, and moved in with his wife at Emahhashini royal kraal. During this period of hardship, Seme relied on friends to assist him, as he had earlier with Locke. Seme was apparently not very involved in raising the three sons he sired outside marriage; the eldest, Zwangendaba, was raised by Seme's brother, Mbekwana, whose only son had died while young.[18]

A friend in need

Seme's friendships were mostly with members of the Swazi and Zulu royal families. They included Swazi princes Malunge and Jaha ka Mancibana. He was also quite close to the queen mother, Labotsibeni, who helped him with many projects, including financial support for *Abantu-Batho* in 1912. His relationship with Sobhuza II was not only personal but also professional, spanning many years. When Seme was struck off the roll of attorneys in the 1930s, Sobhuza was one of several people who pleaded with the court to reinstate him as a lawyer. And when Seme died in 1951, Sobhuza assisted his two sons in Swaziland by giving them large tracts of land to build homes.

In the Zulu royal house, Seme's interactions with Dinuzulu and his successor, Solomon, went beyond the usual bounds that separated king and subject or attorney and client. There was a familiarity that suggested a fair degree of intimacy. It is no wonder that when Seme was interviewed by James Stuart in London in December 1924 and again in May 1925, he could speak so knowledgeably and passionately about Dinuzulu, the way he had grown up, and his fundamental beliefs:

> He had a heart which quickly cast away and forgot unhappy things. He greatly liked to create happiness; he liked amusements (*imidhlalo*). Where he was present, dancing took place; until dawn people would be on their feet. He himself was a great performer (*igagu*); he would go among the people and sing and dance and point with his great

knob-stick (*iwisa*). The songs which he composed were many, both for war and for entertainment. They were nearly as many as those of the times of Mpande and Dingane and Tshaka.

Aware that he could not do full justice to the man he knew so intimately, Seme apologised for having 'failed fully to show you all that Dinuzulu was'. He added that it was impossible to tell Stuart everything about Dinuzulu 'for even those who know finish by saying, "You are beyond understanding, Ngonyama (*Ulibinda, Nkosi, ulibinda, Ngonyama*)"'.[19]

Seme's best-known friendship was of course with Alain Locke, and their correspondence from the early to mid-1920s is central to how Seme came to be known and perceived. Seme valued Locke's friendship, and held him in high esteem. In Locke he had a friend to whom he could pour out the hopes and the dreams he held for South Africa, Swaziland, the African continent, and the black race as a whole. Seme felt strongly that Locke should participate in his endeavours, and at one point he declared:

> During my whole time in South Africa I have never been able to think about the education of the race without your name standing clearly before my vision. All our great Councils know of you already. The native press is ready to carry your message into every home in South Africa ...[20]

For some time he had been urging Locke to leave the United States and settle in Swaziland. Claiming to have convinced Sobhuza that Locke should be given the task of designing an education system for Swaziland, Seme proposed that '[a]fter studying the local needs of the country [i.e. Swaziland] you would make out your own curriculum for the approval of the King and his Chiefs and Councillors'.[21] Locke did not, however, take up these offers.

Seme was also keen for Locke to assist him in his attempt to be awarded a doctoral degree in law by an American university. The first time he raised the matter explicitly was in a letter dated 8 December 1922. He told Locke that he was 'polishing' a thesis on 'The Laws and Customs of the Zulus and the Swazis' and added that he wanted 'a fat LLD [Doctor of Laws] for that'. He then requested Locke to suggest a university to examine his thesis, and asked for information on the required course of study for the LLD degree.[22] However, when Locke sent him catalogues containing information relating mostly to the LLM degree, Seme was disappointed. It seems that Locke then suggested an alternative route: the possibility of a university conferring an honorary degree on him – an idea that Seme found 'gratifying'. He thanked Locke for 'proposing my name to the Academy [for the honorary degree]'. Seme also informed his friend that he was writing a book on 'Native Law and Custom', presumably the same book he had in an earlier letter referred to as 'The Laws and Customs of the Zulus and the Swazis'. He suggested that, were he to receive it, the honorary degree would complement his status as a soon-to-be-published author.[23]

The exchange concerning the honorary degree took place while Seme was in London working on the appeal by Swaziland regarding the kingdom's loss of land. On his way back from London Seme wrote Locke another letter in which he again raised the issue of the honorary degree:

> I shall put myself out as Dr Seme when I get home. So unless I hear from you by cable I shall know that everything is alright ... Don't waste money to cable if things turned alright.[24]

It is unclear whether Locke ever sent the cable. But when Seme returned to South Africa, *Abantu-Batho* published a report on his stay in London, which ended thus:

> Another matter of interest to our readers is to know that while he was in England, Dr Seme wrote a thesis in Bantu Law and custom for which Columbia University offered him the degree of M.A., while Howard University honoured him with the degree of Doctor of Laws. We think we are voicing the opinion of every enlightened African when we say we are proud of this achievement.[25]

From that point on he called himself Dr Seme and signed as 'P. ka Isaka Seme, B.A., LLD'. Although *Abantu-Batho* named the institution that had allegedly awarded Seme the honorary doctorate, *The African Yearly Register*, edited by T.D. Mweli Skota, confused the issue by stating that the degree was awarded in 1928 by Columbia University, not in 1923 by Howard University. The claim has been repeated many times ever since. But it is false. Similarly, *Abantu-Batho* was incorrect in reporting that Howard University had awarded Seme the degree. The university has since explicitly denied that it awarded Seme the honorary LLD degree or any degree for that matter: 'Regrettably, Pixley Seme's name is not among honorary degree recipients at Howard University'.[26] Columbia University has similarly disputed *Abantu-Batho*'s claim about the MA degree, and also insists that the honorary degree did not come from them: 'Seme was never awarded an honorary degree by Columbia University in 1920s'.[27]

Nevertheless, Seme assumed the title Doctor of Laws and flaunted it. Even in his correspondence with Locke – the one person who was aware of the facts – Seme proclaimed his new status: when next he met his friend, he 'certainly ought to look a little more important being a Doctor'.[28] There is no sense of embarrassment at all that he is laying claim to a degree he has not in fact earned. Either Locke was unwilling to dampen his friend's enthusiasm by informing him of the facts, or Seme did not care.

Locke may well have remained silent because he knew Seme was desperate to have a doctorate. Believing that titles enhanced an individual's social standing, Seme had encouraged Locke to gain as many degrees as possible, even if they were conferred by lesser institutions. He told Locke that 'in Africa the big man in your profession is the one who can silence his critics with a powerful pen and organisation as well as please the applauding populace of admirers by printing for them behind his name all the degrees which an ordinary dictionary may define and a few more besides'. Furthermore, the reputation of the institution was of little importance:

> I know you think more of Harvard and Oxford than of any degree which Lincoln University might offer you. I say don't now. You can keep these in your back pocket for good use in Africa. Remember that the African has not even those Southern Universities.
>
> But to inspire Africa you must wear the cap & gown tumbling over a confusion of titles and degrees – these will draw for you the attention and the admiration of the populace. Your utterances will in likewise be clothed with the magic surroundings of an Oracle.[29]

Urging Locke to do whatever he could to assist him in his quest for an honorary LLD, Seme confessed that he had no time to write a thesis since he was occupied with the Swaziland case. He said he was prepared to 'swallow up a stone and take any degree that I may be honoured with', and asked his friend to 'suggest to some University in the South that they honour me forthwith with the coveted distinction M.A., LLD'. In pursuit of his aim, Seme went so far as to suggest exaggerating his achievements: 'You know how to go about the matter of blowing up my merits – do go ahead and fetch the big guns for me I want to fire the enemies' lines with them now'.[30] Given this pressure, it is perhaps not surprising that Locke remained silent when Seme eventually laid claim to the degree. But in the face of available evidence it is more difficult to remain silent when faced with the question as to whether Seme deliberately and knowingly made a false claim.

* * *

At the very least it may be said that Seme placed value on social standing. He firmly believed that having the title LLD would enhance his reputation and status. It is no coincidence that he 'married up', as it were, with his first wife Frances Xiniwe. And while Princess Phikisile ka Dinuzulu was not quite as educated, she was of royal blood, as was Princess Lozinja of the Swazi royal house. Seme's relationships and friendships also demonstrate the two worlds that he straddled: one foot in the new urban educated class and the other firmly planted in traditional royalty. It is testament to his social and political skills that he could so effortlessly move between these worlds.

8

'*Thulasizwe* of the black race'

Seme's re-entry into active politics in the ANC after almost two decades of absence was dramatic. The occasion was the ANC's elective conference, which started on Monday 21 April 1930, in Bloemfontein. It was exceptionally well attended by between 350 and 400 delegates from all over South Africa and the protectorates.[1] The delegates were divided into two main camps, with radicals sitting on the left side of the hall and moderates on the right.[2] Leading the moderate wing was the old guard of the ANC, which had turned out in numbers. All three ex-presidents – Reverend John Dube, Reverend Zaccheus Mahabane and Sefako Makgatho – were present. So too were founding fathers of the organisation, such as R.V. Selope Thema, Thomas Mtobi Mapikela, H. Selby Msimang and Pixley Seme. Leading the radical wing were Cape communists Bransby Ndobe and Elliot Tonjeni,[3] S. Malkenson from Bloemfontein, and Allison W.G. Champion from Natal (who, though not a communist, joined the radical camp at the conference). The battle lines had been drawn well before the conference, and each group was itching for a fight. Both sides got what they wished for – and more.

Right from the start, the conference descended into chaos and disorder over the presidential address delivered by Josiah T. Gumede, president of the ANC at the time. In a fiery speech he charged that the laws General Hertzog's government were spearheading in Parliament were tantamount to a declaration of war against black people. Gumede urged the ANC to adopt a new strategy. Rather than continuing to send deputations to the government and to England, black people should rely on their 'own strength, [and] on the strength of the revolutionary masses of white workers the world over with whom we must join forces'. The object of their struggle should be to 'demand our equal economic, social and political rights'. Those rights could only be attained through a 'South African Native Republic, with equal rights for all, but free from all foreign and local domination'.[4] Moving to the international front, Gumede expressed his support for Soviet Russia and exhorted delegates to support peasant workers in their battle against what he called the 'onslaught of the ene-mies of the oppressed peoples of the world'. He then urged the conference and the ANC in general to adopt the slogan 'Defend the Soviet'.[5]

Gumede's proposal for a South African Native Republic and his plea for support of the Soviet Union confirmed the moderates' belief that he was trying to turn the ANC into a political front for the Soviet Union and the Communist Party of South Africa (CPSA).[6] The moderates fiercely protested that Gumede's speech did not reflect ANC policy and that the executive committee had not been consulted when it was drafted. The radicals in turn shouted down the moderates. Thomas Mtobi Mapikela, a veteran leader from the Free State and speaker of the ANC, could not control the conference from the chair. At one point William G. Ballinger, advisor to the Industrial and Commercial Workers Union (ICU), was requested to quieten down the radical section of the conference, but he too failed.

Pixley Seme's moment arrived when a president general had to be elected. Together with Reverend Mahabane and Gumede, Seme was nom-inated for the position.[7] Before the voting began, Mahabane withdrew from the contest, ostensibly to prevent a split of the moderate vote between himself and Seme. That left Gumede and Seme as candidates. Ballot papers were issued to the delegates, but when they were returned the speaker, Mapikela, declared that they exceeded the number originally issued. He called for the vote to be declared null and void and for a revote to take place. This drew loud protests from the radicals, who called Mapikela's decision unconstitutional. They called for Mapikela to step down as the chair, chanting 'Chuck him out, chuck him out'.[8] It was only after Gumede's intervention that they quietened down and a fresh vote was taken. The results of the election were clear and decisive: thirty-nine votes for Seme and only fourteen for Gumede. Pixley ka Isaka Seme had returned from the political wilderness to lead the organisation he had founded in 1912.

If anyone expected that the decisive result in favour of Seme would settle the conflict between the moderates and radicals, they were mis-taken. The next point of contention was the appointment of persons to serve on the executive committee under the leadership of President General Seme. Gumede had amended the constitution to allow the presi-dent to appoint members of the national executive, instead of their being elected at an elective conference. Accordingly, Seme appointed T.D. Mweli Skota (secretary general), S.M. Makgatho (treasurer general), Dr A.B. Xuma (assistant treasurer and chairman of the Committee of Health), Reverend J.L. Dube (chairman of the Education Committee), H. Selby Msimang (chairman of the Commerce and Labour Committee), Reverend Z.R. Mahabane (senior chaplain and parliamentary reporter), Chief Stephen Mini (organiser of chiefs), R.V. Selope Thema (chief organiser of Congress and corresponding secretary), T.M. Mapikela (speaker and assistant treasurer), D.S. Letanka (organiser of chiefs),[9] S.P. Matseke (deputy speaker and organiser), A.Z.D. Mazingi (clerk and chief organiser for the Cape Province), and Mrs Matambo and Mrs Mahabane (chairwomen of the Women's Auxiliary of the ANC).[10] There was not a single communist in the executive. The exclusion of Gumede, whom the radicals had supported, provoked them into a chorus of protests. They threw down the gauntlet to Seme's executive and vowed to organise against it. Seme took up the challenge, declaring that the ANC would not serve as a refuge for communists and that his executive would introduce measures to root them out. While making the statement, Seme was heckled and booed.[11]

On that dramatic note Seme's improbable ascendance was complete – improbable partly because he had been absent from the ANC for almost two decades. However, his election as president general was a sign of the depth of the crisis that the ANC faced under Gumede. Later on, the question of Seme's return would become a major debating point, but for now the founder of the ANC was seen as its saviour.[12] For his part, Seme later contended that an ANC resolution had unanimously been passed, inviting him to 'come back to re-organise the African National Congress and to lead them as their President General'.[13] However his return would later be explained, Seme had been brought back primarily to unite and guide the organisation after the deep divisions of Gumede's presidency.

There is a second reason why Seme's ascendance was improbable. A few months before his election, Seme had written to Allison Champion, acting general secretary of the ICU at the time, suggesting that the two of them work together to 'organise The African Union and swallow up the defunct Congress [i.e. the ANC] in course of time'. So committed was Seme to establishing a political party that would compete with the ANC that he was ready to enter into a discussion about the 'term and the constitution of such a body as I propose herein'. He outlined the approach that needed to be followed in dealing with the ANC by proposing that the African Union 'may be started not as in opposition to the existing Congress but as an independent party within Congress but bidding openly for the reformation of the Congress along certain definite lines'. What those lines were Seme did not explain, though it appears that one area of complaint was that the ANC had become too provincialised and its organisational machinery too cumbersome.[14]

Nothing came from Seme's overtures to Champion – instead, their relationship deteriorated during Seme's presidency. Moreover, his initiative to form a political party to replace the ANC probably petered out because of his election as ANC president. But the divisions so dramatically displayed at the conference that elected him were to dog him for his entire presidency. The seeds of those divisions had, however, been planted in the years when he was in the political wilderness, especially in the 1920s.

Moderates v. radicals

The 1930 conference reflected the ANC's attempt to respond to pressures arising from two main sources: changes in black politics on the one hand, and in white politics on the other. These changes brought about contradictions and convulsions in the ANC that culminated in the showdown of the 1930 conference. The most notable change was the presence of a small but significant faction within the ANC that advocated for a more assertive and radical response to white minority rule. This faction had begun to engage more directly in popular struggles of workers and other subaltern sectors of the oppressed, a practice which ran counter to the preference for deputations to white authorities in South Africa and England.

Signs of a turn to radicalism in certain sectors of the ANC were already evident in the aftermath of the First World War. For a time, the Transvaal Native Congress (TNC) was the enclave of the radical wing, as demonstrated by its open support for several workers' strikes especially between 1918 and 1920.[15] Numerous factors lay behind the upsurge of the strikes. They included an influx of workers to the Rand due to labour shortages during the war and the deteriorating socio-economic conditions in the native reserves; the rising cost of living coupled with stagnant wages for black workers; repressive measures such as the colour-bar policy and pass laws; and the worsening living conditions in black slums.[16] Those conditions, together with the agitation of workers by the TNC, led to the eruption of strikes throughout the Rand. For instance, in 1918 several strikes were called across Johannesburg by black municipal sanitary workers. Black miners followed, with strikes in the period 1915 to 1920.[17] In 1919 the TNC coordinated and led anti-pass protests across the Transvaal. This radical ferment on the Rand, though ultimately suppressed and defeated by the state, drew the TNC closer to workers and also pushed the ANC under Sefako Makgatho towards radical politics.[18] Although the ANC under Makgatho demonstrated its support for popular struggles, it was only towards the end of the 1920s that the radical wing sought to capture the political centre in the ANC through the election of Josiah Gumede as president general in 1927, and Thibedi William Thibedi, a prominent member of the CPSA, as secretary general.

The early 1920s also saw the emergence of other political forces that sought to mobilise the working class. Notable in that regard was the formation of the ICU in 1919 and the CPSA in 1921. The influence of the two organisations in the emergence of more radical forms of politics in the ANC, as well as in black politics in general, was significant. This was especially the case for the ICU, which expanded its scope from its origins in traditional trade unionism to organising in other sectors of society across a broad range of issues. The ICU had by the mid-1920s become the largest organisation coordinating black people in South Africa. By 1927 it had a paid-up membership of between 50 000 and 80 000,[19] a number far larger than anything the ANC had achieved since its founding in 1912. While the ICU's ideology and politics were not overtly communist, and were drawn from different strands, it 'drew heavily on socialist tenets, particularly the class struggle and antipathy to the capitalist system',[20] which in turn resulted in the radical bias of black politics.

The ICU's radical turn was due to the influence of prominent communists in its leadership such as James A. la Guma, Johnny Gomas, Eddie J. Khaile and Thomas Mbeki. Although small in number in the executive committee, these leaders shaped the tenor of politics in the ICU. Through their influence they offered a balance to the moderate leadership and reformist politics of Clements Kadalie (the founder of the ICU) and lieutenants such as Alexander Maduna. It was in fact a power struggle over the direction the ICU should take which led to the communists' expulsion from the executive in 1926.[21] After their expulsion the communists moved to the ANC, where they would play an important role in the election of Gumede as president general in 1927. They were also at the forefront of Gumede's battles with the moderate wing leading up to the 1930 conference and at the conference itself. Long associated with the moderates, Gumede seems to have undergone a political transformation when, in 1927, together with James la Guma, he attended the Brussels Conference where the League Against Imperialism was established; following this, he visited the Soviet Union and then Berlin at the invitation of the German Communist Party. Converted to radical politics,[22] Gumede referred to the Soviet Union as a New Jerusalem.

Gumede's alliance with communists was not accidental. It coincided with the CPSA's determined effort to organise in the black community and to build a closer working relationship with African political organisations.[23] By the late 1920s that strategy seemed to be bearing fruit, with the emergence of a small but significant number of black communists such as Johannes Nkosi, Gana Makabeni, Albert Nzula, Thomas Mbeki, Edwin Thabo Mofutsanyana, Moses Kotane and John Beaver Marks. These communists played a significant role in the politics of the ANC. Thibedi William Thibedi became the secretary general during Gumede's presidency, while Eddie Khaile, another prominent communist, was a member of the national executive. In later years, J.B. Marks and Moses Kotane would become prominent leaders of the ANC.

The CPSA also sought to appeal directly to the 'native masses over the heads of their leaders'.[24] The organisational vehicle for mobilising the black masses was the League of African Rights, formed by the CPSA after a decision of the 6th Congress of the Communist International (Comintern). By mobilising the black masses and drawing up a petition that addressed matters such as the Cape black vote, extension of voting rights to the whole country, and the abolition of pass laws, the League of African Rights became a direct rival to the ANC and the ICU. It did not help matters that when the league was eventually established in 1929, Gumede was elected president; other office bearers were veteran ICU leader Doyle Modiakgotla (vice president), veteran CPSA leader Sydney Bunting (chairman), Nimrod Tantsi (vice chairman), and Albert Nzula and Edward Roux (secretaries). Also emanating from the Comintern was the decision that the CPSA should adopt the slogan of an Independent Native Republic in South Africa. It was the same native republic that Gumede called for in his address to the ANC conference in 1930.

The increasing penetration of the CPSA into black politics and its encroachment into a territory that had been a preserve of the ANC's moderate wing made confrontation inevitable. Gumede's decision to become president of the League of African Rights at the same time he was president of the ANC, as well as his embrace of radical politics advocated by the CPSA and the league, exacerbated an already tense situation in his executive. So opposed was the executive to Gumede's embrace of radical politics that it resigned en masse in January 1930. Included in the reasons for resignation was the fact that Gumede was president of the League of African Rights, an organisation which allegedly 'had its headquarters in Moscow'. The moderates also accused Gumede of being more concerned with 'Communism than with the affairs of the National Congress'.[25] By resigning en masse the executive forced Gumede also to resign, with the result that Thomas Mapikela, the speaker, became acting president.[26] The fight at the 1930 conference thus reflected divisions between the moderate and the radical wings which had been simmering for years.

Although Gumede had become the lightning rod in the battle between radicals and moderates, what really lay behind divisions in black politics, especially in the ANC, was the question of how to respond to an increasingly repressive white state. Ever since the establishment of the Union of South Africa in 1910, which excluded black people from full citizenship, to the passing of the Natives Land Act in 1913, which took away their land, to ever more oppressive legislation, black people's response to exclusion and oppression had largely been spearheaded by the moderate wing of the ANC with its preference for deputations and petitions. More oppressive measures would be introduced after the coming to power in 1924 of a coalition government of the National Party led by General Barry Hertzog and the South African Labour Party. Among the oppressive measures during Hertzog's premiership was an unfair and onerous law on the taxation of black people, passed in 1925.[27] In 1927 the Native Administration Act made the Governor General the 'supreme chief of all Natives in the Provinces of Natal, Transvaal and Orange Free State' and conferred on him power over almost every aspect of black people's lives, including land ownership and the administration of their justice system.[28] In 1926 the Hertzog Native Bills were introduced, the principal elements of which were a bill that sought to abolish the black franchise in the Cape and another that dealt with the allocation and ownership of land by black people, a successor to the Natives Land Act of 1913. The 1930 Riotous Assemblies Amendment Act gave the Governor General the power to prohibit free speech and the publication of material which he considered to 'engender feelings of hostility between the European inhabitants on the one hand and any other section of the Union on the other hand'.[29] A section of the same law gave the Minister of Justice power to ban any person who in his view was engendering feelings of hostility between Europeans and other sections of the population. Allison Champion, for instance, was banned from Durban under the provisions of this law.

The biggest question facing the ANC was how to respond to this increasingly oppressive state. While the answer would have been straightforward before, the entry of the working class into politics and the turn to radicalism by certain factions had created rifts in the ANC. While these divisions led to Gumede's defeat in 1930, they would dog Seme for the whole of his presidency.

First term: 1930–1933

The start of Seme's term as president general of the ANC was inauspicious. Shortly after his election he fell ill and was ordered by his physician, Dr A.B. Xuma, to rest for a period of time. Following this, *Abantu-Batho* made an announcement and suggested that Seme's name be mentioned in people's prayers.[30] More ominous though were the deepening divisions in the ANC. After the radical faction was defeated at the 1930 conference and again in the Western Cape branch where it was concentrated, it decided to form the so-called Independent ANC in November the same year.[31] Although this splinter group made significant inroads in organising workers in the rural Western Cape, it soon suffered the same fate as the League of African Rights: it collapsed. There were political divisions in other provinces too, and these persisted. In Natal the ANC was divided between Reverend John Dube's Natal Native Congress and Chief Stephen Mini's Natal African Congress, which was affiliated to the national ANC. Divisions in the Transvaal had led to the resignation of Sefako Makgatho as TNC president in 1926.[32] Seme tried to heal the various divisions, though without much success. However, his biggest challenge was uniting his executive, which seemed to have come together with the sole purpose of defeating Gumede, splintering again once it had achieved its objective.

Vision and programme

Seme's first order of business was to outline a vision for his presidency and a programme for his executive. While he had attempted to sketch its outlines at the 1930 conference, the confrontation between the radicals and moderates had prevented him from doing so. Because the task of mending the ANC rift was so enormous, it would take several months for a policy and programme to be developed.[33] Eventually, on 11 July 1930, Seme announced the political programme for his presidency. It differed substantially from anything that the ANC had done during Gumede's term of office. Gone were calls for mass mobilisation; instead there were proposals to support black people to start their businesses and to participate in the economy as farmers, shoemakers, storekeepers, tailors and other trades. Native farmers and other producers, Seme announced, 'would also be directed how to find a better market for their products. In order to do this, the Congress would encourage the establishment of native markets or bazaars in all towns where there was a large native population'.[34] Seme also called for black people to be preferred over other racial groups when it came to the allocation of licences for trading in areas where they lived.

Regarding workers organising themselves in trade unions, Seme offered an alternative: workers 'should be organised into clubs or sections with a view to developing the efficiency of the members, and promoting better relations between the worker and his employer'. In keeping with this, he cautioned black people against 'dangerous' doctrines such as communism.[35]

With that manifesto, the trajectory for the ANC during Seme's presidency was set. He would return to these themes and elaborate on them over the course of his presidency. For all the conflict and disagreements that he and his executive would encounter, the differences were never about the substantive elements of his programme. Instead, the source of their conflict was Seme's leadership style.

Divisions emerge

It was not long before Seme and members of his executive clashed. The first conflict took place at the first meeting of ANC leaders on 5 January 1931, and the source of disagreement was, on the face of it, petty. Most delegates wanted the meeting to be adjourned so that they could attend the Third Non-European Conference, which was taking place in Bloemfontein simultaneously.[36] Seme was deeply opposed to ANC participation in the Non-European Conference, whose mission he said was to 'throw dust in our [the ANC's] eyes with its proposed unification of all non-European organisations'.[37] He then said, 'Who are we going to unite – the Coloureds?' and declared that the 'whole thing [i.e. the conference] strikes me as a conspiracy against the Europeans and we are not going to be a party to this'.[38]

His attempt to prevent members of the ANC from participating in the Non-European Conference was met with utter dismay and opposition. It did not help matters that in his conference address he had alienated delegates by praising General Hertzog's policies regarding black people, calling him a 'man of conviction' who would stand by his commitment to 'assist the Natives by his policy of segregation, according to which they would be given the opportunity to develop on their own lines'.[39] The ANC delegates had strongly criticised Seme for supporting Hertzog's native policy without a mandate. So hostile was their reaction to his support for Hertzog that it seemed his presidency had barely begun before it would end. On the heels of that political faux pas, Seme was preventing delegates from attending a meeting they considered important in bringing about unity among black opposition forces ranged against government policies.

It was barely nine months after his election in April 1930, and Seme was already becoming isolated from his executive. In open defiance of his leadership, stalwarts such as Reverend Dr Walter Rubusana, Sefako Makgatho, James Thaele and Chief Stephen Mini, all of whom were ANC delegates, spoke in favour of the Non-European Conference. To make matters worse, R.V. Selope Thema, seconded by Reverend James Calata, moved for the adoption of a motion supporting both the aims and objectives of the Non-European Conference as well as the endorsement of the spirit of cooperation it engendered. The motion was carried by a large majority.

A standoff with the delegates was only averted when Dr Abdullah Abdurahman arrived to explain that the purpose of the Non-European Conference was not to supplant the ANC as a leading organisation representing black people, but was instead intended to unite the forces opposed to white minority rule. Clearly sensing that his presidency was in danger, Seme stood down from his opposition to the Non-European Conference. However, he then took a step that proved extremely destructive and would haunt his presidency for years to come. Without any notice, and after most delegates had left for home, he announced that he was ejecting certain members of the executive. His reason, he declared, was to 'make room for younger men'. The four members he sought to replace were T.D. Mweli Skota (general secretary), R.V. Selope Thema (corresponding secretary and chief organiser), D.S. Letanka (organiser of chiefs) and Cleopas S. Mabaso (financial secretary).[40] Once again, Seme's attempt was opposed by the conference and he was asked to take the matter back to the executive for consultation.

By the time the executive committee met later that year in May, Seme had climbed down from his attempt to dismiss the four members and was instead preaching unity and cooperation. Perhaps mindful of the confrontation at the meeting in January, Seme extended an olive branch to the executive, asking it to 'build afresh'. He also declared: 'This is not the time to quarrel but to stand together as one man and fight for the freedom of our race.'[41] Present at the meeting were executive members such as Sefako Makgatho, R.V. Selope Thema, H. Selby Msimang, Cleopas S. Mabaso, Simon P. Matseke, Daniel S. Letanka and Reverend Elijah Mdolomba. The meeting had been called to discuss the amendment of the ANC constitution, as well as reorganisation and the unification of various splinter groups especially in provinces. So encouraged was Seme's executive by his talk of unity that it sent several of its members to various provinces to bring about this aim. Thema, for instance, was sent to the Cape to broker peace, while Seme himself undertook to visit Natal to unite warring factions there.

The spirit of unity demonstrated at this executive meeting had also been evident on 7 May 1931 in Johannesburg when Seme, Thema, Msimang and Job R. Rathebe appeared before the Native Economic Commission to give evidence on behalf of the ANC. Other leading figures in the black community gave evidence at various other places across South Africa. The Native Economic Commission had been established by the government in 1931 to consider 'the economic and social conditions of Natives especially in the larger towns of the Union'.[42] Seme gave extensive oral evidence, touching on several subjects that were of interest to the commission and elaborating on certain points in his presidency programme. For instance, he called for healthy competition between black people and white people and suggested that this could only be achieved if all discriminatory legislation were to be removed. He advocated that every person in South Africa should strive for equal rights to be extended to 'all civilised men' and that all legislation should be geared towards the achievement of that goal. In his opinion the United States of America was a country where such a philosophy was being implemented and he believed that much of the progress in that country was a result of 'this spirit of healthy competition'. South Africa was losing its 'greatness' in the world because it did not practise the policy of equal rights for all citizens. Seme went on to express his opposition to various laws, including the Masters and Servants Act, which he characterised as most demoralising to the farmers of the country. Another law he strongly criticised was the Native Service Contract Act, which was designed to cause 'endless trouble and most serious mischief between the farmers and the Natives'. Seme concluded his evidence by

touching on a subject that was obviously dear to his heart: land ownership by black people. Although the subject would be addressed by other
members of his delegation, Seme made sure that his own views were on
record:

> [T]he good policy to follow is to encourage the Native to own property
> wherever possible. This would encourage thrift and enterprise amongst
> them. There is a great need for developing this class of Native in urban
> areas, in order to counteract the evils of rowdyism. The existence of a
> fixed property-owning class within the urban areas would certainly
> have the desired effect of raising the heads of other Natives up and, as I
> have said, encourage thrift and enterprise amongst the Native workers.[43]

Seme's evidence at the Native Economic Commission is significant because
it succinctly captures certain fundamental beliefs he held, especially regarding relations between black and white people in South Africa and how
these might be structured. When pressed by members of the commission
to refute his belief in equal rights for all civilised men, and the importance
of competition between blacks and whites in achieving equality, Seme
hardly changed his position.

The other matter on which he held strong views was the extension of
property rights to black people. Writing in 1929 in a different context, he
had expressed a firm belief in the importance of property ownership
in general and home ownership in particular: 'I am one of those who
often think that a man (unless he is a real Saint) cannot be really good
to himself and his children unless he has a home.' Employing the poetic
language for which he was deservedly famous, Seme argued that home
ownership 'shapes the mind and character of every growing child and it
is the dream of every maiden and a delightful heaven on earth to the sick
and the aged'. Not until Africans owned land and their own homes could
they 'hope to develop a civilisation which shall be our own, a civilisation
which shall be more spiritual and humanistic'.[44]

However, the newfound unity did not last long, and by November Seme
and his executive were at each other's throats. Leading the assault on Seme's
leadership was Thema, the corresponding secretary of the ANC and one of
those whom Seme had planned to dismiss. Thema accused Seme of trying
to change the constitution in order to 'vest all power of administration in
the President-General [i.e. Seme]'. Thema further charged that Seme was

trying to become a 'Mussolini, a Lenin, a Mustapha Kemel or a Stalin', but mocked him for not knowing that 'these men became dictators after years of hard work, during which they organised men through whom they carried their programme'. Voicing an accusation that would haunt Seme, Thema accused him of not believing in team work but in acting alone, denouncing Seme as 'a man who will take nobody's advice'. For all his grudging acknowledgement of Seme's skills, Thema slapped him down: 'a brilliant man, a hard-working man of action but he lacks tact. He is a clever man but not a wise man'.[45]

It was an extraordinary public attack on a sitting ANC president by a member of his executive. What seems to have provoked Thema's ire were Seme's unrelenting attempts to change the constitution of the ANC in order to enable the president general to appoint or fire members of the executive at will. Thema's assault on Seme's leadership marked the beginning of an open civil war in the national executive. What followed was even more extraordinary. On 26 April 1932 several senior members of the national executive met in Johannesburg, without informing the president general, in order to discuss what they referred to as the state of the ANC. At the end of the meeting they issued a statement which they then sent to *Umteteleli wa Bantu*. Contained in the statement was an 'appeal to all African leaders, Chiefs and the people generally to ponder seriously on the present economic and political situation and the misfortune of having not a single active organisation to lead African thought and aspirations'. This was followed by a damning accusation:

> The members of the National Executive have been perturbed by the culpable inertia of the President General who, since his election, has given very little attention and time to the most vital questions affecting the well-being of the race, and has failed to give the lead rendered necessary by the present situation.[46]

The phrase that has come to characterise Seme's presidency is 'culpable inertia'. In the opinion of the national executive, the unprecedented situation facing the black race included: high levels of unemployment (mostly due to the Great Depression and the white government's response to it); a plethora of oppressive laws which were being enforced, one of which classified an unemployed black person in an urban area as a vagrant; mass evictions of unemployed black people from urban areas due to failure to pay rent; and deepening poverty and growing insecurity in urban and rural areas. Having outlined these intolerable conditions and Seme's inertia in addressing them, the executive declared it their duty 'to convene a special emergency convention of the African National Congress and to issue this appeal to *all* African leaders, Chiefs and people generally and to every organisation, society or fraternity, to sink their personal ambitions and rally around as never a race did before'. The signatories to the statement were T.D. Mweli Skota (secretary general), R.V. Selope Thema (corresponding secretary and organiser), Reverend Zaccheus R. Mahabane (senior chaplain and former president general), J.S. Likhing (assistant senior chaplain), H. Selby Msimang (chairman of the Labour Committee), C.S. Mabaso (financial secretary), L. Bud M'belle (a senior leader from Transvaal), Abner Mthimkhulu from Natal and Chief Mandhlesilo Nkosi of Wakkerstroom.[47]

The meeting in Johannesburg, together with the accusatory press statement and the convening of a special emergency convention without Seme's knowledge and approval, constituted an open rebellion against his leadership. The special convention was held in Kimberley on 2 July 1932. It was presided over by Reverend Mahabane, and signatories to the statement included Reverend James A. Calata, Sol Akena and H.M.J. Masiza (Cape); W.F. Bhulose (Natal); S.B. Macheng and Morris Somtunzi (Transvaal); Thomas Mapikela (Free State); ten delegates representing Griqualand West and Bechuanaland; and five delegates from the Women's Section of the ANC. In addition, the African Christian Ministers Association sent five delegates, while the Teachers Association sent four.[48]

Reverend Mahabane assumed the duties of president by delivering an opening address at the special convention. Arguing that clause 21 of the constitution gave the executive council the authority to convene a special convention, he went on to decry the fact that several oppressive laws had been passed by the Union Parliament without protest from the ANC. The purpose of the emergency convention was, thus, to devise a means of reviving the ANC.

While the meeting was still in session, a telegram from Seme arrived. Addressed to Reverend Likhing, it read as follows:

Revd Likhing, care Mahabane, Kimberley, Greetings I don't know Kimberley meeting/ am summoning General Conference Bloemfontein first August/ consider final constitution African National Congress/ Expect your copy next week.

The telegram did not, however, stop proceedings. Instead, delegates appointed Reverend Likhing to ask Seme 'by respectful address not to summon the general conference in August' but to convene it in April 1933. The delegates further appointed Msimang and Thema to assist Skota, the secretary general, in taking steps to reorganise the ANC. Furthermore, the delegates decided to develop a manifesto for the revival of the ANC as well as for addressing the pressing economic and political conditions facing black people at the time.[49] Through these decisions, Seme's attempt at derailing the Kimberley convention was foiled. The question was: what would be his next step?

'The African National Congress: Is it Dead?'

Seme's response to his detractors in the national executive as well broadly in the ANC came in the form of a sixteen-page pamphlet titled 'The African National Congress: Is it Dead?'[50] The pamphlet was remarkable in that it contained Seme's most comprehensive vision yet for the ANC. Not since his inaugural address at the founding conference of the ANC had he outlined his vision for the organisation in such a broad manner. The pamphlet covered a wide range of subjects and its messages were directed at different constituencies, including his opponents in the national executive, traditional leaders who had historically supported the ANC, young educated men and women who were critical of him in the media, the general membership, and supporters of the ANC and the black race as a whole. Seme also presented far-reaching proposals as to how the constitution of the ANC might be amended. Many of these ideas constituted the backbone of his programme for the ANC, and never again in his presidency would he produce anything close to their depth and scope.

The reference in the title to the death of the ANC was a direct response to the many critics who accused Seme of killing the ANC. As early as April 1930, an editorial in *Umteteleli wa Bantu* had posed the question 'Should Congress Die?' It followed up with the same question, framed slightly differently, in an editorial of 20 May 1933: 'Is Congress Dead?'[51] But Seme ignored the question and instead put forward a strong plea for the survival of Congress. The first part of his argument obliquely addressed his detractors by conceding that there were strong demands for the revival of the ANC: if the 'persistent personal attacks from my friends and enemies' including 'my supposed inertia can cause such a widespread desire for unity to arise, then I am glad'. Expressing doubt that he personally was responsible for the focus on the ANC, he suggested that it was 'the dreadful vision of chattel slavery which has so easily passed unopposed in both Houses of the Union Parliament under the guise of the Service Contract Bill, which has opened the eyes of the natives in this country'. He argued that black people would indeed be made slaves unless they united and became one nation. That unity could only be achieved if the ANC was formed 'into a solid and impregnable fortress for the defence of our Liberty, even on this Continent, which is our birthright'.[52]

Seme then addressed directly the breakdown of his relationship with the national executive. He claimed that the 'work of organising the Congress has been seriously retarded by the want of cooperation between the leaders and myself, more especially through the want of cooperation between the members of my own National Executive and myself'.[53] Seme contended that no 'member of the Executive should be allowed to defy his chosen leader and then simply stand in the way and refuse to resign', and pointed out that '[t]he well-known rule which is observed amongst all the nations is that the subordinate in the Cabinet should readily resign if so requested by the Head of his Government'. To prevent a recurrence of such defiance, Seme recommended that the ANC constitution be amended to allow the president general to dismiss members of the executive at will. A further amendment was needed to enable the president to 'appoint members of his Cabinet from the list of Senior Provincial Officers submitted to him by the General or Annual Conference'. In addition, 'Members of the Cabinet or the National Executive shall hold office during the pleasure of the President-General or for three years.'[54]

In support of these proposed amendments, Seme argued that there 'can be no unity amongst us until we shall acquire the habit and the will to recognise one man as head over us. Until we shall learn to do this we shall continue to be slaves'.[55] His proposal for a constitutional amendment that would allow him to unilaterally fire members of the executive earned him the disparaging moniker '*thulasizwe*' – a man who 'wants to sing bass alone against 600 000 voices'.[56]

Seme turned his attention to what was, for him, a very important constituency: the chiefs. He strongly contended that the ANC would not be successful if chiefs were not accorded special status in the organisation. That special recognition could only be achieved if the ANC reverted to its original constitutional arrangement whereby the chiefs had their own house, the upper house, 'wherein they can meet alone as Chiefs and without being inconvenienced by strangers'. Seme proposed that the chiefs 'should feel through this Great House that it is their duty to meet with the other Chiefs of the Nation for the purpose of exchanging views in connection with the new problems which face them today, the problems of employment for their people, the problems of conserving national pride, customs and traditions'.[57]

Members of the upper house would be 'hereditary Chiefs in charge of their own tribes and in accordance with the Native Laws and Customs'.[58] Seme proposed that the upper house be 'the Great House "Indhlunkulu" of the Congress'; as such, it would 'enjoy full appellate jurisdiction in connection with all affairs of the Congress affecting finance, jurisdiction or policy'. The upper house would be led by a chief called a governor, who would in turn chair the treasury committee of the ANC. Joining the chiefs as members of the proposed upper house would be members of the 'High Episcopal Council', another body Seme proposed, comprising bishops and other selected religious leaders representing the independent black churches. Former presidents of the ANC would also become members of the upper house.

Moving to the reorganisation of provinces, Seme proposed that the number of ANC provinces be increased to sixteen. The Transvaal would be divided into three provinces: Pretoria (Northern), Johannesburg (Eastern) and Potchefstroom (Western). The Orange Free State would also be divided into three: Bloemfontein, Kroonstad and Bethlehem. Likewise, Natal would be divided into Pietermaritzburg (Middle), Durban (South) and Vryheid (North). The Cape Colony would retain its four divisions, i.e. Western Cape, Transkei, Bechuanaland and Griqualand West, and Griqualand East, while the three protectorates would remain, with each being treated as a province. Seme claimed that this proposed plan would bring about effective supervision and administration of the ANC, and that it reflected 'the natural divisions of our people' which, he argued, could not be ignored.[59]

Turning to the subject of women and children, he proposed that the League of African Women be established, which would be affiliated to the ANC. Its purpose would be to 'assist in the administration of the Congress generally and to supervise the interests of the African women and the children'.[60] Senior office holders would, by virtue of their positions, be eligible for office in the national executive. He also suggested a 'Junior

League of the Congress' to represent the interests of younger members of the ANC.

In conclusion, Seme addressed the pertinent matter of relations between blacks and whites. It was especially relevant as the Hertzog government's policies were causing consternation and discomfort in the black community. Interestingly, Seme's response to the general unease in the black community was this: 'We really don't need much of that common agitator, who only wants to create strife and class hatred.' In the same vein, he urged: 'We need the white man in this country as much as the white man really needs us. Our welfare as a nation can never be served by sowing hatred between whites and blacks in this or any other country or by disseminating cowardly slanders against the Government, who have no means of knowing what our wishes as a nation may be'.[61] While the message of racial unity was laudable, Seme used it to dissuade black people from openly challenging the oppressive laws being implemented by government.

In a single pamphlet, Seme had outlined his vision for the ANC. The question was whether he had the support of the ANC leadership for his scheme. To mobilise support, he decided to call for a conference to be held in Bloemfontein on 17 December 1932. He proceeded to issue a notice calling all chiefs, leaders of the African peoples, and ministers of religion to attend. The conference's purpose was to consider the following: Seme's proposals regarding the reorganisation of the ANC; the Hertzog Native Bills; the establishment of an ANC headquarters in each province; and, finally, to authorise Seme to tour the country to organise ANC branches – and, presumably, to communicate his constitutional amendments. The notice was issued in his name and that of the secretary general, T.D. Mweli Skota.[62] In addition to calling for the conference, Seme wrote to several newspapers explaining his scheme to reorganise Congress, and exhorting all and sundry to attend the conference in Bloemfontein.[63]

The conference was postponed, but rescheduled to take place from 31 December 1932 to 2 January 1933. In the meantime, several more of Seme's pieces were published in black newspapers.[64] The substance was always the same: he exhorted chiefs, ministers of religion, and leaders of the ANC and other associated groupings to attend the conference. In addition, he urged black leaders to unite behind the banner of the ANC and to support his programme of reorganisation. Unfailingly, Seme preached a message of unity; on 24 December, for instance, he stated: 'We meet in this Congress not as Zulus, Xosas, Swazis, Matebeles, Basutos or Coloured, but as Africans, a new nation on the Continent'.[65] At the conference, Seme repeated the same message of unity in his presidential address. He issued the following call to the 'African nation':

> Tell them all and all over South Africa that this conference proclaims that every African home and every young man and young woman in South Africa shall take out a membership card in the African National Congress once every year. If you will do this, I can promise the African nation, as the executive and administrative head of the Congress, that I will set you free from the political grievances which oppress you all today.[66]

Seme then invited delegates to attend the general conference in April 1933 where his proposals would have to be approved. Optimistically, he expressed the hope that the conference would be attended by a thousand delegates.

One leader

The April 1933 conference was critical for Seme. He was up for re-election as president of the ANC and his scheme for reorganising the ANC was up for approval. Originally scheduled to begin on Good Friday, the conference was postponed to Saturday at the insistence of Reverend Mahabane who protested that no meeting should take place on so sacred a day as Good Friday.[67] When it reconvened the following day, Seme refused to deliver the presidential address, and the minutes of the previous conference were not read out. Instead, Seme ordered delegates to leave the conference venue and to move to an adjacent room. Once there, he constituted them into a committee to receive complaints he claimed came from provinces. One such complaint was from Mr J. Ngcezula of Kimberley, who accused ANC leaders in his province of tribalism. Once various complaints had been received and either dealt with or deferred for later discussion, the conference attended to the matter of credentials of the delegates. That opened a Pandora's box. Thomas Mtobi Mapikela, ANC president and speaker in the Orange Free State, rose to question the delegation from Bloemfontein, his own branch. It comprised thirty-seven delegates, mostly women, compared to the twenty-seven delegates from each of the other provinces. Mapikela questioned the credentials of the Bloemfontein delegation and argued that they not be permitted to vote at the conference. Seme, however, gave the order that those delegates should vote. After that unilateral decision, there was a call for nominations for the position of president. The Kimberley branch sent a telegram seconding the nomination of Seme, as did the Randfontein branch. Reverend Dube, who was absent from the conference, sent a letter pleading with delegates to give Seme another chance. However, the Bechuanaland chiefs opposed Seme's nomination, accusing him of tribalism.

After the nominations, Seme requested an adjournment until the following Monday. Gilbert Coka, a veteran of the ANC, the ICU and the Communist Party, stood up and vigorously opposed Seme's proposal, pointing out that the conference had started a day late and that delegates would not tolerate what he called Seme's autocracy. Seme ignored this and forged ahead with the adjournment. When the conference reconvened on Monday, Thomas Mapikela, who was acting as speaker,[68] declared that because there was no quorum the conference should be closed. Seme ignored him and appointed J. Ngcezula, a delegate from Kimberley, to take over as speaker. He then gave an order that the election of the president should commence, in the process overriding protests from Reverend Mahabane and Gilbert Coka about the unconstitutionality of the election. When, later, the ballots were counted, Seme had received twenty-seven votes, twenty-two of which were from the Bloemfontein women. From there, Seme appointed members of his executive committee, who included Halley Plaatje as secretary general, S.B. Macheng as financial secretary, S.M. Makgatho as organiser of the National Church, and Reverend Dube as education secretary.[69]

When Seme delivered the presidential address he announced that he had expelled all 'unfaithful leaders' from the ANC. These veteran leaders had opposed Seme, and among them were Thomas Mapikela and Reverend Zaccheus Mahabane. In justifying his decision to expel these leaders, Seme said: 'The behaviour of the expelled leaders at this Conference yesterday made them think that they believed that the African National Congress could not exist unless they were returned to office. Your unanimous vote is a clear challenge to such deception and impertinence.' He then claimed that he had given Mahabane ample opportunity to run against him, even allowing his supporters to pray for his election, but still Mahabane had failed to oppose him.[70] To make it clear how he thought the ANC ought to be run, Seme declared: 'There can be but one constitution for the Congress and only one leader of this House. And since you have elected me I tell you that I depend upon your cooperation. The unfaithful leaders having now been expelled there is bound to be greater progress made in the work of organising the Congress.' With a flourish, Seme then exclaimed, 'Viva la Congress'.[71] With that, his first term came to an end and his second began.

Second term: 1933–1937
Seme's re-election through a fraudulent voting process deepened the crisis in the ANC and worsened the divisions. A faction of the Transvaal African Congress led by Simon P. Matseke convened a provincial conference in June 1933 where it condemned the manner in which Seme was re-elected; passed a resolution rejecting the new ANC constitution; and decided to break away from the national organisation. Although the legitimacy of the Transvaal conference and the resolutions it took were hotly contested by other Transvaal leaders, including the secretary, Moses Mphahlele, the contestation was symptomatic of worsening problems under Seme's leadership.[72]

The crisis rendered the ANC dysfunctional, provoking cries of despair in the black press and a widespread search for a saviour. Among those regarded as being worthy of emulation were King Khama II of the Bangwato nation and African Americans Booker T. Washington and W.E.B du Bois, while others viewed former president John Dube as a possible saviour.[73] Across the land questions were being asked as to what had happened to the ANC. A letter to one of the major black newspapers of the time was typical, as it demanded '*UKongolose lona Ubulawa Yini Na?*' (What is killing the Congress?).[74]

While the ANC under Seme was in the doldrums, conditions for black people were growing ever worse. Large numbers of people had lost their jobs due to the Great Depression, while others had been displaced from their employment in order to make way for newly unemployed white workers. The Natives Land Act ensured that land shortages in rural areas became even worse, and for those who had access to the land in reserves, the condition of the land had acutely deteriorated as a result of over-population and overgrazing. To compound an already difficult situation, a severe drought made subsistence agriculture in the reserves all but impossible. There were reports of widespread hunger and poverty, especially in rural areas.[75]

In the midst of all the difficulties facing the black population, Seme's presidency was becoming ever more troubled. The first major problem surfaced in September 1933, a few months after his re-election. His attempt to appoint members of his national executive was unsuccessful; he ended up appointing Halley Plaatje as acting secretary general – the only executive member apart from Seme himself. Four months later Plaatje resigned, leaving Seme as leader of the national ANC, though with no executive. In his letter of resignation Plaatje informed Seme that he had decided to sever all ties with the ANC. He gave as his reason Seme's failure to provide leadership on issues such as convening a conference of provincial leaders to address divisions in the provinces; redefining the relationship between ANC branches and their provincial counterparts, as well as the relationship between provinces and the national ANC; and the implementation of an agreement that the ANC would abandon Seme's project of constituting a National Church to which all black churches would affiliate.[76]

Plaatje's resignation further isolated Seme. As national leader, Seme was left alone to lead an organisation riven by conflict. But he soldiered on. He convened an ANC conference in December 1933 which was well attended. Delegates debated at length how to deal with the Transvaal ANC, which had decided to openly oppose Seme's leadership and become an opposition enclave.[77] There was no national executive, and so Seme attempted to appoint people to the executive. Some delegates questioned this, arguing that members should be elected by the conference instead of being appointed by the president. That view was defeated, however, and Seme announced a list of eighteen executive members, which included himself. In an attempt to reach out to different constituencies and broaden his support base, he brought back members of the old guard such as Reverend J.L. Dube, S.M. Makgatho, T.D. Mweli Skota, Professor J. Thaele, Chief Stephen Mini, J. Ngcezula, A.D. Mazingi and S.B. Macheng. Holding out an olive branch to dissidents in the Transvaal ANC – though this may well have created further divisions – he appointed its president, S.P. Matseke, as deputy speaker and head organiser of the ANC. He also appointed Moses Mphahlele, who was at the time secretary of the Transvaal ANC, as secretary of chiefs in the upper house. In addition, Seme created a new post, African Commander in Music and Chief Band Master, appointing Mark S. Radebe to the position.[78]

By April 1934 Seme was once again publishing newspaper articles popularising his vision for the ANC and the black race as a whole. From Volksrust in the eastern Transvaal, he wrote that he had been asked by members of his executive to issue a public statement outlining his policy as leader of the ANC as well as his plans for reorganising the ANC under the new constitution. The article rehashed arguments he had been making ever since becoming president. Among these was a passionate plea for the recognition of traditional leaders in the ANC, on the basis that the 'African Race has always been led by its hereditary chiefs from time immemorial'. He elaborated:

> My policy and advice as President of the African National Congress is that the Executive Committees of the Congress in every district and in every Province should try to be the best of friends with the chiefs in their districts. They should attend all their own tribal Councils wherever such exist and make themselves personally known to their own chiefs and members of their tribal Councils as being officers of this Congress. We can as a Congress show them how to make the better use of their land, their cattle and their Native Courts.

He returned to another subject which he had addressed many times before. Condemning what he termed 'sedition', Seme had the following to say on the subject:

> No Native Commissioner in charge of a district or Location Super-intendent will want to see any leader of the Congress stirring up strife and other trouble for the authorities among the Natives. The African National Congress must condemn the spirit of sedition in any form. The leaders who preach sedition and insubordination are a disgrace to the Congress whose noble aims are to lift up the Africans by helping them to build up economic foundations for their support in every tribe or district in South Africa, and to win public sympathy in favour of the amelioration of all our economic and political disabilities in this country.

Seme's vision for black economic upliftment was to establish 'national supply stores' in each province to provide goods and services to black people. He planned to work with chiefs to help black entrepreneurs sell and distribute goods and foodstuffs via these supply stores. Because black people might not be equipped to run this proposed scheme on their own, Seme suggested that, initially, there should be white supervision. Another instrument he proposed was the establishment of African Congress Clubs (ACCs). These clubs would support black business entrepreneurship by encouraging black people to start their own businesses, and provide support through skills and funding. ACCs would be established in each branch and district of the ANC, with members also joining the local ACC. They would be funded through a proposed national fund, also administered by the ANC, and black people who wanted to start businesses would be encouraged to apply for loans from their local ACC. Each ACC would also function as a supplier of goods and services; it would 'help the Native shopkeeper, the hawker and the pedlars by giving them supplies through the wholesale departments. The chiefs will be able to get their motor cars more cheaply and the Native transport services will be much improved owing to the supervision of the motor car mechanics of the ACC'.[79]

Seme expanded on the functioning of an ACC: in the case of automobiles, a Congress Automobile Club would assist taxi owners and mechanics to establish a 'general African Garage'. The garage would be owned by black people who work in the automobile sector. Its purpose would be to sell new or second-hand cars as well as automobile spare parts. The garage would have branches across the country, and black people would be encouraged to buy cars and spare parts from these garages, which would also service their cars. He suggested that the same scheme could be applied in other trades and sectors such as carpentry, cabinet-making, tailoring, shop-keeping, or owning a butchery.[80]

He also proposed the establishment of a national fund – which he termed 'isivivane' or 'isithabathaba' – for the ANC. All members would be required to make a monthly contribution to the fund, with chiefs being requested to contribute an amount of £5. Seme motivated his argument by pointing out that the ANC had no money in its treasury, which was the reason why not a single office bearer received a salary. He requested ANC members to act as volunteers for collecting money for the fund from the branches.

For several months, Seme continued writing articles in the black press. His main message remained the same: the unity of black people and support for the new ANC constitution as well as its programme. With growing divisions, especially in the provinces, Seme's appeals for cooperation and unity became increasingly earnest and desperate. In June 1934 he saw fit to write a special memorandum to ANC presidents in the provinces, as well as other senior office bearers, appealing for unity and cooperation.[81] The following month he directed his appeal for unity to

Matseke and Makgatho, leaders of the rival factions of the Transvaal ANC, and expressed regret that the leadership divisions had not been addressed.[82] The Transvaal feud had deteriorated to the extent that the two factions were even fighting over ownership of the New Congress Butchery in Marabastad – which, the town clerk of Pretoria revealed, was owned by Simon P. Matseke.

Probably urged by Reverend Elijah Mdolomba, the veteran Cape leader who was now ANC secretary general, Seme reached out to the Transvaal ANC. He called members to a special conference which took place in Johannesburg from 3 to 7 August 1934. It was well attended and among those present were some of Seme's harshest critics, such as Thema. Considering Seme's autocratic leadership style, the conference outcome was surprising. Seme entered into an agreement with the Transvaal leadership, and its essential elements went to the heart of the criticism that had been levelled against him. The agreement included the following: the ANC would be run along democratic lines; members of the national executive would each have defined duties and would be required to perform their duties according to the constitution; it would be the duty of the president general to act with the advice and approval of the majority of the national executive; members of the national executive would be required to wholeheartedly cooperate with one another in carrying out the work of the ANC; provincial executives would be required to carry out all resolutions and decisions of Congress; and the national executive would be recognised as having full rights, powers and authority to organise, re-organise and represent the Congress Federation of the African National Congress in any part of South Africa subject to the given authority of the general conference or the annual conference of the ANC and its constitution.[83]

Accompanying the *Bantu World* report on the ground-breaking agreement was a photograph of the 'leaders who helped bring about the spirit of unity'. Sitting in the centre is Seme, and on his left are Reverend Elijah Mdolomba and Chief Benjamin Nxumalo, an associate of King Sobhuza II, who had started an ANC branch in Swaziland. On Seme's right are Simon P. Matseke and R.V. Selope Thema. Others in the photograph are T.D. Mweli Skota, C.S. Ramohanoe and Moses Mphahlele, who was at the time secretary of the Transvaal ANC.[84]

Following the agreement, Reverend Mdolomba convened another meeting with the Transvaal leadership to discuss the state of affairs in the ANC in general and in the Transvaal in particular. With the majority of leaders in the provinces favouring the old constitution, the leadership agreed to the proposal with the proviso that the status of the ANC constitution drafted by Seme be clarified. When Mdolomba gave them the assurance that the latter did not supersede the old ANC constitution, the leadership was 'considerably relieved and at once decided to throw in their lot with me [Mdolomba] in the reorganisation of the Congress'.[85] The Transvaal leaders committed to convene a meeting for rival factions to address divisions among themselves. Accordingly, at the end of October 1934, a meeting presided over by Skota resolved the leadership dispute, with Makgatho declaring that he no longer wished to be president, thereby leaving Matseke as president of the Transvaal ANC.

Having succeeded in his efforts, Seme took his message of unity to the Orange Free State. He wrote to John Mancoe, acting secretary of the Orange Free State ANC, requesting him to ensure that divisions were healed and that the provincial conference due to be held on 7 October 1935 would 'elect the very best man as the Provincial President of the Congress in that Province'.[86] He informed Mancoe that he had received nominations for the Orange Free State presidency with the candidates being Jacob Nhlapo, Dr James Moroka, C. Moikangoa and Sam Leshoai.[87] Seme also underlined the importance of the Orange Free State province, calling it 'the heart and centre of the political life of the Union of South Africa'.[88] Seme's outreach was a follow-up to an agreement he had signed with the Native Advisory Board of Bloemfontein at the twenty-third annual conference of the ANC where the board and the ANC had agreed to work together to advance matters that were in the interests of black people.[89]

At the beginning of March 1935, Seme took his message of black unity, under the banner of the ANC, to Cape Town where he addressed enthusiastic crowds over two consecutive days. The first meeting took place at the Cape Town City Hall and was presided by James Thaele, president of the Western Cape ANC. Seme exhorted his audience – made up of people from the African and coloured communities – not only to unite, but also to 'stand with your brothers in the north', thereby supporting the political struggles of black people in the northern provinces of South Africa. In an address that was described as inspiring, Seme preached a message of economic independence for black people at the African Methodist Episcopal Church the following day. There too he was enthusiastically welcomed 'by the great audience who had come to see and hear the Head of the Congress for the first time'.[90]

Puzzling as it was, Seme's sudden turn towards inclusive leadership is likely to have been driven largely by Elijah Mdolomba, a respected leader who had served as president of the Cape ANC in the 1920s and for many years afterwards as a prominent ANC leader. His appointment as secretary general of the national ANC and his initiative to reach out to leaders who were disillusioned by Seme's leadership appear to have brought them back into the fold. Seme may have also realised that he was completely isolated as president, with members of his executive constantly abandoning the ship soon after being appointed by him. But whatever lay behind Seme's tactic, it was clearly successful.

Mdolomba's success in uniting the Transvaal ANC did not, however, mean that the ANC was out of the woods. It had to face the gathering storm of the Hertzog Native Bills which were on the brink of approval by the Union Parliament. The four bills outlining the government's broad policy towards black people were first introduced in Parliament in 1926 and included the Representation of Natives in Parliament Bill, the Union Native Council Bill, the Natives Land Act Amendment Bill and the Coloured Persons Rights Bill. Because a two-thirds majority was needed to abolish the Cape native franchise and the Hertzog government did not have that support in Parliament at the time, the bills were sent from one parliamentary committee to another without much success.[91] It was only with the fusion of the National Party and the South African Party in the early 1930s, and the government that resulted from that union in 1934, that there was the necessary majority to finally pass the Native Bills. By then they had been rationalised and reduced from the original four to two: the Representation of Natives Bill and the Native Trust and Land Bill.

The Representation of Natives Bill abolished the Cape black franchise and proposed in its place that black people across the country be represented by four white senators who would be voted in by chiefs, headmen, native advisory boards, black local councils, and members of the reserve boards of management. No black person in the Cape or anywhere else in the country could be registered on the common voters roll. The bill also created a statutory body called the Native Representative Council consisting of twenty-two members, some of whom were officials from the Department of Native Affairs (including the Secretary for Native Affairs who chaired the council), while others were appointed by the Governor General, with the rest being elected by black people. The purpose of the NRC was to advise government on matters affecting black people.

The second piece of legislation was the Native Trust and Land Bill, a successor to the 1913 Natives Land Act which had allocated just over 7 per cent of South Africa's land to black people and prohibited them from buying land outside of this. In August 1913 the government had appointed a commission of inquiry to identify land in South Africa that would not be permitted to be acquired or hired by black people or other race groups apart from whites. William Beaumont, a former administrator in Natal, was appointed to chair the commission. The Beaumont Commission had recommended a limited increase in land allocated to black people but left it to provinces to make final decisions, following which most provinces decided to reduce the recommended allocation for Africans.[92] The Native Trust and Land Bill, which was ultimately passed into law in 1936 (together with the Representation of Natives Act), made provision for the creation of a trust that would buy land for settlement by black people. It proposed an increase in the percentage of land allocated to black people to about 13 per cent, though that was never reached.

The two Hertzog Native Bills provoked consternation and outrage in the black community. They were condemned by black leaders across the political spectrum, with Reverend Mahabane stating that they demonstrated the failure of the white rulers to recognise a black person 'as a human being with feelings, aspirations and powers of thinking and reasoning'.[93] Adding his voice to the condemnation, Dube stated:

> Prior to the coming of the whites to South Africa we had our great leaders – our empire builders – who mean as much to us as [Cecil John] Rhodes means to Europeans. We had our Councils and we ran our own government. Yet when we came under the white man were treated worse than children. We are repressed, not controlled as children should be.[94]

Nimrod Tantsi, another ANC veteran and former leader in the League of African Rights, described the bills as a direct challenge to the black race, whose future was at stake.[95] Meetings were called across the land to discuss the bills. For instance, Ciskei chiefs held a meeting in King William's Town and resolved, inter alia, that the bills be translated into African languages so that they might be widely understood. They also resolved that the Cape native franchise rights 'be preserved undisturbed, while new and long overdue political privileges are instituted for the Bantu in the Union as a whole'. Significantly, the chiefs also decided that 'land areas projected for Bantu occupation be increased to an extent that will enable all aboriginal peoples and their future descendants to make an adequate living on the land'.[96]

There were calls for a national convention of black leaders from all political and non-political formations to discuss responses to the bills. At the same time, the government was crisscrossing the country promoting the bills before they had even been published for public comment. For instance, on 8 August 1935 the Department of Native Affairs invited chiefs and black leaders from the Free State and Transvaal to a meeting in Pretoria to discuss the bills. Prominent leaders on the Reef such as Seme, Xuma, Thema, J.R. Rathebe, S.G. Senaoana and A.S. Vil-Nkomo were nominated to attend that meeting. Such government-sponsored meetings were met with resistance, with Professor D.D.T. Jabavu, president of the Cape Native Voters' Convention, warning black leaders against attending them. In his view the government meetings were calculated to divide black leaders 'into sections so that we may contradict each other'. Jabavu counselled that it was important for black leaders to 'stick to our original intention to stick together and die together'.[97] Here, Jabavu was referring to the intention to hold a national convention of all black leaders, and proposed that it take place in Bloemfontein on what was known as Dingaan's Day (16 December 1935). He suggested that Seme chair the convention, though not in his capacity as president of the ANC. Jabavu then went on to state: 'I have not written to Dr Seme, for I do not even know where he lives nor am I concerned with his faults if he has any. All I desire is someone able to carry our message to its destination free from the entanglement of business ties, able to express our feelings and loyal to the race.'[98]

Jabavu's statement was revealing, for it touched on two important matters: Seme's location and his character. Jabavu's confession regarding Seme's location was odd, since Seme was the leader of a prominent organisation. Seme's supposed 'faults' included his frequent absence from South Africa in the early to mid-1930s after he was struck off the roll of attorneys, which was contributing to the weakness of the ANC; also, by now his autocratic leadership style was widely acknowledged, even by leaders outside the ANC such as Jabavu.

The All-African Convention

While other black leaders were calling for a national convention where all political formations could discuss the Hertzog Native Bills, Seme and Mdolomba convened a special ANC conference from 3 to 5 August 1935 to discuss the very same bills. Seme and Mdolomba argued that the ANC was the only legitimate body that had the right to convene a special meeting to discuss the bills. They argued that the ANC was 'the national organisation for all Africans and as such [had] to direct all their interests and defend all their rights in this country'.[99]

These attempts to put the ANC at the forefront of the fight against the Hertzog Native Bills received little support. Although Seme had been enthusiastically received in Cape Town, he did not enjoy the same level of support elsewhere. Black leaders were pulling the carpet from under Seme and Mdolomba by publicly arguing for a national convention of all parties, not necessarily led by the ANC. For instance, in May that year, Thema had given a public lecture at the Bantu Men's Social Centre in Johannesburg where he argued that 'a national convention could not be left in the hands of any one organisation'.[100] Working together with the Joint Council Movement (an organisation funded by the Chamber of Mines to quell political and industrial discontent), prominent ANC leaders, including Thema, formed a committee to convene the national convention to discuss the bills and the incorporation of the protectorates into the Union of South Africa.[101]

The national convention did eventually take place on 16 December 1935, as planned. It was a historic meeting, drawing black leaders from all over the Union of South Africa and the protectorates. But Seme, who was expected to preside over the convention, was not present at its start. The explanation given by Mdolomba was that transportation difficulties had prevented Seme from travelling from 'the wilds of Eastern Swaziland'. This led delegates to proceed without Seme, and to choose Jabavu to preside owing to the 'supreme popularity and respect' he enjoyed.[102]

After travelling for three days and nights by train and by car, Seme eventually arrived, accompanied by chiefs representing Sobhuza II.[103] His contribution at the convention appears to have been minimal, though he did call for a meeting of the ANC to be held afterwards, on 18 December 1935. Among the leaders present at that meeting were R.V. Selope Thema (who was chosen to chair the meeting), L. Mvabaza, J. Dunjwa, T.D. Mweli Skota, S. Leshoai, J. Thaele, chiefs Nxumalo, Moloi and Monafela, Mrs Bhola, Mrs Manoni, and thirty other female representatives.[104] Seme expressed appreciation for the ANC national executive's participation in the convention and proposed that the annual general conference be postponed in order to allow the officers of the All-African Convention, an organisation created by the convention, to fight the two Hertzog bills. And then, commenting on the drought and widespread famine, and doing so in a manner typical of his obsequious posture towards the government, Seme thanked government for providing maize to black people 'on very easy terms so that no one should starve or die from starvation'. He then stated that 'these were those things which made the present Minister of Native Affairs, Mr Grobler, much loved and trusted by Africans. He was always ready to come to the relief of the Africans in their distress.' Seme went on to urge the national executive to pass a vote of confidence in the minister, which it duly did.[105]

Seme's presence at the AAC's inaugural convention did not indicate the ANC's full approval of the formation of another organisation. The ANC was still fiercely contesting the matter, with Seme himself not being particularly supportive of the idea. The defection of certain prominent leaders to the AAC was partly a reflection of divisions in the ANC itself, especially over its leadership concerning struggles against the Hertzog Native Bills. But there was more to it than this. Confidence in Seme's leadership of the black race under the banner of the ANC had declined to such an extent that, when faced with a choice concerning which organisation should take the lead in the fight against the Hertzog Native Bills, the majority of leaders chose rather to form a new organisation. The acceptance of leadership positions by ANC figures such as Xuma, who became vice president of the AAC, with Jabavu as president and Msimang as secretary general, was another indication of the degree of discontent. Mahabane and Thema became executive members of the AAC. Although Msimang, Thema and Mahabane were well-known opponents of Seme's leadership, it would have been offensive even to Seme that they chose to occupy prominent positions in the AAC under the leadership of Jabavu, a man who, for all his accomplishments, had, like his father before him, always distanced himself from the ANC.

As the ANC's star under Seme waned, the AAC's star shone ever brighter as Jabavu became the leading voice articulating the concerns of black people. He headed delegations to meet with Prime Minister Hertzog to protest the bills, and the AAC provided financial support to challenge them in the courts.[106] By the end of 1937, urgent questions were being asked about the future of the ANC. One newspaper editorial, in particular, captured the prevailing mood:

> The African National Congress has undoubtedly laid the foundation stones of the progress that has been achieved by our race in many spheres of activity. But we would like to know what is going to be its future? Is it the intention of its leaders to so reorganise it that it shall become a force that will make white South Africa realise that as human beings we are entitled to a place in the sun and to participation in the government of this country?[107]

Seme was not there to answer important questions about the organisation he had founded as a young man in 1912, and whose future had become bleak under his watch. In any event, his own fate as president would soon be decided at the elective conference due to begin on 16 December 1937. The conference coincided with the ANC's twenty-fifth anniversary, and the silver jubilee became the main focus, filling the entire programme of the first day. Ralph Bunche, an African American who was visiting South Africa at the time and who was invited to attend, kept a diary of events which formed the basis of a vivid report. Proceedings began with a brass band leading a procession of delegates around the location in Bloemfontein. From there, delegates moved to the conference venue where the whole morning was dedicated to religious services, the singing of hymns, the delivery of sermons and the reading of scripture. Two oxen were slaughtered for the 'Jubilee Feast' – despite Seme's claim that the ANC lacked funds.[108]

After the religious services and much singing, Seme took to the podium to deliver his presidential address. He was dressed in a frock coat and white spats, wearing his famous stovepipe hat, and clad in morning pants. He covered familiar territory, calling for black people to unite and cooperate, exhorting them to establish his economic upliftment scheme of the African Congress Clubs, and decrying the ANC's lack of financial resources. Bunche observed that Seme seemed nervous at the conference, speaking hesitantly and displaying no force of personality.

The evening of the first day was dedicated to a celebration party, which was, however, poorly organised. The next day was also badly organised, with Congress leaders scouting around for people to give speeches in order to fill up a barely existent programme. A car was even sent to fetch Bunche to give a speech, an invitation he declined as he had received no prior notification. Delegates blamed Seme for the chaos at the conference, vowing that they would not vote for him again.[109] When it came to the election of the president, Seme tried to delay this, sensing, according to Bunche, that he faced defeat. Half an hour to midnight, the election finally took place – a two-horse race, with Seme against the former president, Mahabane. The result went heavily against Seme, who gathered only nine votes to Mahabane's twenty-six, with one spoilt ballot.[110] Mahabane's victory was met with much applause, as delegates sang '*Nkosi Sikelel' iAfrika*'.

After this devastating loss, Seme did something unprecedented: he requested to withdraw from the contest altogether in order to give Mahabane a unanimous vote. The delegates rejected his proposal, arguing that it was too late; they had already voted and he had lost. Bunche claimed that Seme then told him he was happy that Mahabane was his successor because Mahabane was 'sane' and 'moderate' and not a 'radical' and a 'fire-eater'. Moreover, Mahabane's election would appeal to white people 'who can do much for us'.[111] There is no evidence that Seme discussed any of this with Mahabane, though it is likely that he was trying to console himself after what could only have been a painful loss. In the early hours of the following day the conference finally came to an end, and delegates left for their homes. The curtain had fallen on the presidency of Pixley ka Isaka Seme, and the ANC moved forward without its founder at the helm.

A problematic presidency

It is indisputable that Pixley Seme was not a great president of the organisation he founded. But what is perhaps debatable is whether his presidency was as disastrous as some have asserted.[112] After all, Seme was not the only president to have led the ANC in a turbulent period. What is often overlooked when assessing Seme's presidency is the fact that he was brought back to lead the ANC after almost two decades of absence primarily because the organisation had virtually collapsed under the leadership of Josiah Gumede. So opposed was the executive to Gumede's leadership that it had resigned en masse in January 1930, leaving the ANC rudderless in the lead-up to the elective conference. It should also not be forgotten that the ANC was deeply divided under Dube's leadership, which resulted in his ousting as president and of Thema as secretary general. This is not to suggest that Seme's presidency was a success, which it was not, but rather that it be assessed from a broader perspective.

It is evident from the manner in which Seme led the ANC that his autocratic style contributed to the problems he encountered. The same attributes that led him to found the organisation – a supreme confidence in his intellectual capabilities coupled with single-mindedness – turned out to be a major weakness in leading a deeply divided ANC that faced an implacable foe in the Hertzog government. Where a more consultative and accommodating approach was needed, Seme opted for an imperious style, with the frequent refrain that he was president and his views and authority were therefore beyond debate. This soon alienated other leaders of the ANC, distinguished persons in their own right, who were constantly reminded that he alone was leader and if they wanted their views to carry the day they themselves should contest elections and become president. A clear demonstration of his intolerance was of course evident at the 1933 conference where he expelled senior leaders of the ANC, including a former president, simply because they had dared question the manner in which he had ensured his own re-election. This intolerance was actually evident much earlier on, and is demonstrated in a letter he wrote to Allison Champion in October 1930. Seme had been attempting to recruit Champion to write for *Ikwezi le Afrika*, which he hoped to establish as the official organ of the ANC. Instead of attempting to persuade Champion, he haughtily instructed him:

> You must recognize that I have written as President-General of a senior organisation urging all other organisations to fall into line and cooperate as one under our banner. It is for the best that all should recognise this principle. We cannot all be equal under Congress. I must command all under me. Your turn and that of other leaders must come by election. No chieftainship or hereditary principle – democracy must elect under a free constitution.[113]

It was in the same letter that Seme accused prominent leaders such as Thema of being 'spies and nothing else'; if one wanted information to reach 'the ears of the Government', he asserted, these people should simply be told certain things.[114] The ANC suffered a great deal as a result of an arrogance and domineering style that earned Seme the moniker '*thulasizwe* of the black race'. It alienated many of his colleagues in the ANC, undermined his efforts at bringing about the unity of black people, and led to his reputation for high-handedness.[115]

There were, however, other factors that negatively impacted on Seme's presidency. The 1930s were a tremendously difficult period in Seme's personal life. In September 1932 he was struck off the roll of attorneys after losing a case brought by the Law Society of the Transvaal for overcharging some of his black clients. The Supreme Court of the Transvaal found him guilty in absentia, with the result that he was unable to practise as an attorney and therefore deprived of a major source of income. Also, for all Seme's forays into business, there is no evidence that he generated much income from them. So desperate was his financial situation that at one stage the Zulu regent, Prince Arthur Mshiyeni ka Dinuzulu, felt compelled to write to the Native Commissioner in Nongoma, pleading for Seme to be readmitted as an attorney. In the letter, Prince Mshiyeni stated that Seme had tried everywhere to find work, but without success, and his wife and three children were so poor that they neither had clothes to wear nor food to eat.[116] It is unclear whether the prince consulted Seme before writing the letter, but it would undoubtedly have been humiliating to find himself in a situation where he was unable to provide for his family. It partly explains why Seme spent so much time in Swaziland: he was dependent on Sobhuza's patronage for his very survival. One might therefore imagine that his dire financial situation affected his duties as president of the ANC.

In addition to financial woes, Seme may have been dogged by personal demons. Apart from having 'bad debts', Seme was allegedly 'beset increasingly by alcohol'. In February 1929 he landed up in jail after a conviction for being drunk and disorderly: he had crashed a cart by driving in the wrong direction up Joubert Street in Johannesburg.[117] At the time, Clements Kadalie was with him in the cart.[118]

The incident that landed him in jail appears not to have been an isolated one. Seme had gained a reputation for indulging in alcohol, whiskey being his drink of choice. Just over a month after Dinuzulu's death, Seme decided to visit Rietfontein, where Dinuzulu had been resident. Harriette Colenso, who was already at the farm, heard that Seme was coming and wrote him a letter in which she warned him not to bring alcohol to the farm. 'I must ask you not to bring any whiskey with you,' she wrote. 'To do so would be fatal in more than one way.'[119] H.M. Basner, who was Seme's contemporary and his colleague in the legal profession, described Seme as 'a drunk' and went on to suggest that 'liquor had begun to destroy him even before he came back from England. By 1912, he was a burnt-out wreck, run to fat, with a hoarse, asthmatic voice and speech so rambling that it was difficult to follow him at all.'[120] I have not been able to corroborate Basner's account of Seme's perceived alcoholism. From available evidence it appears that the judgement is rather harsh. It is inconceivable to imagine that the delegates at the 1930 conference would elect as president general an alcoholic who had become a 'burnt-out wreck'. In any event, there is no evidence to suggest that Seme's 'alcoholism' hampered his leadership of the ANC.

There were also other factors beyond his personal circumstances that undermined Seme's presidency. As with his predecessors, Seme led an ANC that had significant organisational weaknesses – a fact that is clear from Skota's statement in his report to the 1930 conference:

> Last year [1929] was perhaps the worst year of the African National Congress I ever experienced. This obviously is due to the fact that all Provincial Congresses failed hopelessly not only by violating the Constitution, but also in disregarding the resolutions arrived at in the Convention. Orders and instructions of the President-in-Council have been treated with contempt. The expulsion by the Convention of officers who failed to carry out the Constitution were disregarded and open rebellion was manifested.[121]

Skota also decried the paucity of funds, which meant that elected officers could not visit branches in their provinces. This was an ongoing complaint. Historically a reliable source of funding for the ANC, the chiefs had, over the years, gradually withdrawn from active participation in its affairs, including providing financial support. Seme's constant pleas and invitations to the chiefs to participate in the ANC, and his constitutional scheme to revive the upper house, were partly motivated by a desperate need for financial support. At one point he openly pleaded with chiefs: 'I must depend upon your financial assistance and patriotism. I depend upon every Chief in South Africa to help me in the difficult task of inviting the African people to come into their own inheritance and become a nation'.[122] But Seme's pleas went largely unheard, which contributed to the weakness of the ANC.

Further compounding the problem was the fact that ANC provincial congresses were for all intents and purposes independent fiefdoms of leaders who had no actual obligations to the national ANC. Indeed, the provinces themselves experienced divisions and faced difficulties in exerting control over local branches.[123] In part, Seme's determination to amend the ANC constitution was an attempt to address this problem by centralising power at the national level so that the national ANC could, for instance, have access to membership dues collected at a provincial level. Gumede had faced the same problem during his presidency and had similarly tried to centralise power; he failed, however, when the provincial party bosses revolted against his scheme.[124]

Neither before nor during Seme's presidency might the ANC have been described as organised, unified or disciplined. But another factor was membership: even though no accurate records were kept regarding paid-up membership, estimates suggest that the numbers were low, varying perhaps between 1000 and 4000 during the inter-war period.[125] In 1930, when Seme was elected president, only fifty-three delegates of the over 300 present were eligible to vote, suggesting that even then numbers were small. And by the end of Seme's term in December 1937, membership seems to have declined even further.[126]

The divisions during Seme's presidency were not so much divisions among ordinary members as among the leaders. What is striking is that these divisions were not even over ideology, for Seme's politics were no different from those of his opponents in the ANC executive. Leading opponents such as Mahabane, Msimang and Thema advocated for the same self-help economic programmes for which Seme is renowned. For instance, *The Bantu World*, under the editorship of Thema, repeatedly carried the message of economic self-help for black people in its leader and editorial pages.[127] Msimang similarly endorsed this vision, proposing the establishment of a national fund he called *umfelandawonye*.[128] These same opponents also preferred a moderate approach to challenging black political exclusion. Most of Seme's opponents in the executive were in fact prominent participants and leaders in the Joint Council Movement, which brought together liberal white and black leaders and advocated for a moderate path to political reform in South Africa. It is an often forgotten fact that Seme chose not to participate in the Joint Council Movement because, in his view, such organisations undermined leading black organisations such as the ANC. Likewise, his opposition to the 1931 Non-European Conference should be viewed through the prism of his belief that black political organisations should maintain their independence. With the exception of Gumede's temporary embrace of radicalism,[129] moderate (and conservative) politics was the political mainstream in the ANC in the first three decades of its existence. To portray Seme's presidency in a negative light on account of his moderate politics is to ignore this history.

Finally, in assessing Seme's presidency it is important to bear in mind that he presided over the ANC during the bleakest period for black people in South Africa. The Great Depression that started in the late 1920s disproportionately affected black people, with large numbers losing their jobs or falling victim to the Hertzog government's scheme of retrenching black workers in order to employ white people who had lost their jobs. The government then forcibly removed unemployed black workers from urban centres and sent them back to the rural reserves where most black migrant workers came from. Further aggravating the situation was a drought that gripped South Africa during the 1930s, thrusting many black families in the rural reserves into debilitating poverty and famine. It was only in the 1940s that job opportunities began to open up for black people, with large numbers being drawn back to the main economic centres. By then Pixley Seme's presidency had run its course. However, throughout his time as president, Seme had to provide leadership to a community that was going through its darkest days. The decline of the ANC during that period was a tragedy not only for Seme and black South Africans, but perhaps also for the black race as a whole.

* * *

Looking back at Seme's tenure as president one cannot but be dismayed at how tragic the whole affair was. For here was the man who had founded the ANC as a thirty-year-old – its moving spirit – nearly killing it when he was brought back to save it during its moment of crisis. And of course the tragedy engulfed black people during a particularly bleak period in a long history of suffering.

History has justifiably been very harsh on Seme, not only for what he did, but also for what he failed to do as president. Brilliant as he was, his personality was not suited to leading an organisation as complex as the ANC was then – and indeed continues to be. That he was allowed to become its fifth president despite demonstrating early on that he lacked an accommodating temperament and a willingness to be inclusive is a clear indication of how desperate and frustrated its leaders had become with the radical leadership of Gumede and the increasingly oppressive white minority government of General Hertzog. But his missteps as president cannot and should not eclipse the fact that Pixley ka Isaka Seme was – and indeed remains – a towering intellectual and political figure.

9

Fall from grace

On 22 September 1932 the Transvaal Provincial Division of the Supreme Court of South Africa removed Seme from the roll of attorneys and interdicted him from practising as an attorney. Presiding over the case were Justice Barry and Justice Maritz, who ordered Seme to hand over his certificate of admission and enrolment as attorney to the registrar of the Supreme Court; he was also ordered to pay legal costs. The court had found Seme guilty of unprofessional and dishonourable conduct, and also of conducting himself in a manner that was contrary to the duties and expectations of an attorney. Seme was not present when judgment was passed – he later used this as a basis for appealing the court's decision.

The matter which resulted in Seme losing his status as an attorney concerned a case involving a group of black people who lived in Waverley Township on the north-eastern outskirts of Pretoria. The matter itself had a very long history. On 24 October 1902 a firm owned by Frank McIntosh and John Moffat acquired a piece of land (just over 500 hectares in extent) from a farm called Hartebeestfontein in north-eastern Pretoria for the sum of £17 546 and ten shillings.[1] When Moffat and McIntosh bought the land they found living on it a substantial number of black people. In a petition submitted to the Governor General of the Union of South Africa in November 1918, Moffat estimated the number of black people living at Waverley Township to be 250 and stated that 'a considerable number of them have been there for 20 years or more'.[2] Upon acquiring the farm, Moffat entered into verbal lease agreements with the black people who lived on the land. According to the lease agreements each family was to pay rent of £3 annually. The original leases were agricultural; however, over time Waverley Township became a residential settlement occupied mainly by black people who worked in Pretoria and Johannesburg. The leases were renewed automatically every year, even for those occupants who did not pay rent. Gradually, other black families came to settle in Waverley Township.[3] Moffat characterised the black community living in Waverley as law abiding, with three-quarters of the males employed as labourers in Pretoria and the surrounding areas as well as in Johannesburg.[4] It is important to note that Moffat's characterisation of the black community was not shared by the authorities. For instance, the Head Constable of the South African Police in Pretoria, W.F. du Plooy, claimed that only a quarter of the black community of Waverley Township was gainfully employed as labourers. The rest, he claimed, 'simply roam about during day-time, steal or deal in liquor and return to Waverley during night-time'. His characterisation of the women in the township was worse. He claimed that half a dozen of them 'have been convicted for possession of liquor on more than 10 occasions each, several have been convicted for theft, Robbery, Assault, etc., and nearly all under the Pass Laws'.[5]

In 1906 Waverley Township was zoned and declared a township for white settlement. The declaration, however, did not affect the black residents as they were told by Moffat that it would take many years for white people to start settling on the township land. He advised the residents to remain in the township for as long as white people were not there.[6] This continued occupation of the land was also enabled by a lack of interest by white people to buy plots at Waverley. Only one white person, Mr R.T. Brown, bought land there, purchasing a total of eight lots. Other white people cited distance from Pretoria as a negative factor, and so they opted not to buy.[7]

Problems began for the black community at Waverley Township with the enactment of the Natives Land Act of 1913. The act identified certain areas in South Africa as scheduled for occupation, purchase and/or selling by black people only, with others being reserved for occupation by white people. Waverley Township fell outside the areas reserved for occupation by black people: it was a 'white area'. This presented a difficulty for the owner, Moffat, as well as for the black community living there. The problem was particularly acute for Moffat because white people were choosing not to buy the plots, while the black people who were eager to buy were prevented from doing so by the Natives Land Act. Moffat then wrote a petition to the Governor General requesting that Waverley Township be declared an area for black settlement. His petition exposed a split in the government. In a letter to the Secretary for Native Affairs dated 12 December 1918, the Pretoria magistrate to whom the petition had been referred recommended that the Governor General approve Moffat's request; the magistrate contended that he did not 'think that [the] township will ever be suitable for anything save a native township'.[8] When the Secretary for

Native Affairs solicited the view of the Secretary for the Transvaal Provincial Administration, the latter agreed that Waverley be declared an area for black settlement. He stated that 'so far as this office is concerned there is no objection to the proposal so long as it is understood that the lots in the township would be sold to natives only'.[9]

There was, however, fierce opposition to the proposal of making Waverley a township for black settlement from the South African Police in Pretoria, supported by the head office. The National Police Commissioner declared the state of affairs in regard to black people living in Waverley 'unsatisfactory' and urged the Secretary for Native Affairs to take 'action'. It was, however, the Pretoria District Commandant who lay down the argument of the South African Police: Waverley was located between the European townships of Villieria and East Lynne and it would be 'unfair to the Europeans of Villieria & Eastlynn to allow a native Township in between them, and also to Europeans that may have already bought ground in the Township of Waverley'. Moreover, if Waverley were to become a black township it would be very difficult to control, especially since there already existed 'three native townships Eersterust, Riverside, and Dispatch' on its western side. So opposed were local officials to the presence of black people in Waverley that they prosecuted Moffat on several occasions for contravening the Natives Land Act by permitting black people on his property. The public prosecutor, F. Glen Leary, went so far as trying to get a convict by the name of Marr, allegedly Moffat's associate, to 'give a true statement implicating Moffat'– this in exchange for not being prosecuted for aiding the continued presence of black people in the township.[10] That ploy seems not to have succeeded, however.

The opposition to turning Waverley Township into a settlement for black people gathered momentum throughout the 1920s. The council of the Innesdale Municipality, a local authority adjacent to Waverley Township, threw its weight behind the forces opposing the settlement of black people. The town clerk of Innesdale Municipality wrote that he had been instructed to inform the Pretoria magistrate 'that the Council strongly protests against the establishment of this township, it being of the opinion that the establishment of a coloured township on the boundaries of Innesdale will be a menace to public Health'.[11] He then took the matter a step further, issuing a public notice calling for a meeting of white residents from surrounding areas to be held at Villieria School on 20 December 1927 to discuss the proposal that Waverley become a native location. In all,

437 residents signed a petition opposing the idea, claiming that the continued presence of black people at Waverley was not only detrimental to the health of white people, but also jeopardised the safety of their families: 'most of the natives have bad records and the area is well-known as the centre for illicit beer-brewing'; furthermore, at weekends 'hordes of natives usually congregate here for a drunken brawl'. The petition was addressed to the Minister of Native Affairs, who, through the Secretary for Native Affairs, pleaded with the area's Sub-Native Commissioner to work with the police to address the matter as soon as possible. The Secretary for Native Affairs proposed that consideration be given to moving the black residents of Waverley to the 'Native townships of Eerste Rust, Riverside, etc. where the Natives could without difficulty make arrangements for their future settlement'.[12] So strong was opposition to the proposal that not even an inquiry by the Minister of the Interior on behalf of Moffat regarding the matter of Waverley was successful. The Minister of Native Affairs merely responded that Moffat's petition was 'carefully gone into by the Native Affairs Department which found the proposal strenuously opposed by the Innesdale municipality, the Police, and local officials'.[13] He may well have added to his list the white residents who were bitterly opposed to having black people as their neighbours.

At the same time as white people were opposing the Waverley proposal, the Transvaal Native Congress was vigorously campaigning on its behalf. E.H. Chake, a leading official of the TNC, wrote several letters to the Minister of Native Affairs pleading the case for Waverley to become a black township. On 4 March 1920 Chake urged the Minister of Native Affairs to treat the matter with urgency. Sefako Makgatho, who was TNC president at the time, also made representations to the government on behalf of black residents of Waverley Township. Makgatho argued that a section of those residents 'only know Pretoria as their only home', and they 'have sons and daughters born and married in Pretoria'. He offered to buy the land where Waverley Township was located, claiming that he was 'the holder of an option for the purchase of the Township "Waverley"'.[14] Pressing his case, Makgatho wrote another letter on 4 December 1922, to which the Secretary for Native Affairs replied that 'no definite decision has yet been arrived at in regard to the matter'.[15] Makgatho persisted, and a week later he again wrote to inform the minister of '7 or 8 hundred native families who are at present tenants in the Indian Location' and who were likely to be ejected from their homes and therefore needed a place where they could build new homes, which he suggested could be done at Waverley.[16] He received a reply the following year, on 5 February 1923; but once again he was told to wait,[17] and later still he was informed that his proposal had been turned down.

Driving these constant official refusals was strong white opposition, which pushed the Secretary for Native Affairs to seek assistance from the Attorney General in Pretoria. The Secretary for Native Affairs described the continued presence of black people in the area as constituting 'a serious menace to peace, order and good government' and requested the Attorney General to take steps 'against Mr Moffat to compel him to put an end to the existing unsatisfactory state of affairs'. He then accused Moffat of allowing 'Natives indiscriminately to enter into residence on plots within the township with the result that a large uncontrolled settlement exists today'. He revealed that there had been several attempts to prosecute Moffat for permitting black people to live on his land in contravention of the Natives Land Act, but such attempts had failed on account of lack of evidence. While it was indeed the case that black people lived on his property, there was no evidence that their presence was sanctioned by Moffat. As a result he could not be found guilty of any crime. The Secretary for Native Affairs pleaded with the Attorney General to find some evidence that would lead to a successful prosecution.[18] However, there was nothing much the Attorney General could do as long as there was no evidence proving that Moffat was actively involved in the continued presence of the black community at Waverley Township.

White campaigning reached a crescendo towards the end of the 1920s, as white women, especially those from surrounding neighbourhoods, joined attempts aimed at removing black families from Waverley. Nine months after the signing of the first petition, white female residents declared: '[W]e, the women of this district, feel we are in duty bound forced to make some movement to ensure the safety of ourselves and our families, which has been severely threatened by the close proximity of hundreds of native squatters, who are under no authority or control.' In terms clearly aimed at spurring the authorities into action, the women declared: 'Our menfolk are away at employment by day, and we have all been made to realise the grave danger which unprotected women and children may suffer from these Kaffirs.' They charged that Waverley Township was a 'well-known centre for illicit liquor-brewing', and claimed that 'at week-ends huge crowds of natives gather and drink themselves into a terrible condition, when they are no longer responsible, or even aware of their actions, causing us an immeasurable amount of anxiety and worry'. While the language here is highly emotive, the sentiments are reflected in many of the letters and memoranda concerning Waverley Township.

One proposal in the women's petition proved consequential: if there was no law that could be used to evict black people from Waverley Township, the Minister of Native Affairs should 'introduce some measure at the next Parliamentary Session which will cope with the situation, which is in fact becoming intolerable, to prevent any more native squatters being allowed to settle, and to have those removed who are already established there'.[19] The proposal to enact a law that would give the white authorities power to evict the black residents seemed to strike a chord. There had been ongoing frustration concerning the authorities' inability either to successfully prosecute the owner of the land, or to prosecute the black people who lived there. In July 1928 the Pretoria Sub-Native Commissioner expressed regret that the police were not able to successfully prosecute Moffat under the Native Urban Areas Act of 1923.[20] Four months later, similar frustrations were expressed by the Secretary for Native Affairs in a letter to the Attorney General.[21] And on 10 December 1928 the Attorney General pointed out that the prospects of successfully prosecuting Moffat for contravening section 6 of the Native Urban Areas Act of 1923 were remote.[22]

Section 6 of the Act made it a criminal offence for an owner of land situated within three miles of a boundary of an urban area to allow black people to reside on that land without express approval of the Minister of Native Affairs. Waverley Township fell exactly three miles outside the urban white municipality of Innesdale, and was therefore subject to the law. The Minister of Native Affairs had not given approval for black people to reside there. In fact, he had repeatedly rejected Moffat's petitions to have the area declared a township for black settlement, thereby making the presence of black people on the land a clear violation of the law, though the state had of course repeatedly failed in its attempts to prosecute Moffat. Furthermore, while the Act made it a criminal offence for landowners to keep black residents on their properties without the minister's authorisation, it did not expressly make it an offence for black people themselves to occupy the land. So the black residents of Waverley Township could not be prosecuted in terms of section 6 of the Native Urban Areas Act of 1923.

The proposal to enact a law was meant to address that gap in the existing law. Indications that the authorities were considering the introduction of a new law appeared in a letter written by the Secretary for Native Affairs to Mr R.T. Brown, the sole white landowner at Waverley Township. Brown was opposed to turning the land into a black township, and was also opposed to the continued presence of black people on the land. The Secretary for Native Affairs informed Brown that his question regarding the introduction of a new law to address the Waverley situation was being considered by the minister.[23] By December 1928 a decision had duly been taken to amend the Native Urban Areas Act. The Secretary for Native Affairs informed the Additional Native Commissioner for Pretoria that there was a proposal to 'insert a special clause which will enable the present matter to be dealt with'.[24] The private secretary to the Minister of Native Affairs explained to the town clerk of Innesdale Municipality that the clause would make it 'an offence for Natives to congregate upon land within three miles of an urban boundary and secondly by restricting the application of the saving clause in so far as townships are concerned to such as may be specially exempted by the Minister'.[25] The special clause was inserted in the amendment of the Native Urban Areas Act in a bill that was passed by Parliament in 1930. From then on, it was a criminal offence for black people to congregate or reside on land which was within three miles of an urban area. With the gates opened for prosecution, the Secretary for Native Affairs informed the Police Commissioner that he had 'the honour to point out that machinery now exists which can be utilised to put an end to the unsatisfactory state of affairs obtaining in Waverley Township'.[26]

With the amended law in place, the authorities no longer had their sights on Moffat, the owner of the land, but rather on the black residents. Soon, hundreds of black residents were arrested for contravening the law, and prosecuted at the Pretoria Magistrate's Court. The most famous case was *Rex* v. *Seshele*, and Pixley Seme would lead the defence.

The Seshele case

The white authorities made their first move against the black residents of Waverley Township in August 1930. Summonsed to appear before the Pretoria Magistrate's Court for contravening the Native Urban Areas Amendment Act passed that year, the residents were duly charged. According to Tom Ntuli, one of the accused, the residents decided to seek a lawyer to defend their case. They consulted Petrus Matseke, a prominent leader of the Transvaal Native Congress, who for a fee of £1 offered to introduce them to Seme who was at the time practising as an attorney in Johannesburg. Seme agreed to take up their case at a fee of £2 and five shillings per person. If they lost the case, he undertook to take it to the Transvaal Supreme Court, and if necessary to the Appellate Court in Bloemfontein. He however stated that he would charge an additional £3 per person for taking the case beyond the Magistrate's Court.

Seme's terms were agreed to by over a hundred residents and confirmed at a subsequent meeting with the residents where Moffat, Makgatho and Matseke were also present. Money was collected from the residents and handed over to Seme, who issued a receipt confirming the amount given to him at that meeting.[27]

Acting in his capacity as legal representative of the accused, and upon their consent being given, Seme entered into an agreement with the state that all the accused would be tried in one case, *Rex* v. *Seshele*, and that the verdict in that case would apply to all the accused since the charges were all the same. Presiding over the case was Mr K.R. Thomas, the additional magistrate at the Pretoria Magistrate's Court. Representing the state was Mr Plewman, a public prosecutor, with the defence counsel being Seme as well as a Mr Fourie, who represented two of the accused. The proceedings began with the accused entering a plea of not guilty. The state called two witnesses: the Innesdale Municipality town clerk, Mr Frederick Carl Wegerle, and Mr Johan de Villiers de Beer, an attorney of the Supreme Court who for many years had acted as Moffat's legal representative in his dealings with the state on the matter of Waverley Township. Both witnesses repeated the known facts about the history of Waverley Township and confirmed that black people resided there.

The defence decided to call no witnesses. Instead, Seme addressed the court. He argued that the state had failed to prove that his clients had not been given permission by the Minister of Native Affairs to reside at Waverley Township, as required by section 6 of the Native Urban Areas Amendment Act. In any event, he contended, the Act did not apply to existing rights, thereby implying that his clients had rights to reside at Waverley Township before the law was passed. Since that law could not be applied retrospectively, Seme argued, its provisions could not be applied to his clients. Seme also argued that the accused were protected by the 1913 Natives Land Act, which ensured that, before the Act was passed into law, black people who already lived in the Transvaal were protected from being removed from the areas where they resided. The provisions of the Native

Urban Areas Amendment Act, Seme averred, were 'not sufficient to deprive natives of rights under Act of 1913 [Natives Land Act]'.[28] When Fourie stood up to address the court, he associated himself with Seme.

Despite the spirited defence, the accused lost the case, with each one being given the option of a £5 fine or imprisonment with hard labour for five days. The sentence was suspended for one month, during which time the accused were to leave the township and be on good behaviour. Preparations for appeal began immediately. Money was collected by various parties, including some of the accused – Petrus Mapela in particular – and by Petrus Matseke. The appeal was heard at the Transvaal Provincial Division of the Supreme Court in May 1931. Assisting Seme was John Murray, K.C., with Joseph Liebson as junior counsel. Murray's fee, including consultation, was £25, while Liebson's was slightly over £16. The combined legal fee for senior and junior counsel was just over £47 after other costs were incurred during preparation for the case.[29]

Judgment was handed down by the Transvaal Provincial Division of the Supreme Court in June 1931. The black residents of Waverley had lost the appeal. The next stop was the Appellate Division in Bloemfontein. As agreed with his clients, Seme was expected to lead the charge. But he neglected to do so, and that is when his legal troubles began. There is a dispute about the reasons behind Seme's decision. His clients argued under oath that after they lost the case at the Transvaal Supreme Court they were under the impression that Seme was preparing for the appeal in Bloemfontein. However, they only learnt that Seme had abandoned them when Matseke advised them to see Liebson, who informed them that 'Seme had altogether neglected the appeal' and that 'their rights were in serious danger'. To make matters worse, on the day they visited Liebson they discovered that that was the last day for lodging the appeal. They requested Liebson to file papers on their behalf and to apply for condonation for the delay in filing the appeal within the stipulated period.[30]

Seme's version of events was different. In a letter addressed to Messrs De Beer and Liebson dated 5 August 1931, he stated the following:

> I told the clients that the appeal costs had to be paid in before I could take the matter of Bloemfontein. I made several trips to Waverley in order to explain this to them. On one occasion I met your Mr Liebson at the Railway station and I told him that I was going to Waverley and would come back to see him that afternoon and give him final

instructions. But I failed to come as I was delayed by the natives not turning up in time to find your office still open. That was my last day in the Transvaal and I left instructions with the leaders to collect the money and come to pay in your office the following day so as to enable you to proceed with the appeal to Bloemfontein.[31]

Seme went on to caution the two lawyers against his clients: 'Don't let them be trying dodges as before. I think that you know them well enough already.' The residents disputed Seme's claims, which were also challenged by the legal firm, De Beer and Liebson, to which the Waverley Township residents had turned for legal representation at the Appellate Division. What lay at the heart of the dispute was Seme's apparent abandonment of his clients in the middle of a case without informing them and, crucially, whether he had overcharged them for legal services and left them in the lurch before all their legal options had been exercised. De Beer and Liebson were of the opinion that Seme had overcharged his clients, and they said as much in a letter to him. They rejected Seme's explanation for not pursuing the appeal, expressing amazement 'that you could have brought yourself to submit the explanation you did'. They also accused him of withholding the funds that were meant for the appeal in Bloemfontein and charged that his conduct put the lives of Waverley Township residents 'in serious jeopardy' since the failure to appeal would lead to their eviction and cause them to 'suffer great hardships'. Seme was informed, furthermore, that affidavits were being prepared to report him to the Incorporated Law Society of the Transvaal for unprofessional conduct[32] – which duly occurred.

The Incorporated Law Society of the Transvaal v. Pixley ka Isaka Seme

In May 1932 the Incorporated Law Society of the Transvaal petitioned the Transvaal Supreme Court in Pretoria to strike Seme's name off the roll of attorneys on the basis of his conduct in handling the Waverley Township matter. In an affidavit signed by its president, Hendrik Lodewyk Malherbe, the Transvaal Law Society accused Seme of charging his clients, the black residents of Waverley Township, excessive and unreasonable legal fees; of failing to fulfil the duties owed to his clients in his capacity as their legal representative; of failing to account to his clients for the money paid to him when asked to do so; and of failing to pay counsel's fees from the money paid by his clients for that purpose. The Law Society argued that, collectively, the accusations constituted 'unprofessional and dishonourable conduct unworthy of the dignities and duties of the Attorney of this Honourable Court'. It further charged that Seme was unworthy and unfit to practise as an attorney.[33]

In support of its case the Law Society submitted affidavits from two residents of Waverley Township, Tom Ntuli and Petrus Mapela, and from two lawyers, John Murray and Joseph Liebson. What proved crucial to the case was the matter of Seme's legal fees, which the Law Society argued were excessive and unreasonable. The two black residents submitted to the court separately that the money collected from the residents and paid to Seme was approximately £400.

Seme disputed the substantive claims in the affidavits, and also the claim from Ntuli and Mapela that he was paid £400 to defend the case all the way to Bloemfontein. In a reply to De Beer and Liebson, Seme conceded that the agreed fee per person was £3, but disputed that he had been paid the amount claimed by the residents of Waverley. He claimed that he had charged a special fee for the case because he was not at the time conducting his usual legal practice owing to his election as president of the ANC, which took him to various parts of the country. He had informed the residents that he would take up their case as long as they were prepared to pay his travelling expenses, which in his view were high and warranted the unusually high fees. He claimed, furthermore, that he had told the residents that his approach would involve exercising political influence on the authorities in Pretoria, and that the estimated cost of this would be approximately £100. Seme stated that his 'man has interviewed all the authorities that have the powers to intervene in the matter, including the Minister, the Police, the Provincial Departments, the Municipality of Innesdale, the Commission on Native Locations etc.' His 'man', he said, also 'had to make a run to Cape Town to interview the Minister'.[34]

Seme neither disclosed the identity of this man nor indicated whether or not he had been successful, but his claim to have incurred costs in wielding political influence was emphatically disputed by the Waverley residents. Ntuli baldly stated: 'I have heard that Seme now says that we engaged him to exercise influence of various kinds and that part of the money was for this purpose. This is altogether untrue. We engaged Seme from start to finish as an attorney and as an attorney only.' Seme's explanation for charging high fees, Ntuli said, was the high cost of engaging advocates to represent them in court. Ntuli's version was supported by Mapela.[35]

Seme's claim ran into problems when the two advocates he had engaged complained of not being paid. As a result of the non-payment, Murray, the senior counsel in the appeal case, put Seme on a blacklist. The junior counsel, Liebson, similarly complained that Seme had paid him only a small proportion of his fee.

Denying that his fees were excessive, unreasonable and unconscionable, as argued by the Law Society, Seme contended that 'taking into consideration the difficulties which I had in this case and the number of full and part days I spent thereon and the disbursements I had in connection therewith fully justified my charging a much higher fee'. He went on to claim that had it not been for the political interest he had in the case he would not have taken it on. He blamed his failure to pay counsel on his inability to collect the full fees from the Waverley residents. Concerning his failure to inform his clients about the need to take the case to Bloemfontein, Seme offered the following defence:

a number of educated members of Waverley Township were present in Court and the result [of the appeal at the Transvaal Supreme Court] was widely discussed by them and other natives in the vicinity. The results of the Appeal were also published in the local newspapers. I held a public meeting of Natives after the case and told them that the Appeal had failed in the Provincial Division and that it was necessary to prosecute same further in the Appellate Division.

He claimed, furthermore, that he had discussed the matter with the senior counsel, De Beer, and arranged with him to lodge an appeal, promising also to pay the necessary fees. Seme expressed regret at not having honoured his promise and offered to pay £25 when he lodged his responding affidavit.[36]

It was left to the judges of the Transvaal Supreme Court to adjudicate on the claims and counterclaims contained in the affidavits. The Transvaal Law Society's application to have Seme's name removed from the roll of attorneys was made at the Transvaal Supreme Court on 9 August 1932. Presiding over the application were Justice Barry and Justice Maritz. Seme requested postponement of the proceedings so that he could prepare his responding affidavit, and the next hearing was set for 24 August 1932. On the day of the hearing, Seme was accompanied by Advocate Joseph Liebson, who represented him pro Deo. Liebson's presence probably surprised everyone because he had written a damning affidavit against Seme for the same case. Seme requested another postponement, and the court again granted his request. The hearing was set for 21 September 1932. However, Seme failed to turn up. There was no explanation for his absence – or indeed that of his representatives, who likewise were not at the hearing. The two judges postponed the case to the following day, 22 September, and gave instructions that Seme be ordered to come to court. Once again, Seme and his legal representatives were nowhere to be found on the appointed day. The court proceedings went ahead in his absence, with Advocate C.W. de Villiers, K.C., arguing the case of the Transvaal Law Society. Having listened to the arguments and having read the affidavits from both parties, the two judges passed the verdict: Seme was guilty of unprofessional and dishonourable conduct. Accordingly, they ordered that he be struck off the roll of attorneys and be interdicted from practising as an attorney. He was further ordered to hand over to the registrar of the court his certificate of admission and enrolment as an attorney, and to pay the costs of the application.

Seme's absence from court on 21 September 1932 was not only surprising but also baffling. After all, he had been present in court when the new date for the hearing was set after his request for a postponement. The explanation Seme gave was as simple as it was staggering. He claimed that he had 'misheard the date to which it [the hearing] was postponed'. He said that he thought the hearing had been postponed to 24 September instead of 21 September. Seme explained that he had left for Swaziland on the day the hearing was postponed, i.e. on 24 August 1932. He said he only returned from Swaziland on the evening of 22 September to prepare for the hearing that he had thought was set for 24 September. It was only the following day, 23 September, that he learnt from his attorney, Mr A. Basner, that the hearing had taken place the previous day and that he had been struck off the roll of attorneys. Mr Basner had shown him a copy of the *Rand Daily Mail* which carried the story of his being removed as an attorney. Seme claimed to have gone to the offices of the Transvaal Law Society the very next day, 24 September, accompanied by Mr Basner. The purpose of the visit was to explain his absence from court and also to inform the secretary of the Law Society of his intention to apply for a re-hearing of the case.

Seme went ahead and filed papers: in his affidavit he informed the court that he had erroneously believed the date of the hearing to be 24 September instead of 21 September, as set down by the court. He also expressed his belief that the court would not have struck him off the roll had he been present at the hearing, given evidence, and cross-examined witnesses. Seme informed the court that he was, moreover, a 'poor man, aged 52 years', had 'no assets either in cash or property', and was 'dependent on the proceeds of my professional activities' for livelihood. He had a wife and three minor children to support, as well as a mother-in-law and an aged aunt, and he pleaded that the court's decision would render him and his dependants 'destitute'.[37]

Basner confirmed that Seme had come to see him on 23 September, and that he had accompanied Seme to the offices of the Transvaal Law Society the next day. However, the crucial aspect of Seme's version that Basner did not corroborate was the reason for his absence from court on 21 and 22 September. In fact, the Law Society questioned Seme's claim that he was unaware that 21 September was the date of the hearing, producing two letters it had written to Seme on 2 and 6 September respectively on matters related to the hearing. The first was sent to Seme's postal address, while the second was sent to his office address, 188 Marshall Street. Notably, the Law Society claimed that the letter sent to Seme's office was duly signed for by a clerk. Furthermore, the Law Society had written to the registrar of the Supreme Court asking Seme to file a missing document, and Seme's office had replied to the request on 15 September 1932.[38] It is a significant fact, though, that the clerk who sent this reply had indicated that Seme was in Swaziland, and that the office had not been able to communicate with him.

Seme's application to have the order striking him off the roll of attorneys set aside was heard at the Transvaal Supreme Court on 21 February 1933. Presiding over the case were the same two judges, Barry and Maritz. Seme appeared in person while the Transvaal Law Society was once again represented by C.W. de Villiers, K.C. Seme argued that the court's judgment was granted by default and the default was inadvertent. He repeated his version, that he had mistakenly believed the date for the hearing to be 24 September 1932. Counsel for the respondents argued that the judgment was not by default, and contended that Seme had been negligent in failing to appear in court on the appointed date.[39]

Delivering the judgment, Justice Barry stated that it was difficult for the court 'to come to the conclusion that the appellant is free from blame' for not appearing in court on the appointed date in September 1932. Yet even if he were blameless, 'in his application he should have entered into the merits of the case and shown to the Court that he had good defence to the charge made against him by the witnesses and that it might be possible for the Court to come to a different conclusion to the conclusion to which it came on the 22nd September'. It was not enough for Seme to contend that 'had he given evidence on his own behalf and cross-examined the witnesses who appeared against him, this Court would not have granted the petition of the Law Society against him'. Justice Barry noted Seme's belief that the order to strike him off the roll was not based on sound reason; he was not present to defend himself, and he had made a bona fide mistake by not attending proceedings on the appointed date. Accordingly, Barry's finding was as follows: 'In those circumstances I think the Court should make no order, but the applicant will have to pay the costs.' Justice Maritz concurred, adding however that he did not believe a 'bona fide mistake was made as to the date of postponement'.[40]

The court's decision was a blow to Seme's career and was an extraordinary reversal of fortune. Since his admission in 1910, Seme had acquired a reputation as a distinguished lawyer with impressive achievements, acting as a legal advisor to royal families and kings, and even representing the Swazis at the British Privy Council. As sitting president of the ANC, he would have been stung by the court's finding. Had he been struck off the roll for pursuing a worthy political cause he would have been praised as a hero. But instead he was being removed for essentially taking advantage of the very people the ANC was committed to defend, at a moment they most needed its support.

However, this decision was not the last word on the matter. Five years later, Seme lodged another application with the same court seeking to be reinstated as an attorney. In an affidavit filed on 9 December 1937, Seme informed the court that he was fifty-seven years old with a wife, four children and a mother-in-law to support. When the case was heard in 1938, he disputed statements in Tom Ntuli's affidavit, especially the claim that he had been given money by individual residents of Waverley Township. Seme stated that his legal fees were collected by a committee of residents and paid to him by that committee. He also accused the Transvaal Law Society of discrimination by not affording him an opportunity to explain his conduct when it accused him of acting improperly in his business dealings with the Waverley residents.[41]

Seme submitted a supporting affidavit from Sefako Makgatho, who stated that, in his capacity as senior vice president of the ANC in the Transvaal, he had attended several meetings Seme had held with the residents.

He corroborated Seme's claim that a committee of residents had been established, through which Seme's legal fees were collected and handed over to him. Furthermore, Makgatho claimed that he had heard no complaints regarding Seme's alleged failure to issue receipts. In any event, Makgatho stated, if the residents had anything to complain about they would have come to him because he was their leader.

There were two more affidavits in support of Seme's application. One was from Father V.C. Mayabas, the priest in charge at St Cyprian's Anglican Church in Johannesburg. He testified to Seme's good character and his good standing in the church. The other was from Piet Marema, a former resident of Waverley Township, who had been a member of the committee established to collect money for legal fees. Marema stated that he had been one of the persons who went to see Seme in Johannesburg when charges were laid against the residents. He supported Seme's claim that the money for legal fees was collected by the committee and paid over to Seme.[42] However, neither Makgatho nor Marema addressed the question of Seme's exorbitant fees, or the issue of whether the money was also intended for representation at the Appellate Division in Bloemfontein.

A date for the hearing was set: 22 April 1938, in Pretoria. Presiding over the case was Judge Solomon. The proceedings began with the Law Society's counsel, Mr Findlay, pointing out that Seme had not paid the costs of the 1932 proceedings, as the court had ordered him to do. The rules of the court required that, before Seme's application for reinstatement could be considered, Seme should pay these costs. If he failed to do so, Findlay argued, the matter could not be heard by the court. Seme's counsel, Mr Reitz, swiftly responded with a request that Seme's application be changed: that it sought instead an order to set aside the court's decision.

Judge Solomon was not pleased with the request to strike down the court's decision. He pointed out that the request was 'made five years after the last application to re-open was made, heard and dismissed'. The judge further stated that if there was 'any valid ground for re-opening the case the applicant must have been aware of it long since and able to produce the evidence which was necessary'.[43] Seme was also reminded that the judges in the February 1933 case had informed him that he needed to produce evidence that dealt with the merits of the case if he hoped to overturn the decision of the court. Judge Solomon stated that, having read all the relevant papers, he could 'see no material difference between the excuses for misconduct put up by the applicant in the present application and the evidence he filed some years ago'. He expressed surprise that Seme had challenged Tom Ntuli's claim regarding the collection of money for his legal fees, and that Seme was challenging this in 1938 when he could have done so in 1932 and again in 1933. While the judge rejected the application to set aside the 1932 decision of the court, he decided to make no order regarding the application for reinstatement, and ordered Seme to pay the costs of the proceedings, with Judge Grindley-Ferris concurring.[44] Seme was back to square one.

Vilakazi's cattle

Devastating as these court judgments were for Seme's career, it is important to remember that he had run foul of the law on previous occasions, and for similar reasons. The most notable case of course involved Seme's refusal to pay back money entrusted to him by Manana for the purchase of a piece of land in Daggakraal. The Wakkerstroom Magistrate's Court had found Seme guilty of theft.

Another case, though one that seems not to have reached the courts, involved Johannes Vilakazi from Springbokkraal in the Piet Retief district. From his earnings as a manual labourer, Vilakazi had bought seven head of cattle, which he kept at Springbokkraal while working away from home. He intended to use the cattle to pay *ilobolo* for a woman he wanted to marry, but discovered that his uncle, Mbulawa Vilakazi, had taken his livestock. After several failed attempts to get his cattle back, Johannes Vilakazi approached Seme for legal assistance. Seme took the case on condition that he was paid £15, of which Vilakazi claimed to have paid £7 as a first instalment. Seme then demanded that Vilakazi pay an extra £5 and five shillings before commencing with legal representation. On 21 March 1917, Seme wrote to his client:

Ngizokwedhlula lapo ngolwesihlanu ekuseni, 23rd March 1917. Kuhle ke ungilungisele imali u 5 pounds 5 shillings imali yaleli cala. Lizoba likuni lona ngoba umfowenu use tate u Mmeli. Kuhle ke wenze njalo sibonane esiteshini ekuseni.[45]

[I will come by on the morning of 23rd March 1917. It will be good if you prepare to pay me 5 pounds 5 shillings, which is for the case. The case will be difficult because your brother has hired an attorney. You must bring the money and be at the train station in the morning.]

Johannes Vilakazi claimed to have given Seme £3 when they met on the appointed date, at the Transvaal Hotel in Volksrust. The clerk of the Wakker- stroom Magistrate's Court confirmed that the case was indeed heard at the court, with Seme appearing for Johannes Vilakazi, and Mr Sausenthaler, an attorney, appearing for Mbulawa Vilakazi. The outcome of the case was that Mbulawa Vilakazi was ordered to hand over eleven head of cattle to his nephew, Johannes, or pay the monetary equivalent of £60. Mbulawa Vilakazi was also ordered to pay the costs of the proceedings, including the legal fee that his nephew had paid to Seme. Seme then promised to pay back the £15 fee to Johannes Vilakazi, but he failed to do so. He also failed to return the cattle that his client's uncle had given back after losing the case. Seme merely said that the 'cattle are in his [Seme's] farm' with the promise that he would 'send them to [Vilakazi's] home'. On other occasions Seme informed his client that the 'cattle are running on his [Seme's] farm'. Some months later, Johannes Vilakazi arranged to meet Seme at Daggakraal. However, Seme refused to discuss the matter with him. Instead, he allegedly challenged Vilakazi to take him on, going so far as to declare that there was no one who could win against him in a court of law.

It was then that Johannes Vilakazi sought the assistance of Ben Boshoff, who was, however, unsuccessful, and therefore returned a portion of the fee his client had paid him. Undeterred, Johannes Vilakazi reported the matter to the Secretary for Native Affairs, who in turn referred it to the Chief Native Commissioner. Sadly, Vilakazi's efforts at getting Seme to return his money and his cattle proved fruitless.[46]

* * *

The Waverley Township case and the consequent court decision to remove Seme from the roll of attorneys was a significant blow to a brilliant legal career and also to a life that shone with achievements. Were it an isolated case it could easily be dismissed as a lapse of judgement. But alongside Seme's impressive legal and political contributions lay a disturbing his- tory of rule breaking and taking advantage of those who came to him for assistance. Seme had few qualms about exploiting poor people's desperate hunger for land, and the Waverley Township and Vilakazi cases serve to show that at times his ruthlessness knew no bounds.

It is important to mention that Seme was not the only one who was accused of taking advantage of his clients. Early on in his career, Mangena was accused of overcharging his clients. His case did not reach the courts because the Transvaal Law Society felt there was insufficient evidence to lodge a successful prosecution. Richard Msimang also faced the same accusation. In the early 1930s, he faced a charge of defrauding a black woman by the name of Saliswa Mbanjwa. Msimang admitted that he owed her money and committed to pay it back. The Transvaal Law Society expressed an intention to institute legal proceedings against him for defrauding Mbanjwa. What saved Msimang from suffering the ignominy of possibly being struck off the roll of attorneys was his untimely death in 1933.[47]

The dark side of Seme's life could therefore be said to be the underside of an emerging middle class with limited opportunities for material wealth, a middle class whose hold on its new status was extremely tenuous. To be fair to Seme, it is important to note that almost all leading figures in the ANC at the time had business interests of one sort or the other – whether it was (foiled) plans for land speculation in Waverley Township, as with Sefako Makgatho, or charging the poor of Waverley a fee for services, as with Petrus Matseke, the Transvaal president of the ANC, when he introduced the residents to Seme in Johannesburg. So Seme's case was not unique: like other leaders at the time he was expected to provide leadership to the very same people he looked to for economic survival. That often presented a conflict of interests – not only for Seme, but for other leaders as well.

For all this, however, Seme's behaviour in the Waverley Township case cannot be explained away. It was clearly driven by greed, and Seme and his family would pay dearly for this and other transgressions.

10

In from the cold

Seme's court defeats were echoed in the political arena. His crushing defeat by Reverend Zaccheus Mahabane at the ANC conference in December 1937 reflected delegates' despair, frustration and their low regard for Seme's presidency. This was probably the only time in the history of the ANC where a president's defeat was followed by singing of the anthem, '*Nkosi Sikelel' iAfrika*', to express delegates' relief that they had reclaimed their organisation and the aspirations it embodied. Once again, Seme would have been stung. His vanquisher, Mahabane, whether out of generosity or sentimentality regarding Seme's role in the formation of the organisation, appointed him to the national executive. He gave Seme the portfolio of secretary for the chiefs and added another responsibility, namely legal advisor to the national executive. The inclusion of a former ANC president in the executive of another was not unprecedented. John Dube and Sefako Makgatho, for instance, had both served in Seme's national executive when he was elected in 1930.

Appointing Seme as secretary for the chiefs was an inspired choice. Right from the start of the ANC, he had been a moving spirit behind the establishment of an upper house for chiefs. He had also been instrumental in the appointment of prominent traditional leaders as honorary presidents. Eventually, though, the upper house had become inactive and Seme had attempted to resuscitate it during his presidency. He had also organised his law practice to focus most of its work on servicing traditional leaders, the most prominent case being the one that concerned the Swazi royal house. Although Seme's name had been struck off the roll of attorneys for several years when Mahabane gave him the additional portfolio of legal advisor to the national executive, he was still recognised as one of the preeminent black lawyers of the time. By giving him the two responsibilities, namely secretary for the chiefs and legal advisor, Mahabane was acknowledging Seme's twin passions.

Seme took to his role as secretary for the chiefs like a duck to water, particularly in the cruel aftermath of the 1936 Native Trust and Land Act.

Though the Act marginally increased the percentage of land allocated to black people, it also entrenched the process of land dispossession set in motion by the 1913 Natives Land Act. The land law was accompanied by the Representation of Natives Act, also passed in 1936, which removed African voters in the Cape Province from the common voters roll, thereby firmly shutting the door to equal political rights for black people in South Africa. Instead, Africans were to be represented in Parliament by white members; a Native Representative Council was also created, comprising six white officials as well as four nominated and twelve elected Africans.

Seme had readily adapted to the changed circumstances, though he was not the only ANC leader who seemed to accept the new arrangements imposed by the white government. In fact, some of the leading figures in the ANC stood for election as members of the NRC, and when Thema, for instance, won the badge of being a member of the Representative Council, he proudly added 'MRC' to his name. As president of the ANC, Mahabane seemed fairly comfortable operating within the status quo and continued with the politics of leading deputations to the government and operating within the structures it had established.

Taking to his new position with gusto, Seme communicated with chiefs and white representatives on various matters affecting black people and chiefs in particular. In fact, throughout his term as president, but especially during his last year in 1937, Seme had invited members of the NRC and white senators representing Africans in Parliament to mass meetings he called from time to time to discuss matters such as the scarcity of land. His favourite white representative was J.D. Rheinallt Jones, who represented Africans from the Transvaal and Free State in the Senate. In October 1937, two months before his ousting, Seme invited Rheinallt Jones, Thema and Richard Baloyi – treasurer general of the ANC and also a member of the NRC – to attend a community meeting in Daggakraal to discuss the Commission on Native Farm Labour. Ever wary of offending those in authority, Seme gave the assurance that the meeting would be held on a Sunday because he was aware 'that the farmers need all their Native labour at this time'.[1]

This cautious approach to those who wielded power, both within and outside of government, would shape the manner in which Seme executed his duties under the Mahabane presidency. His main occupation during his tenure as secretary for the chiefs was convening a conference of chiefs. On 8 April 1939 he wrote to Mahabane and other members of the national executive, informing them that the Transvaal African Congress[2] would be hosting the conference, which would take place in Marabastad on 24 May 1939. He pleaded that their attendance would help to make the conference a success, as well as induce chiefs in other provinces to attend. Matters to be discussed included the position of African chiefs, their rights to land and their powers; the economic needs of Africans in towns, on private farms, and in the native areas; the education of black children; how to make the representation of Africans in Parliament more effective; the 'Native cattle and their market'; and the establishment of a 'Congress Monthly Magazine of Review for the Chiefs'.[3] The agenda is unsurprising, considering the conservative nature of Seme's politics. It is also not surprising that the first item concerned the rights and powers of chiefs, which Seme strongly felt should be increased.

The conference appears to have taken place as planned. Seme had tried to convene another conference for the chiefs of the Transvaal province, but this was postponed. In August 1939, Seme wrote to the Chief Native Commissioner for the Northern Areas (comprising the northern region of the Transvaal) to inform him that he and the Transvaal ANC president, Petrus Matseke, had visited Pretoria on ANC business; they had taken the time to visit the commissioner's office to explain the purpose of the upper house and the role of chiefs in the ANC. Seme seemed anxious to dispel the commissioner's perception that the ANC upper house wanted the protectorates to be incorporated into South Africa – a position that ran counter to that of the government. Seme firmly stated that 'the Upper House has never taken part in the question of the transfer of the protectorates to the Union of South Africa', and added that the matter had not been discussed at the conference of chiefs in Marabastad. He gave the assurance that it was not on the agenda for the planned September meeting, and said that the chiefs would never discuss a matter if the Department of Native Affairs did not wish them to do so.[4]

He went on to outline the ANC's position regarding the chiefs, and in doing so Seme revealed not only his own position vis-à-vis the chiefs, but also his broader political view:

It is the policy of the Congress to to [sic] help the chiefs to retain their prestige and to advance their usefulness to their own people under present conditions when all the young people have to live away from their reserves and among members of other tribes, in industrial areas and other places where they must go in search of employment. The African National Congress was established for this purpose in 1912 and it has retained its very good name with the native Africans, the South African public and I hope with the Government also. This clear record of the Congress in the past and its administration under the present leaders in every Province, I hope is sufficient assurance as to our continued good sense and responsibility.[5]

Seme also sought to distance the upper house from the activities of the lower house, informing the commissioner that the upper house had no 'executive functions in connection with the propaganda and political work of the Congress'. That role, he said, belonged to the lower house. The upper house, in his view, should have a close and constructive relationship with the government. He was grateful to the government for granting the chiefs more powers through the Representation of Natives Act and reminded the commissioner that the government could work with chiefs effectively as partners. Seme also pleaded with the commissioner to influence the government to recognise the ANC as a 'non-official Body representing the chiefs and their people'. This would 'open very rich opportunities for many unofficial contacts between the leaders of the Africans and the Department [of Native Affairs] on a higher scale and make its officers wiser about what is really going on in the native mind'.[6]

Seme would accommodate the government in this obsequious manner for the entire period he was secretary for the chiefs – and, indeed, throughout his dealings with it. He did not seek equal rights. Rather, he wished simply to accommodate Africans within the system of inequality in which he had settled and in which he seemed comfortable. As time went on, his preferred position was to distance the upper house from the very ANC of which it was a part in order to create the impression that it was non-political. In late 1939, as he again sent out a call for the conference of the chiefs, he went so far as to issue the following proclamation: 'The Upper House of the Congress is a none [sic] political body, in the sense that it will not support any political party or political parties in the country nor be drawn into any controversy against the Government.' Its role was to 'create a feeling of brotherhood among the Chiefs and to break down tribal prejudices'. In line with this, the only items up for discussion were: 'What the Government expects the Chiefs to do'; 'What the Africans expect the Chiefs to do'; 'The Native Representation & Trust Acts of 1936';

'What Co-operative Societies can do for Africans'; and the establishment of a monthly magazine for chiefs.[7]

But then the Second World War broke out, and the conference did not take place. Seme told Rheinallt Jones that he had postponed it on his own initiative because he 'could not accept the responsibility for holding such a conference during war time'. He implies that he had not been pressured, yet in the very next sentence Seme says that the 'Government was anxiously concerned in the matter of keeping the Chiefs quiet', fearing no doubt that the conference would provide the chiefs with a platform for expressing opposition to South Africa's participation in the war.[8] That was a likely expectation given the experience of the First World War, where fierce opposition had been expressed, especially regarding the participation of Africans on the battlefields. After the sinking of the SS *Mendi* and the scores of black volunteers who had drowned, as well as the large number of casualties at Delville Wood, black people were unwilling to participate in another war. Seme, however, was firmly behind the government's decision to fight in the war and in fact thanked Jones and other parliamentary representatives for supporting the war effort.

Boldly, he suggested that Britain might take a leaf from France's assimilation policy and apply it in South Africa, encouraging its subjects to adopt the English language and culture. In doing so, Seme suggested that Britain would thereby 'gain new wealth and power among the Africans'. In statements that are especially controversial by today's standards, Seme went on to deride those who called for social equality between Africans and whites, dismissing their view as 'silly'. He declared: 'We Africans don't waste time thinking about that. Just look at Lourenco Marques [Maputo] where there is not even a bit of restrictions, there is no invasion of European hotels and places by the B [i.e. blacks] – In the French colonies the same.' The implication was that if restrictions were lifted, the colour bar would nevertheless stay in place as black people chose not to mingle with whites, whom they regarded as their superiors. Thus it was that Seme could make the following assertion: 'It is the undoubted spiritual and intellectual forces and higher moral power which give the Whiteman his prestige – his great sense of justice and not his lynching mob or resolutions "to keep the natives down"'. Naively entertaining the hope of many black soldiers in the First World War, Seme declared, 'I can see a good opening for the Africans if they will be allowed to assist Great Britain in this war.' He expressed the optimistic belief that 'British statesmen may open the gates of liberty to the slaves'.[9] History would of course show that Seme's faith in the goodwill of white people – in South Africa and Britain – was entirely unfounded.

When Alfred Xuma became ANC president in 1940, he kept Seme on as a member of the national executive. However, Seme's relationship with Xuma and the secretary general, James Calata, was not an easy one. While Mahabane had let Seme do as he pleased as secretary for the chiefs, Xuma and Calata kept him on a tight leash. In one particular instance, Seme was forced to climb down after publishing an article in *Umteteleli wa Bantu* urging chiefs to vote for Rheinallt Jones as a Senate representative, a position that ran counter to that of the national executive. Xuma forced him to publicly rescind his endorsement of Jones by stating that his earlier letter 'was not consistent with the policy of Congress concerning the present election'. In addition, Seme wrote to Xuma apologising for publishing the original article and avowing that he did not 'want to oppose the policy of Congress or to play solo in any shape or form'. He declared furthermore that the 'President General must be supported by all our people' and pledged that he would 'do the same'.[10]

The disagreement over the election of white Senate representatives was just the tip of the iceberg. In December 1942 Seme wrote a long letter of complaint to James Calata, the secretary general. What seems to have triggered this was Calata's letter informing Seme that he was too busy to meet with him. Grudgingly acknowledging that their 'administration has raised the status of the Congress more especially the leadership of Dr. Xuma which is most outstanding in the whole Union', Seme went on to express dismay that they had not convened a national conference, which he thought was long overdue. He listed several things that Xuma and Calata were failing to do, such as the establishment of a national newspaper, a subject close to Seme's heart. He disagreed with the removal of national executive members' names from the ANC letterhead on the basis that it 'injure[d] the dignity of the National Executive Committee'. Clearly distressed, Seme levelled further accusations at Calata:

> Your notions have no constitutional support and you seem to violate congress traditions wherein all officers of the Congress are members of Cabinet or National Executive Committee. You seem to like creating classes. You used to have 'Additional Members of the Cabinet'. Now these have disappeared without any apology or explanation and you have 'Advisors' in their place! What are you really after? The African

National Congress like every national organisation draws its inspiration from the mother of parliaments – the home of democracy! All the officers share a joint responsibility in the direction of the affairs of the Congress. All the present officers of the Congress are very distinguished men. Please don't call them your 'Advisors'. You have also omitted to add 'B.A.' title after W.B. Ngakana.[11]

Seme was also upset that the ANC motto had been replaced, as the old motto respected the 'last warnings of Moshoeshoe and the Prophet Ntsikana'. He did not, however, say what these warnings were. He made his position clear: 'I personally hate changes especially when they are unwarranted', declaring a 'love and respect [for] tradition wherever I find it'.[12] It was quite clear from the letter that there were fundamental disagreements between Seme and the two leaders, Xuma and Calata. Even so, Xuma appointed Seme to join a group tasked with drafting the African Claims document, a set of political demands and rights drawn up in response to the Atlantic Charter which was considered to fall short of addressing the political status and demands of black people in South Africa and the African continent as a whole.[13] Nevertheless, Seme did not last long in the national executive, and his influence waned.

Reinstatement
The period from 1932 when Seme was struck off the roll to his eventual reinstatement in 1942 was probably the most difficult in his life. It coincided with his presidency of the ANC, which was itself very challenging. In 1940, Prince Mshiyeni ka Dinuzulu, acting paramount chief of the Zulu nation, wrote to the Nongoma Native Commissioner:

Ngiyacela Nkosi ngokutobeka pambi kwako ukuba ungidlulisele loku uku-kala kwami kuye eNkosini yetu enkulu uNdabazabantu eMgungundlovu, ezwe ukukala kwami ngikalela umuntu wake u-Dr. P.I. Seme, B.A., L.L.D. owayenguMmeli wamacala, wavelelwa yiziposiso ekuzipateni kwake-ke wayesekishwa emsebenzini wobumeli, akabe esatola msebenzi wokuzondla kanye nomuzi wake, engikuluma nje Nkosi, usewaba ngumdingi nomham-buma ezweni.

Nkosi, usebuyate umpuyaza-pi eti uzama ukutola okokukohlisa izingane angapumeleli ndawo; nomkake udadewetu izibulo likababa uDinuzulukanye nezingane zabo ezintathu sebehlupeke kabi beswele

*nokokwembata nokokudla, okuze kwati ngokudliwa umunyu ngabatata
mina ngabagodla lapa kimi pezu komtwalo nami ongaka wezintandane
engiwupete.*[14]

Essentially, Mshiyeni was pleading for assistance in reinstating Seme as an
attorney. Admitting that his brother-in-law had done wrong, he explained
that the family was by now so destitute that he had invited them to live
with him. But it was difficult to continue supporting them as he had the
additional burden of looking after orphans (presumably his late brother
Solomon's children).

In February 1942 Seme filed a third court application seeking reinstatement. In his affidavit he stated that he was sixty-one years old and had lost
a child since his last court application in 1938. His material circumstances
had also greatly diminished. He described how he had supported his family
by farming, but in 1938 his farm plots in Daggakraal had been taken over
by the bank because he had failed to meet his mortgage repayments. His
family now relied on financial assistance from various parties, including
Sobhuza II, who, Seme said, had provided occasional financial assistance
from the time he was debarred. After losing their home in Sophiatown and
being forced to leave Johannesburg, he stated that his family had sought
refuge with his brother-in-law, Prince Mshiyeni.[15] For a while they had
also stayed with Seme's family in Nongoma.

Crucially, he informed the court in his affidavit that he had paid the
legal costs he owed the Transvaal Law Society; having settled this, he could
now make another appeal. He argued that the court could trust him with
handling his clients' money because he had 'collected large sums of money
for and on behalf of Zobhuza II [*sic*], Paramount Chief of Swaziland, which
monies were used to discharge obligations incurred by the said Zobhuza II,
and the Swazi nation, to their satisfaction.'[16] Given the fact that he had been
struck off the roll for overcharging his clients, calling into question his
trustworthiness, this was an important point.

Supporting Seme's petition for reinstatement were several prominent
names. Among them was Sobhuza II, who stated that he believed Seme to
be an honest and conscientious person who could be trusted with money
because he had always handled the money of the Swazi nation with care
and honesty. He added that Seme was a 'sober and hardworking person in
the interests of all his people and our chiefs, who all regard him as a very
able leader indeed'. Father V.C. Mayabas of St Cyprian's Anglican Church

in Johannesburg added his voice by attesting to Seme's good character, as did Albert William Lee, the Anglican bishop of Zululand and Swaziland, who also expressed concern about the future of Seme's family. Seme's friend, Rheinallt Jones, also wrote a supporting affidavit, as did Edgar Brookes, another African representative in the Senate.[17]

The Transvaal Provincial Division of the Supreme Court delivered its judgment on 14 April 1942, a full ten years after Seme was struck from the roll. Justice Barry delivered the court's decision. In an application such as Seme's, the court considered whether it was satisfied 'that since the applicant's name was struck off he has led an honest and honourable life and that he has held positions of trust since the application for striking him off'. Justice Barry stated that weight had to be given to the supporting affidavits, singling out those of Jones and Brookes who held particularly prominent positions as parliamentary representatives. Moreover, Sobhuza's affidavit held important evidence for the court because it dealt with the manner in which Seme had handled money entrusted to him. Having considered all the evidence before the court, Justice Barry stated: 'I have come to the conclusion, in all the circumstances, the applicant should be reinstated.'[18] Justice Maritz concurred.

Seme was once again free to practise his profession – one that had made it possible for him to meet some of the most prominent people in southern Africa, and that had brought fame and fortune. But when he veered off the rails, it had brought shame and embarrassment, and destitution for him and his family. His reinstatement opened a new chapter in Seme's life that included meeting a young lawyer who would change the politics of the ANC in a short space of time. This young firebrand was none other than Anton Muziwakhe Lembede.

Seme & Lembede Attorneys

Whether coincidence or not, it is of undeniable significance that the man behind the formation of the ANC and the one behind the founding of the ANC Youth League ended up as partners in the same law firm. There were few practising black lawyers at the time, a situation that had been aggravated by two premature deaths – that of Alfred Mangena in 1924 and Richard Msimang in 1933 – and this may explain Lembede's presence at the firm. Whatever the reason, on 25 January 1944 Anton Muziwakhe Lembede entered into articles of clerkship with Pixley ka Isaka Seme, and for two full years he served under his tutelage.

The road that took Lembede to 2–3 Rosenberg Arcade, home of Seme's Johannesburg law firm, was a long one. Born on 21 March 1914 at a farm in Eston, Natal, he was the eldest of seven children. His father, Martin Mbazwana, was a farm labourer while his mother, Martha MaLuthuli, was a school teacher. Lembede was home-schooled by his mother until he was thirteen years old, when he started formal education. Although both parents were employed, the family was not well off, and at one point young Anton had to work as a 'kitchen boy' for a white family to help finance his studies. In 1933 he enrolled at Adams College at Amanzimtoti to train as a teacher. When he completed his course he taught in the Orange Free State, though it soon became clear that other things attracted him. He enrolled for a BA degree at the correspondence University of South Africa and chose Roman law, logic and metaphysics as his major subjects. He also took Latin, English, Dutch, native law, Roman-Dutch law, South African criminal law, and education. He completed the degree in 1940 and immediately enrolled for a Bachelor of Laws, which he obtained soon afterwards in 1942. Armed with the two degrees, he signed up with Seme in January 1944.

After serving two years of clerkship and being admitted as an attorney, Lembede became a partner in the new firm Seme & Lembede Attorneys – Prokureurs & Conveyancers. True to Seme's earlier record, the firm focused mostly on the issue of land. Significant migration into urban centres in the 1940s had made the scarcity of land acute. Seme & Lembede Attorneys defended cases that dealt specifically with the issue of insufficient land for settlement by black people. One such case was *Albertyn* v. *Kumalo and Others (1946 WLD 529)*, which involved an application for confirmation of an interim order to eject a group of Africans who had occupied a piece of land in Johannesburg that belonged to what the court papers referred to as 'a Cape Coloured man'. The group of African occupants, led by William Kumalo, claimed that they had bought the land in question from a group described as the Albertyn Syndicate. The owner of the land disputed that he was part of the syndicate even though one of his partners, a white lawyer, was shown to have been present when certain transactions were concluded. The court had granted an interim order for the ejectment of Kumalo and his group, and the application was for the confirmation of that order. Seme and Lembede were the respondents' legal representatives. After considering the evidence before it, the court ruled that the matter needed to be examined further to determine whether the landowner's associates had indeed been involved in the sale of the land.

A similar case was *Johannesburg City Council* v. *Monongoaha and Others* (*1946 WLD 509*), involving a group of Africans who had occupied a piece of vacant land in Orlando Township. The City of Johannesburg claimed that it had surveyed the land in question for building houses for Africans and suggested that its illegal occupation by Monongoaha and his associates was interfering with those plans. The city also claimed that the same group of Africans had been ejected from another piece of land at Pimville, which they had illegally occupied. The city manager for Non-European Affairs claimed in court papers that in the ten-year period from 1936 to 1946 there had been a massive influx of Africans into Johannesburg, which had increased their number to 166 000. He claimed that the city was battling with what he termed 'squatting movements' by Africans. From the period 1944 to 1946 alone, there had been five major 'squatting movements', each involving 7 000 people, as well as three minor movements. The city complained that the effort it took to deal with the illegal land occupations was putting a strain on its senior officials and disturbing efforts aimed at 'the efficient prosecution of the plans in hand for non-European housing'.[19] The legal representatives for the affected occupants argued that the City of Johannesburg had an obligation to provide housing for Africans who resided in the city. But Judge Roper who presided over the case disputed that assertion, stating instead that such an obligation did not exist in law, and the responsibility on the city's part was thus discretionary. He found that the Africans had broken the law by occupying the land in question. There were other cases concerning land occupation involving either Seme or Lembede, for example *African Congregational Church Co., Ltd., and African Congregational Church* v. *Dube* (*1944 WLD 204*), a case that Seme defended.

Seme & Lembede Attorneys was, however, not only involved in land occupation cases. For instance, Seme represented James Sofasonke Mpanza when the latter was ordered to leave his home in Orlando Township to live on a farm called Coldplace in the district of Ixopo in Natal, and to do so within three days of the order being served on him. Mpanza was, furthermore, not permitted to leave Coldplace without permission being granted by the Secretary for Native Affairs. When Mpanza did not comply with the order to leave Johannesburg, he was arrested and forced onto the 3:40 p.m. train to Natal on 28 February 1946. That same afternoon Seme filed a petition asking the court to prevent Mpanza's removal from Johannesburg until his appeal had been heard. The court granted the application as an interim interdict against the state, pending the hearing of the case. In *Mpanza v. The Minister of Native Affairs and Other (1946 WLD 225)*, the court agreed with Seme's contention that Mpanza's rights could not be interfered with as the appeal had not yet been concluded. Judge Price decided in Mpanza's favour and ordered that the state should in the meantime refrain from deporting him from Orlando Township. He also ordered the state to pay costs.

Even though the partnership between Seme and Lembede was going well, Seme appears to have developed an interest in moving back to Natal. It is unclear what motivated him to move, although it has to be said that his family had not returned to Johannesburg after relocating to Nongoma following Seme's disbarment. Moreover, Seme was intimately involved in the establishment of Clermont Township outside Durban, in which his brother-in-law played a leading role. In fact, Seme bought two plots of land in Clermont, though there are indications that he wanted to open a legal practice in Richmond, near Pietermaritzburg. His intention to leave Johannesburg became apparent when he decided to sell his share of the practice to Lembede. According to the memorandum of sale, Seme committed to sell his legal practice to Lembede for the sum of £500, which Lembede was expected to pay upon signing of the agreement. The terms of the agreement included the following: Seme would hand over to Lembede all office equipment, though not the law books and journals, which Seme would retain; Lembede would pay Seme a commission of 5 per cent for each case, as from the date of signing to 31 December 1947, with the commission deemed part of the selling price but exclusive of the £500; and Seme would be entitled to practise in the Transvaal in order to take cases that concerned chiefs and other traditional leaders and their tribes. In the event that Seme undertook such work in the Transvaal he would pay Lembede a third of the legal fees. Because of his intention to continue practising in the Transvaal, a clause was included that a room would be kept in the offices for Seme's exclusive use.

Although the agreement was signed on 2 August 1946 it seems not to have been implemented. The following year, on 30 July 1947, Lembede suffered a fatal heart attack. The status of the sale agreement came into question when Lembede's brother Nicholas – legal heir to his estate since Lembede was unmarried at the time of death – asked the Native Commissioner to assist him to effectively reclaim the legal practice from Seme, which Nicholas claimed belonged to his late brother. In a letter dated

10 October 1947, just over a month after Lembede's death, Nicholas claimed that his brother had paid the £500 purchase price for the practice and Seme had failed to issue him with a receipt. He told the commissioner that he was anxious to know about the disposal of the practice.[20] This letter is surprising because, exactly two weeks after his partner's death, Seme had in fact written to the Native Commissioner to say that he had discussed the matter of the partnership with Lembede's mother as well as his brother Nicholas. The Lembedes wished to have the partnership discontinued and had asked him to wind up its operations and pay any monies owing to Lembede's heirs. Seme informed the commissioner that winding up the business entailed taking over several cases that had already been paid for. He had made an undertaking to the family that he would do so, without billing Lembede's estate.[21] It is clear from this correspondence and several other letters that Seme was of the firm view that the sale of his practice to Lembede had not been concluded – despite the fact that the sale agreement had been signed, as Nicholas correctly informed the commissioner.

Nicholas's letter reflects a deeper distrust that had developed between the Lembede family and Seme over the disposal of Lembede's estate. What seems to have complicated matters is the fact that the family had appointed Seme executor even though he was an interested party in a major aspect of the estate. It is clear from the correspondence that members of the Lembede family, especially Nicholas, became suspicious that Seme was short-changing them. This suspicion lingered for some time. In December 1948, for instance, a year after his brother's death, Nicholas again wrote to the commissioner seeking assistance for an outstanding amount of £150 that he claimed was owed from his brother's estate. He informed the commissioner that upon his brother's death the family had drawn £300 from the estate and a balance of £150 remained in the account. He claimed that Seme had not honoured his pledge to pay this amount at a later date, despite several entreaties from the family.[22] Nicholas was also interested in the fate of a 1941 Chevrolet that his brother had bought six months before his death and was still paying off at the time. Initially, Nicholas had wanted the car to be exchanged for a truck, but both Seme and the salesman had allegedly advised against this.[23] Seme's response to the family's suspicions that he was somehow hiding the money was to detail the account, thereby proving that not much money was left in the estate. Though several parties lodged claims against the estate, Lembede had not left any substantial assets. He had no immovable property and his only substantial movable assets were the car and three heads of cattle. The suspicions of the Lembede family that Anton had left substantial amounts of money or assets were baseless.

Apart from the £300 paid to Lembede's family soon after Anton's death, Seme does not appear to have handed any large sums of money to them.[24] It was not irrational to believe that a lawyer's estate was substantial; it should be recalled that there were few black people in the profession at the time, and there was a perception that lawyers were wealthy. However, the reality was – and indeed remains – far more disappointing.

* * *

After Lembede's death, Seme decided to change his plan to relocate to Natal, and continued his practice in Johannesburg. There is no indication that he handled any big or spectacular cases, as he had when he started out in 1910. Indeed, no case could be compared to the Swaziland one, which had consumed him and attracted much fame, though little fortune. Furthermore, Seme's political career effectively ended when Xuma failed to reappoint him to his executive. Looking at his life in the 1940s one cannot but conclude that its best days had already passed. The winds of change were gathering, and they would blow in a barely recognisable manner. The ANC was becoming more radical and more mass-based. Young arrivals such Anton Lembede had begun to lay claim to its leadership. Seme, in contrast, was increasingly yesterday's man shouting in the wilderness for an era that was long gone. What Seme made of Lembede's radicalism and his influence is one of the interesting mysteries of South Africa's political history. It is often assumed that Seme shaped his legal protégé's Africanism as he was himself an Africanist. But there is no evidence to support this view. Indeed, looking at Seme's political views and his overall record, it is doubtful that he shared Lembede's assertive Africanism. After all, as he once said to James Calata, he hated change and admired tradition whenever he found it. The 1940s and beyond were a period of radical change, and this would surely have sat uncomfortably with a professed traditionalist. It is perhaps as well that Seme did not live long. As his partner had in 1947, Seme also succumbed to a sudden death, passing away just four years later, in 1951.

11

'We are one people'

The death of Pixley Seme in June 1951 left his wife, Princess Phikisile, with many challenges, the most basic of which was supporting a family that had been entirely dependent on her husband's income. Compounding the problem was the fact that Seme had left little money and few assets. In fact, his estate was practically insolvent and the claims against it far exceeded the money that was left behind.

The problems that lay ahead became clear soon after her husband's funeral. Princess Phikisile had asked the Native Commissioner for Johannesburg, whose office was responsible by law for administering estates of Africans, to advance her some money from Seme's estate to cover her rail fare and living costs while she was in Johannesburg attending to her deceased husband's affairs. The commissioner gave authorisation for the sum of £5 to be withdrawn from Seme's Standard Bank account, and to be given to her. For some unknown reason Standard Bank advanced Princess Phikisile £51 instead of the approved £5 (the princess later claimed it was £50, not £51 as claimed by the bank). That figure alarmed the commissioner, who ordered Princess Phikisile to submit a sworn affidavit explaining why she had withdrawn £51 instead of the approved amount. In a handwritten statement she declared that she had also understood the Native Commissioner to have approved the withdrawal of £5 and 'was very much surprised at this big amount'. She added that Timothy Zulu, her late husband's friend who had gone into the bank to receive the money, simply informed her that £51 'was the amount handed over by the bank'.[1]

Although her affidavit did not shed light on who had altered the amount, Princess Phikisile must surely have realised from her late husband's bank statements that after withdrawing the £51 there was not much left. The manager of the Market Square branch of Standard Bank confirmed that, after the withdrawal of the £51, a balance of just over £388 remained in the account.[2] That amount was handed over to the Native Commissioner's office for distribution among those who had lodged legitimate claims against Seme's estate – claims that began to pour in after his death. Lawyers sent letters on behalf of claimants who ranged from employees who claimed for unpaid wages, to clients who had paid fees for cases that were not yet closed, and newspapers claiming for unpaid advertisements relating to Seme's various business dealings.

Other lawyers sent letters of inquiry regarding the identity of the person appointed as executor of Seme's estate. The family had chosen Oliver Reginald Tambo, a young lawyer practising in Johannesburg at the time and future president of the ANC. In a letter to the Native Commissioner, Tambo stated that he had 'been approached on behalf of the relatives of the late Dr Seme in connection with the appointment of Executors in [Seme's] Estate' and added that he was 'willing and prepared to act as co-executor in the Estate'.[3] However, the commissioner decided not to appoint Tambo, and instead appointed a white lawyer by the name of Solomon Goss. After a few months in his role as executor, Goss resigned. Although he did not explicitly state the reason for his resignation he recommended that Seme's estate be investigated by the Incorporated Law Society of the Transvaal as its liabilities far exceeded the assets.[4] The commissioner struggled to find a replacement because, as he explained it, no lawyer in Johannesburg was willing to act as executor of the estate owing to its 'parlous condition'.[5] It became a routine matter to inform claimants that the estate was insolvent and nothing could be done to assist them in their claims. In this, too, Seme was not alone. When he died on 6 December 1933, Richard Msimang, another pioneering black attorney, was for all intents and purposes poor. He had no movable or immovable assets and no money. Claimants on his estate were informed that the estate was insolvent and their claims could not be considered, as was the case with Seme.[6]

All the while, Seme's widow held on to the belief that her late husband had left money to see to the needs of the family. She also believed that certain people, colleagues and friends in particular, had taken advantage of the situation and stolen certain of her late husband's assets. She accused some of his staff of having stolen £50 from Seme's wallet. She also believed that Seme had subscribed to two insurance companies on behalf of two sons sired out of wedlock, Zwangendaba and Dumakude Seme, and that the subscription books had gone missing. Princess Phikisile pleaded with the Native Commissioner to investigate staff at Seme's office for 'the loss of the money'.[7] She also requested assistance in claiming property her late husband had bought in Clermont Township. It transpired that this had not been fully paid for: Seme had paid a £50 deposit for the stand in question, but a balance of £70 was still outstanding.[8] Regarding other assets, Seme had left two guns, a few law books, some office furniture, and just over £400 in his bank account – of which £51 had already been given to his widow.[9] Apart from this, Seme had left a mountain of liabilities. And yet, despite evidence to the contrary, the family continued to believe that Seme had died leaving a fortune. Suspecting that the Johannesburg Native Commissioner was somehow in possession of the wealth, Seme's widow made a desperate plea to the Nongoma Native Commissioner:

> I am writing to let you know of the starving I have in my home and the children, I can no longer bear it. Therefore I am asking you if you can forward this kind of request to the Native Commissioner of Johannesburg that I am asking if he can send me a cheque of twenty five pounds (25) if he please. I really can no longer bear the hunger I have.

But the commissioner was unable to give her any money because there really was nothing left in her late husband's estate. Yet still the perception persisted, and in January 1970, almost two decades after Seme's death, his two sons Zwangendaba and Dumakude got a lawyer to write to the Bantu Affairs Department inquiring about their late father's estate and staking a claim to it. They were informed that Seme's estate was indeed insolvent.

Seme's case was not unique, as Lembede's own makes clear. Although the lifestyles of educated black professionals were an improvement on those of working-class black people in urban areas or black peasants in rural hinterlands, the material foundations remained precarious. As lawyers, teachers or doctors they may have owned cars and some property, but they were not wealthy, and the vulnerability of their situation was often exposed after death. Seme's situation was undoubtedly exacerbated by the ten-year hiatus after being struck off the roll. This resulted in him being stripped of his assets, and eventually being forced to live with his wife's people at Mahhashini. Of course it did not help matters that he had extravagant habits and was inclined to spend rather than save his earnings, with the tragic consequence that his wife and children suffered destitution after his death.

However unfortunate, the numerous claims made against Seme's estate should not have been surprising. He had a long history of careless management of his own financial resources, and of managing the resources of others in a cavalier, if not unethical, manner. This became evident quite early in his career when he colluded with a white-owned company in a scheme that left a group of black people in the Wakkerstroom district landless after paying substantial sums of money to him. When people from Waverley Township faced eviction from land they had lived on for decades, and in desperation approached Seme for assistance, he left them in the lurch after taking significant sums of money from them – a transgression for which he would pay dearly. Bad as they were, these transgressions were exacerbated by the fact that they were committed by a respected black political leader, the founder of the ANC. Instead of assisting his fellow sufferers, Seme saw opportunities for enriching himself. All this suggests that, when Seme was faced with an opportunity for self-enrichment, no political principle or cause was sufficiently strong to act as a deterrent. This is the tragedy of his life. It is a major blot on his legacy.

But Seme's shortcomings, for which he and especially his family paid dearly, were not the sum total of the man. He was a man of extraordinary vision and intellect. His achievements cut across every aspect of South Africa's political and social life. He was also a man of unsurpassed ambition, with the energy to match. Friend and foe alike, both at home and abroad, marvelled at his intellectual acumen. Leaving for America as a youth, he not only gained the education he had crossed the seas to seek, but by the end of his studies he had won Columbia University's coveted debating prize, and at just twenty-four years old he had outlined a vision for the regeneration of a continent and the redemption of a race. It is easy – too easy, sometimes, given the passage of time – to fail to appreciate the full significance of Seme's intellectual and political achievements, let alone his bravery and determination. Few in their lifetime could credibly count Booker T. Washington, W.E.B. Du Bois, Henry Sylvester Williams, Theophilus Scholes and Alain Locke, renowned figures in the African diaspora, as friends, associates or acquaintances. This is not to mention political giants in South Africa such as Rubusana, Dube, Jabavu, Plaatje, Makgatho, Xuma and many others. Even when these historical figures vehemently disagreed with Seme, they conceded that he was a man of extraordinary vision and intellect.

Seme is renowned for his seminal contribution to black politics especially in South Africa. And although his failure as president almost destroyed the ANC as an organisation, the unity of black people that he brought into being was his signal achievement. Let it not be forgotten that many previous attempts had been made to bring together the various black organisations that existed at the time – attempts that mostly failed because of the inability of leaders to overcome regional and tribal identities. Seme, partly inspired by the notion that underpinned the formation of the Union of South Africa in 1910,[10] as well as the centripetal forces that capitalist development in South Africa had unleashed, was able to succeed where most had failed through his galvanising inclusive message of black unity. In an editorial after Seme's death, *The Bantu World* reminded its readers of the mammoth contribution Seme had made in bringing together different black groups, which, in the words of Thema, had often only met on the battlefield: '[I]f today, Basutos, Zulus, Xhosas, Shangaans, Bechuanas and Vendas know themselves as Africans, and that Africa is the land of their fathers, they owe this to the inspiring foundation of African nationalism laid by Pixley ka Izaka Seme.'[11] This black unity, and the organisation that has embodied it for over a century, is without a doubt Seme's greatest legacy.

To restrict Seme's contribution purely to the political realm would be to ignore the breadth of his achievements. His pioneering work in the legal field is also extraordinary. He, together with Mangena, Msimang and Montsioa are founding fathers of black formal legal practice in South Africa. Perhaps because of his colourful personality and his astute choice of cases to defend, Seme received far greater recognition than his peers, with Alfred Mangena running a close second. Seme's most famous case was of course his representation of the Swazi nation in a British High Court. Without Seme's involvement in this as well as several related matters, an independent Swazi kingdom would arguably have been inconceivable. Although to a lesser extent, Seme also exerted an influence on the affairs of the Zulu royal house.

Pixley Seme was a political visionary, a pioneer in his profession, and he was also an entrepreneur. He established several companies, with a number being involved in the buying and selling of land. As he wrote in a newspaper article in 1929, he firmly believed that the road to salvation for black people was through economic empowerment. In a sense, Seme advocated black economic empowerment a century before it became a policy of the post-apartheid democratic government. And even though his conduct may suggest the opposite, Seme's economic vision did not relate to the individual alone. In the 1930s he presented an elaborate programme outlining how black people might build their own enterprises. Essentially, black people would generate wealth through buying goods and services produced by other black people.

This broad vision of empowerment had a fatal flaw, however: it ignored the relationship between poverty and a racialised economic model that was founded on the subjugation of the very people he hoped to empower. Seme believed it possible to engineer black prosperity without radically transforming an economic and political system that was the fundamental cause of black exclusion from the country's wealth. As the political and economic status of black people sank even lower, Seme sought accommodation with the white government of the day. He often lauded the authorities in the hope, perhaps, that they would acknowledge and reward the reasonableness of an educated black elite of which he himself was a torch bearer. But Seme's accommodationist politics failed spectacularly, and he was eventually removed from office in disgrace.

In surveying Seme's life, there is an inescapable sense of wasted talent: a man of his exceptional intelligence and vision could have – indeed should have – achieved so much more. What stood between Seme and the fulfilment of his potential may partially be ascribed to a predilection for opulence. But to leave it at that would do an injustice to the man. His talent and vision withered before the blast of a social and political system that made no concessions and refused to accommodate the needs of black people, however desperate they might be. Seme lived in the hope that a class of educated black men and women could at the very least thrive at the margins of such a system or at best be incorporated into its inner sanctum. This was, however, an illusion.

A new generation of black nationalists quickly realised that the only way white domination could be defeated was to confront it head-on. At the forefront of that cohort of nationalists was Seme's protégé, Anton Muziwakhe Lembede. Though it sounded the call Seme had made in 1912, 'We are one people', this new generation spurned his accommodationism. Instead, it spearheaded a mass-based movement that roused the ANC from its stupor. Mass mobilisation and confrontation would ultimately win the fight that Seme's brand of politics had so dismally lost. Significantly, the new generation of activists planned the first mass-based anti-apartheid campaign during Seme's funeral. The mourners were not only burying the man, they were also burying his politics – and the silence of history about the many achievements of Pixley ka Isaka Seme suggests that they may indeed have succeeded. Nevertheless, from Seme's ashes rose broad-based resistance, which would become a victorious force in the battles he had begun.

Acknowledgements

Letsema is an old African practice in which villagers help one another to perform a task that none of them alone can do. This spirit of collaboration and neighbourliness is common during the ploughing and harvesting of fields, hence the name *letsema* in seSotho or *ilimo* in Nguni languages.

I am the beneficiary of *letsema* of a different kind. The writing of this book would not have been possible without the encouragement, support and assistance of many people and institutions. I am particularly grateful to the descendants of Pixley ka Isaka Seme, the subject of this biography, for their unstinting support. Maxwell Vezindaba Seme, his grandson, joined me on several trips to his grandfather's ancestral home at Inanda and also introduced me to other members of the Seme family, including his aunt and Seme's only remaining child, Princess Helen Mamama Seme. Seme's granddaughters who live in Swaziland welcomed me into their homes and answered many questions about their grandfather. I am grateful to Zodwa Seme in particular for her keen interest in the story of her grandfather and for her unfailing support during my research trips to Swaziland. Joy Ndwandwe, another Swazi national, was also helpful in many ways, including introducing me to members of the Swazi royal house who know about Seme's role in the making of the modern Kingdom of Swaziland. I am indebted to Prince Mangosuthu Buthelezi for sharing memories of the time he spent with Seme, who was his maternal uncle.

Many friends and colleagues at the Presidency of the Republic of South Africa have supported me in various ways. Mac Maharaj linked me with my publisher and read the full manuscript. Cassius Lubisi, Vuso Shabalala and Ashraf Kariem read and commented on each chapter, as well as the completed manuscript. Other colleagues who provided support are Lakela Kaunda, Busani Ngcaweni, Joy Rathebe, Bongani Majola, Zandile Mavundla, Dudu Fakudze, Khanyisa George, Hlengiwe Nkonyeni, Fezile Mamfengwana and Kgomotso Maake.

My gratitude also to Sixtus Sibeta, Nkosinathi Mzelemu and Mcebisi Ndletyana who also read and commented on each chapter and on the whole manuscript. I wish also to thank Tembeka Ngcukaitobi, who provided me with some material on legal cases on which Seme and Lembede worked in the 1940s and brought to my attention the link between Seme and Booker T. Washington. Phumelele Maome provided excellent research support in Pietermaritzburg, especially by making several trips to the Pietermaritzburg Archives Repository to look for information on Seme.

When I informed Peter Limb that I intended to write a biography of Seme, he was very encouraging but cautioned me against writing a hagiography. I hope I have heeded his caution. Moreover, he pointed me to various sources of information on Seme. Robert Edgar has also been a constant source of support. I thank him for bringing along a treasure trove of information on the relationship between Seme and his African American friend, Alain Locke, all the way from the United States to South Africa.

I am deeply saddened by the death of Tim Couzens before the publication of the book. On occasions when I faced some obstacles, Tim encouraged me to push on. Brian Willan, who reviewed the manuscript, gave insightful comments and suggestions on how it could be improved. I have tried as much as possible to incorporate his suggestions. I also thank Christopher Saunders for his helpful comments.

I have also been a beneficiary of *letsema* from dedicated archivists and librarians from various institutions in South Africa, Swaziland, England and the United States, countries with which Seme is associated. I am especially grateful to a group of young members of staff at the National Archives of South Africa in Pretoria, who went beyond the call of duty assisting me to search for obscure information on Seme. The same dedication and support were demonstrated by archivists at the Pietermaritzburg Archives Repository, the Swaziland National Archives, Inanda Seminary, Wits University Historical Papers, the TEBA Collection at the University of Johannesburg, the Archival and Special Collections at the University of South Africa, and the Alan Paton Centre and Struggle Archives at the University of KwaZulu-Natal. I also benefited from the generosity of dedicated archivists at Columbia and Howard universities in the United States, especially Jocelyn K. Wilk at Columbia, and Tewodros (Teddy) Abebe and Joellen ElBashir at Howard. At Oxford University, I thank Chris Jeens, Simon Bailey and Renee Prud'Homme for the support. The dedicated staff at the National Library of South Africa in Pretoria, as well as the staff at the library in the Presidency proved reliable sources of ready support.

A major contribution to the *letsema* came from Marlene Fryer and her colleagues at Penguin Random House South Africa, my publisher. I thank them first and foremost for taking a chance on me by publishing the book. Robert Plummer has patiently and expertly managed the process of its publication from the beginning to the end. Lynda Gilfillan brought to bear her exceptional editing skills, while other staff members pitched in to make its publication the success that it is today.

Finally, my wife, Nondumiso, has been part of the writing of this book from the very beginning. She has read every word and joined me on many research trips. She has also borne the burden of looking after our two young children while I have been absent working on the book. I thank her for all the support. Like everybody who has made this book possible, she should not be held responsible for any errors of omission or commission that may be contained in it, which are all mine.

BONGANI NGQULUNGA
TSHWANE, MAY 2017

Abbreviations

AAC: All-African Convention
ABM: American Board of Missions
ACC: African Congress Club
ANC: African National Congress
BA: Bachelor of Arts
BCL: Bachelor of Civil Law
CNC: Chief Native Commissioner
CPSA: Communist Party of South Africa
CS: Colonial Secretary, Transvaal
GG: Governor General
GNLB: Government Native Labour Bureau
ICU: Industrial and Commercial Workers Union
IFP: Inkatha Freedom Party
KJB: Native Commissioner, Johannesburg
NEA: Native Educational Association
NEC: National Executive Committee
NRC: Natives Representative Council
NTS: Secretary for Native Affairs Correspondence Series
PM: Prime Minister
RCS: Resident Commissioner Secretariat (Swaziland)
SABC: South African Broadcasting Corporation
SANC: South African Native Convention
SANNC: South African Native National Congress
SNA: Secretary for Native Affairs
TIC: Transvaal Indian Congress
TNC: Transvaal Native Congress
TPD: Transvaal Provincial Division (of the Supreme Court)
WLD: Witwatersrand Local Division (of the Supreme Court)

Notes

INTRODUCTION

1. 'Passing of a great pioneer', *The Bantu World*, 23 June 1951.
2. *Ilanga lase Natal*, 16 June 1951.
3. *Inkundla Ya Bantu*, 30 June 1951.
4. The information about Pixley Seme's death and his funeral is drawn from several newspaper reports of the time, especially in *Ilanga lase Natal, Inkundla Ya Bantu, The Bantu World* and *Umteteleli wa Bantu*.
5. Chris Saunders, for instance, repeats these incorrect claims about Seme's law degree and his mother in 'Pixley Seme: Towards a Biography', *South African Historical Journal* 25(1), 1991, pp. 196–217. Heather Hughes also makes a similar incorrect claim about Seme having completed a law degree at Oxford University; see p. 158 of *First President: A Life of John L. Dube, Founding President of the ANC* (Johannesburg: Jacana Media, 2011).
6. Norman Etherington incorrectly identified Pixley Seme's brother, Mbekwana Seme, as his father; see Arianna Lassoni et al (eds), *One Hundred Years of the ANC: Debating Liberation Histories Today* (Johannesburg: Wits University Press, 2012), p. 58. Similarly, Heather Hughes, on p. 15 of *First President: A Life of John L. Dube, Founding President of the ANC* (Johannesburg: Jacana Media, 2011), describes Marsh Isaac as Pixley Seme's father (he was in fact his eldest brother).
7. H. Kuper, *Sobhuza II, Ngwenyama and King of Swaziland: The Story of an Hereditary Ruler and His Country* (London: Gerald Duckworth, 1978).
8. R.V. Selope Thema, 'How Congress Began', *Drum*, August 1953.
9. Moss Mashamaite, *The Second Coming: The Life and Times of Pixley kaIsaka Seme, the Founder of the ANC* (Pretoria: Chatworld, 2011).
10. Richard Rive and Tim Couzens, *Seme: The Founder of the ANC* (Trenton, NJ: Africa World Press, 1993).
11. Peter Limb (ed.), *The People's Paper: A Centenary History and Anthology of Abantu-Batho* (Johannesburg: Wits University Press, 2012). See also Alan Cobley, *The Rules of the Game: Struggles in Black Recreation and Social Welfare in South Africa* (Westport, Conn.: Praeger, 1997).
12. Thema, 'How Congress Began'.
13. Nicholas Cope, *To Bind the Nation: Solomon kaDinuzulu and Zulu Nationalism, 1913–1933* (Scottsville: University of Natal Press, 1993).
14. See www.thepresidency.gov.za.
15. See AD 843, S38.1 in A.B. Xuma Papers, University of Witwatersrand (Wits) Historical Papers.

CHAPTER 1: THE BUSTARD HUNTERS

1. The history of the Seme family as recorded by Masinga consists of twelve handwritten pages. I am grateful to Maxwell Vezindaba Seme, Masinga's nephew,

who generously made a copy available to me. Any reference to the Seme family history in this book, as recorded by Masinga, is drawn from this material.

2. A. Bryant, *Olden Times in Zululand and Natal: Containing Earlier Political History of the Eastern Nguni Clans* (London: Longmans, Green, 1929).

3. NTS 7601, 6/328, National Archives of South Africa, Pretoria.

4. SNA I/1/282, 1987/1898 and SNA I/1/43, 1909/1538, National Archives of South Africa.

5. SNA I/1/476, 3485/1910, National Archives of South Africa.

6. Ibid.

7. See letter dated 7 June 1911, SNA I/1/476, 3485/1910, National Archives of South Africa.

8. I am grateful to Simon Bailey, Keeper of the Archives at Oxford University, for making Seme's matriculation form available to me.

CHAPTER 2: THE EDUCATION OF AN AFRICAN PATRIOT

1. This section is largely drawn from Rive and Couzens's study of Seme's early years, *Seme: Founder of the ANC*, which focuses on his years at Mount Hermon school in Massachusetts.

2. Ibid., p. 14.

3. See Reverend Stephen Pixley to Professor H.F. Cutler, 13 August 1898, Mount Hermon School File, Appendix, in Rive and Couzens, *Seme: The Founder of the ANC*.

4. Ibid. Letter to Professor H.F. Cutler, 28 August 1898.

5. Ibid. Letter to Professor C.E. Dickerson, 22 August 1901.

6. Ibid. Alfred K. Merritt to Professor Henry F. Cutler, 31 May 1902 and 12 June 1902.

7. Female students had to enrol at Barnard College, a sister college to Columbia College.

8. I am grateful to Jocelyn K. Wilk, University Archivist at Columbia Rare Books and Manuscript Library, for invaluable assistance with Seme's academic record. The information in this section is drawn from Seme's academic record, as well as digitised copies of catalogues. See www.wikicu.com/Annual_Catalogue_of_the_Officers_and _Students_of_Columbia_College.

9. *Columbia Daily Spectator*, 12 December 1902.

10. 'Sophomore-Freshman Debate', *Columbia Daily Spectator*, 30 January 1903.

11. *Columbia Daily Spectator*, 23 January 1903.

12. 'Freshman Debating Team Chosen', *Columbia Daily Spectator*, 12 March 1903.

13. *Columbia Daily Spectator*, 29 October 1903.

14. *Columbia Daily Spectator*, 12 October 1904 and 2 November 1904 respectively.

15. For reports of Seme's participation in the activities of the Barnard Literary Association see archives of the *Columbia Daily Spectator* at www.spectatorarchive .library.columbia.edu.

16. See Craig Charney, 'Pixley Seme '06: Father of the African National Congress', *Columbia College Today*. I am grateful to Jocelyn Wilk for bringing this article to my attention.

17. Letter to Professor Cutler, 17 June 1903, in Rive and Couzens, *Seme: The Founder of the ANC*.

18. See Rive and Couzens, *Seme: The Founder of the ANC*.

19. See 'Royal Zulu Willing to Become Valet', www.sahistory.org.za.

20. Letter to Professor Cutler, 26 September 1903, in Rive and Couzens, *Seme: The Founder of the ANC*.

21. See unpublished autobiography of H. Selby Msimang, transcript of tape recordings made in Pietermaritzburg, 1976–1977, in Msimang Papers, John Aitchison Collection, Alan Paton Centre and Struggle Archives, University of KwaZulu-Natal.

22. *The Columbian*, 1906, p. 385.
23. I am grateful to Jocelyn Wilk for bringing the yearbook to my attention.
24. 'Every Continent Contributes to the Student Roll of Columbia University', *New York Times*, 15 April 1906.
25. *Columbia Daily Spectator*, 12 December 1905.
26. *Columbia Daily Spectator*, 20 March 1906.
27. Quotes here and below from 'The Regeneration of Africa', *The Columbia Monthly*, III(6), April 1906.
28. See 'IZulu Elidumileyo', *Ilanga lase Natal*, 13 April 1906. See also 'A Zulu Wins A Prize', in the same edition.
29. Marika Sherwood, *Origins of Pan-Africanism: Henry Sylvester Williams, Africa and the African Diaspora* (London: Routledge, 2011), p. 72.
30. Though delivered by Du Bois, the address was the collective effort of Bishop Alexander Walters, president of the Pan-African Association, as well as Henry H. Brown (vice president), H. Sylvester Williams (general secretary) and W.E.B. Du Bois, who was chairman of the Committee on Address. See www.credo.library.umass.edu/view/pageturn/mums312-b004-i321 for a copy of the address.
31. In A. Crummell, *The Future of Africa: Being Addresses, Sermons, etc Delivered in the Republic of Liberia* (New York: Negro Universities Press, 1862).
32. Wilson Jeremiah Moses (ed.), *Classical Black Nationalism: From the American Revolution to Marcus Garvey* (New York: New York University Press, 1996), p. 171.
33. Ibid., p. 172.
34. Ibid., p. 292.
35. Ibid., p. 293.
36. Ibid., p. 173.
37. Ibid., p. 174.
38. 'The Regeneration of Africa'.
39. L. Harris and C. Moleswort, *Alain L. Locke: The Biography of a Philosopher* (Chicago: University of Chicago Press, 2008), p. 67.
40. David Killingray, 'Significant Black South Africans in Britain before 1912: Pan-African Organisations and the Emergence of South Africa's First Black Lawyers', *South African Historical Journal*, 64(3), 2012, p. 407.
41. It is likely that his passage was funded by his benefactors at Columbia.
42. I am grateful to Renee Prud'Homme, Assistant Librarian at St Catherine College at Oxford University, for information on the history of the Delegacy for Non-Collegiate Students and related matters. Email correspondence, 29 June 2015.
43. I am grateful to Simon Bailey, Keeper of the Archives at Oxford University, for his assistance in obtaining information on Seme as a student at Oxford. Email correspondence, 21 August 2014.
44. Information provided by Renee Prud'Homme. Email correspondence, 29 June 2015. It was possible to take a non-degree course before being admitted to a degree-awarding course; some students took non-degree courses without aiming at a degree.
45. Information provided by Christopher Jeens, Archivist at Jesus College. Email correspondence, 25 June 2015.
46. Ibid.
47. Ibid.
48. Information provided by Simon Bailey. Email correspondence, 21 August 2014.
49. Seme to Locke, 14 March 1907, in Alain L. Locke Papers, Moorland-Springarn

Research Center, Howard University, United States of America. I am indebted to Robert R. Edgar for bringing to South Africa the Seme-Locke collection of letters.

50. Seme to Locke, 21 June 1907, Alain L. Locke Papers, in which he again recommended colleges, and also revealed that the rumours of opposition to Locke's presence at Oxford were false.

51. See Scholes's letter to Locke in Jeffrey Green, *Black Edwardians: Black People in Britain, 1901–1914* (London: Routledge, 1998), p. 150.

52. Ibid., p. 152.

53. Ibid., p. 153.

54. Sherwood, *Origins of Pan-Africanism*, p. 192.

55. Alain L. Locke Papers, undated letter.

56. Ibid. The collection includes several undated letters from Seme to Locke.

57. Green, *Black Edwardians*, p. 151.

58. Alain L. Locke Papers, undated letter.

59. Ibid.

60. Ibid.

61. Ibid.

62. Ibid.

63. Ibid., 27 January 1909.

64. Ibid., undated letter.

65. Ibid., 11 February 1910.

66. *Oxford University Gazette*, 8 June 1909, p. 769.

67. Ibid., 3 August 1909, p. 891.

68. Information provided by Simon Bailey.

69. Alain L. Locke Papers, undated letter, probably written in 1909 while Seme was studying at Middle Temple.

70. Ibid.

71. Ibid., Seme to Locke, 6 February 1910.

CHAPTER 3: THE MOVING SPIRIT

1. 'UPixley Seme', *Ilanga lase Natal*, 7 October 1910. See also the English edition, 'Arrival of Mr Pixley Seme', 7 October 1910.

2. 'Zulus welcome Rev. Rubusana M.P.C.', *Ilanga lase Natal*, 28 October 1910.

3. *Ilanga lase Natal*, 20 October 1911.

4. Ibid.

5. Ibid.

6. *Ilanga lase Natal*, 2 June 1911.

7. Ibid.

8. *Cape Mercury*, 3 August 1911. I thank Brian Willan for drawing my attention to this news report.

9. See *Ilanga lase Natal*, 1 September 1911, and *Imvo*, 5 September 1911. See also André Odendaal, *Vukani Bantu!: The Beginnings of Black Protest Politics in South Africa to 1912* (Cape Town: David Philip, 1984), p. 259, where Odendaal incorrectly claims that Seme and Cleopas Kunene represented Natal at the August meeting. Though born in Natal, Seme attended as a Transvaal representative (see *Imvo*, 5 September 1911). Kunene was present in his capacity as secretary of the SANC. Moreover, he was not a Zulu as Odendaal claims; Kunene was of Swazi origin with Natal connections, as were many prominent Natal leaders at the time. Another incorrect claim is that of Brian Willan who states that Sol Plaatje was present at the August meeting (see *Sol*

Plaatje: A Biography, Johannesburg: Ravan, 2001, p. 151). Plaatje was not present, and instead sent a letter of support (see *Imvo*, 5 September 1911).

10. *Ilanga lase Natal*, 1 September 1911, and *Imvo*, 5 September 1911.

11. Ibid.

12. *Imvo*, 12 December 1911. It is unclear whether a person or a committee was appointed to mediate between the rival groups in the Transvaal. Odendaal suggests that an 'unnamed arbitrator' was appointed at the August meeting to mediate, though he fails to provide evidence for this assertion (see *Vukani Bantu!*, p. 260). A decision was taken to appoint a person or group of persons to mediate, but it is not clear whether that decision was implemented.

13. See Seme's letter to Chief Silas Molema of Mafikeng, Silas T. Molema and Solomon T. Plaatje Papers, Collection A979, Cc9, Wits Historical Papers. Citing the draft constitution in the Molema and Plaatje Papers as his source, André Odendaal claims that the draft constitution for the proposed Congress was presented by Seme to the August 1911 meeting (see *Vukani Bantu!*, p. 259). However, the draft constitution was only presented at the November meeting. The letter Seme sent to Silas Molema and other leaders to which he attached the draft constitution is dated 3 November 1911, so it is not possible that it was presented at the August meeting as Odendaal claims.

14. *Ilanga lase Natal*, 1 December 1911.

15. 'Native Union', *Ilanga lase Natal*, 1 December 1911.

16. *Imvo*, 5 December 1911.

17. Ibid.

18. Ibid.

19. *Ilanga lase Natal*, 20 October 1911.

20. *Imvo*, 5 December 1911.

21. See Silas T. Molema and Solomon T. Plaatje Papers, Collection A979, Cc9, Wits Historical Papers.

22. *Imvo*, 5 December 1911.

23. André Odendaal, *Vukani Bantu!*, p. 235.

24. Ibid., p. 168.

25. Ibid., p. 262.

26. Ibid.

27. Ibid., pp. 151–196.

28. *Ilanga lase Natal*, 12 January 1912.

29. Rive and Couzens, *Seme: The Founder of the ANC*, p. 1.

30. There are discrepancies in the way delegates are identified. In its edition of 26 January 1912, *Ilanga lase Natal* mentions Charles Dube, Seme and Mvabaza as having represented Natal. The *Pretoria News* of 8 January 1912 identifies Seme as a Johannesburg representative, while Odendaal states that only Charles Dube and Chief Majozi represented Natal (see *Vukani Bantu!*, p. 271).

31. For the list of delegates who attended the conference, see *Ilanga lase Natal*, 26 January 1912. See also *Pretoria News*, 8 January 1912, and Odendaal, *Vukani Bantu!*, pp. 270–272. In addition to Rubusana, the Cape was represented by Messrs Zini, Ncezula and Motshumi (see *Ilanga lase Natal*, 26 January 1912).

32. Thema, 'How Congress Began'.

33. Odendaal, *Vukani Bantu!*, p. 274.

34. *Ilanga lase Natal*, 26 January 1912.

35. Odendaal, *Vukani Bantu!*, p. 274.

36. *Pretoria News*, 11 January 1912.
37. See Thema, 'How Congress Began'.
38. *Pretoria News*, 13 January 1912.
39. Ibid.
40. Odendaal, *Vukani Bantu!*, p. 272.
41. See Peter Walshe, *The Rise of African Nationalism in South Africa: The African National Congress, 1912–1952* (Berkeley: University of California Press, 1970), p. 35.
42. *Ilanga lase Natal*, 26 January 1912.
43. Willan, *Sol Plaatje: A Biography*, p. 153.
44. Willan explains Dube's absence as the consequence of an injury sustained after 'a bad fall from a horse', ibid. However, Dube himself claimed he could not attend because of 'educational and editorial calls at home', *Ilanga lase Natal*, 2 February 1912. Dube's explanation seems credible as he had recently been in Johannesburg raising funds for his Ohlange school. It was at one such fundraising event that £4 was raised to cover his brother Charles Dube's costs as a conference representative for Natal and Zululand, *Ilanga lase Natal*, 12 January 1912.
45. *Ilanga lase Natal*, 26 January 1912.
46. Ibid.
47. Odendaal, *Vukani Bantu!*, p. 275.
48. Walshe, *The Rise of African Nationalism in South Africa*, p. 35.
49. Willan, *Sol Plaatje: A Biography*, p. 153.
50. *Pretoria News*, 5 January 1912.
51. *Ilanga lase Natal*, 10 January 1912.
52. Ibid., 9 January 1912.
53. Ibid., 26 January 1912.
54. See Walshe, *The Rise of African Nationalism in South Africa*, p. 37.
55. Ibid., 2 February 1912.
56. In Rive and Couzens, *Seme: The Founder of the ANC*, p. 90.
57. Willan, *Sol Plaatje: A Biography*, p. 151.
58. Ibid., p. 150.
59. *Ilanga lase Natal*, 20 October 1911.
60. Odendaal states that the NEA was formed in 1879 (*Vukani Bantu!*, p. 6). Peter Limb concurs, see *The ANC's Early Years: Nation, Class and Place in South Africa before 1940* (Pretoria: Unisa Press, 2010), p. 76. However, Walshe claims it was formed in 1882 (*The Rise of African Nationalism*, p. 3).
61. Odendaal, *Vukani Bantu!*, p. 7.
62. Willan, *Sol Plaatje: A Biography*, p. 151.
63. Odendaal, *Vukani Bantu!*, p. 10.
64. Odendaal states that *Isigidimi* was established in 1870 (*Vukani Bantu!*, p. 6), while Walshe puts the date at 1876 (*The Rise of African Nationalism*, p. 3).
65. Odendaal, *Vukani Bantu!*, p. 15. Rubusana and these associates would go on to establish the South African Native Congress in 1898.
66. See opening chapters of Odendaal's *Vukani Bantu!* and Walshe's *The Rise of African Nationalism*.
67. See Limb (ed.), *The People's Paper*, where the founding of *Funamalungelo* is recorded as 1888 and also as 1887, see pp. 76 and 93 respectively.
68. Limb (ed.), *The People's Paper*, p. 94.
69. Willan, *Sol Plaatje: A Biography*, p. 151.
70. See undated letter to Locke, probably written in late 1911 or early 1912, Locke Papers.

71. See Limb (ed.), *The People's Paper*.
72. See Chris Lowe, 'Swazi Royalty, the Founding of *Abantu-Batho*, and Pan-Ethnic Nationalism in the Early South African Native National Congress' in Limb (ed.), *The People's Paper*.
73. Thema quoting Lord Rosebery in 'How Congress Began'.
74. The executive at the time included Seme himself, even though he was not active. Other members were: Dube (president); Rubusana, Mini, Makgatho, Mapikela, Letanka and Mvabaza (vice presidents); Twayi (treasurer); Thema (secretary general); and H. Selby Msimang (corresponding secretary). *Ilanga lase Natal*, 13 July 1917.
75. Alice Werner to Harriette Colenso, 12 June 1914, file A204 in Pietermaritzburg Archives Repository.
76. Alice Werner to Harriette Colenso, 21 January 1916, file A204 in Pietermaritzburg Archives Repository.
77. Dube to Colenso, 3 October 1917, file A204 in Pietermaritzburg Archives Repository.
78. For a report on proceedings of the Newcastle meeting see *Ilanga lase Natal*, 26 June 1917.
79. Thema, 'How Congress Began'.

CHAPTER 4: THE SWAZI NATION'S ATTORNEY

1. 'A Native Attorney', *Imvo Zabantsundu*, 17 January 1911.
2. Ibid.
3. '*Pambili Bafana!*', *Ilanga lase Natal*, 20 January 1911.
4. See Msimang Papers in the John Aitchison Collection, Alan Paton Centre and Struggle Archives, University of KwaZulu-Natal.
5. For the report on the court proceedings, see *Imvo Zabantsundu*, 17 January 1911.
6. 'Opposed application: *Alfred Mangena* v. *The Incorporated Law Society of the Transvaal*', TPD 8/4, 123/1910, in National Archives of South Africa.
7. See *Mangena* v. *Law Society*, South African Law Reports, TPD-TPA-WLD-WPA, 1910 (649-650).
8. Seme, 'Alfred Mangena of Lincoln's Inn Esquire and barrister-at-law', *Ilanga lase Natal*, 14 August 1908.
9. *Ilanga lase Natal*, 24 November 1911.
10. 'A Native Lawyer: Sensation in B Court', which also appeared in *Ilanga lase Natal*, 3 February 1911.
11. '*Icala Eliyinkinga*', *Ilanga lase Natal* , 9 February 1912.
12. See Seme's account of the incident in *Ilanga lase Natal*, 15 December 1911. It was written in the form of a letter addressed to his erstwhile benefactor Reverend Pixley in response to the latter's own letter to the newspaper decrying Seme's conduct in the incident.
13. This story first appeared in the *Transvaal Leader*. On 9 April 1915 it was reprinted in *Ilanga lase Natal*. In the English section it appeared under the headline 'I Refuse to Answer'. The isiZulu version, '*Ummeli uMangena no Mlungukazi eGoli*', was more colourful. For instance, the English version states that a black man was charged for making an indecent overture to a white woman, while the isiZulu version reports that he was charged for *ukushela umlungukazi*. Rather than an indecent overture, *ukushela* is the profession of love for a woman. Also, Mangena's cross-examination is reported with clear approval: '*Pho, into ka Mangena, yambuza imibuzo waze wapenduka inkuku.*' ('Oh, the son of Mangena, he peppered her with questions until she turned into a chicken.')
14. J.S.M. Matsebula, *A History of Swaziland* (Cape Town: Longman Penguin, 1988), p. 205. See also Kuper, *Sobhuza II, Ngwenyama and King of Swaziland*, p. 205.

15. See Matsebula, *A History of Swaziland*, p. 205. See also Kuper's official biography, *Sobhuza II, Ngwenyama and King of Swaziland*, p. 47.
16. See Seme's introduction to the 'Petition of the Swazi Tribes of the Eastern Transvaal to the Union Parliament', GG 1569, 50/1443, in National Archives of South Africa.
17. A.N. Boyce, *Swaziland Concessions and their Political Consequences (1876–1908)*, MA dissertation, University of South Africa, p. 3.
18. See R. Davies, D. O'Meara and S. Dlamini, *The Kingdom of Swaziland: A Profile* (London: Zed, 1985), Ch. 5.
19. D. Hugh Gills, *The Kingdom of Swaziland: Studies in Political History* (Westport, CT: Greenwood Press, 1999), p. 48.
20. See Boyce, *Swaziland Concessions*, p. 3.
21. Ibid., p. 8.
22. See Swaziland Concessions Commission Report, PM 1/2/170, PM 48/3C in National Archives of South Africa, pp. 188–190.
23. Ibid., p. 21.
24. Ibid.
25. See notice signed by W.G. Bentinck, PM 43, 104/4/1907 in National Archives of South Africa.
26. See copy of Deputy Resident Commissioner's statement, PM 43, 104/4/1907 in National Archives of South Africa.
27. See copy of Selborne's speech sent to General Louis Botha together with a letter dated 4 June 1909, CS 718, 11245/104/1/1909 in National Archives of South Africa.
28. See Hugh Macmillan, 'A Nation Divided? The Swazi in Swaziland and the Transvaal, 1865–1986', in Leroy Vail (ed.), *The Creation of Tribalism in Southern Africa* (Berkeley: University of California Press, 1991), p. 295.
29. For the August 1921 Swazi petition, see RCS 332/22 in Swaziland National Archives.
30. Initially granted to John Harrington by Mbandzeni, the concession had been taken over by the South African Republic after the 1894 Convention with Britain, and, following the Anglo-Boer War, it was taken over by the British administration in South Africa under Lord Milner.
31. Originally established by Queen Labotsibeni, the fund's purpose was the development of Swaziland, particularly with regard to education and livestock farming. A tax of £2 per annum was imposed on Swazis, and when the British-controlled Swazi Administration took over it became involved in the collection of those taxes, taking control of the administration of the fund and using the money as it saw fit. The Swazis hotly contested this, arguing in the petition that it should be administered by their king.
32. The point about Swazis who lived outside the borders of Swaziland was a sore one for the royal family as the partition of Swaziland and the subsequent redrawing of borders resulted in some areas becoming part of the eastern Transvaal.
33. See Kuper, *Sobhuza II, Ngwenyama and King of Swaziland*, p. 77.
34. See RCS 332/22 in Swaziland National Archives.
35. Other signatories were Ndabezimbi, Ntamo, Mavelativeni, Jabhane and Masumpe. Seme and Benjamin Nxumalo signed as witnesses.
36. See RCS 332/22 in Swaziland National Archives.
37. Ibid.
38. Ibid.
39. See letter dated 15 September 1922, RCS 332/22 in Swaziland National Archives.

40. See Sobhuza II's letter dated 23 September 1922, RCS 332/22 in Swaziland National Archives.
41. Ibid.
42. See Kuper, *Sobhuza II, Ngwenyama and King of Swaziland*, p. 80.
43. See 'Deputation of Swazi Chiefs to the Secretary of State for the Colonies at the Colonial Office on Wednesday, the 10th January 1923', RCS 177/23 in Swaziland National Archives.
44. This may possibly be an erroneous reference to Ben Boshoff.
45. See transcript of the shorthand notes, 'Treasury Reporter, Conference with the Swazi Chiefs and their legal advisors at the Colonial Office on Monday, the 22nd January 1923', RCS 177/23 in Swaziland National Archives.
46. See letter from High Commissioner to Resident Commissioner, 7 May 1923, RCS 332/22 and letter from Secretary of State for the Colonies to High Commissioner, 9 April 1923, RCS 332/22, both in Swaziland National Archives.
47. Sobhuza II to Financial Secretary in Mbabane, 4 August 1923, RCS 332/22 in Swaziland National Archives. There were other expenses the Financial Secretary had inquired about in a letter to Sobhuza II dated 29 May 1923. Sobhuza accounted for each of those expenses, and raised questions about others.
48. See letter from Dr Nathan, 21 May 1924, RCS 333/24 in Swaziland National Archives.
49. Ibid.
50. Resident Commissioner to Dr Nathan, 27 May 1924, RCS 333/24 in Swaziland National Archives.
51. See letter dated 15 April 1925, RCS 333/24 in Swaziland National Archives.
52. This paragraph is drawn largely from Kuper, *Sobhuza II, Ngwenyama and King of Swaziland*, p. 85.
53. Ibid., p. 86.
54. Ibid., p. 87.
55. See letter from Wakkerstroom Magistrate, 1 July 1924, NTS 2716/304/301 in National Archives of South Africa.
56. See letter to Secretary for the Interior, 8 July 1924, NTS 2716/304/301 in National Archives of South Africa.
57. See letter from Secretary for Native Affairs, 19 July 1924, NTS 2716/304/301 in National Archives of South Africa.
58. See Kuper, *Sobhuza II, Ngwenyama and King of Swaziland*, p. 87.
59. See record of court proceedings in F47545, University of South Africa Library.
60. See record of court decision in F47356, University of South Africa Library.
61. See Kuper, *Sobhuza II, Ngwenyama and King of Swaziland*, p. 92.
62. Later on, when the Swazis made land claims in the 1930s, this point was disputed by the South African government. See correspondence between various South African government officials, RCS 258/39 in Swaziland National Archives.
63. See letter from Labotsibeni, 24 January 1918, GG 1547, 50/695 in National Archives of South Africa.
64. See petition in GG 1569, 50/1443 in National Archives of South Africa.
65. Seme to Sobhuza II, 13 July 1936, RCS 604/36 in Swaziland National Archives.
66. See minutes of meeting between Sobhuza II and the Resident Commissioner, RCS 604/36 in Swaziland National Archives.
67. Marwick to Seme, 16 July 1936, RCS 604/36 in Swaziland National Archives.
68. This was in keeping with Seme's general approach to the white authorities, and the Minister of Native Affairs in particular, during his tenure as ANC president in the 1930s.

69. See petition and Seme's covering letter, RCS 604/36 in Swaziland National Archives.
70. Ibid.
71. For a record of Sobhuza II's pleadings, see RCS 258/39 in Swaziland National Archives, where the authorities were again dismissive of the Swazi claims.
72. See Kuper, *Sobhuza II, Ngwenyama and King of Swaziland*, p. 101.

CHAPTER 5: ZULU ROYALS

1. See Jeff Guy, *The Destruction of the Zulu Kingdom: The Civil War in Zululand, 1878–1884* (Scottsville: University of Natal Press, 1979).
2. The Bhambatha Rebellion was known as *impi yamakhanda* among the indigenous population of Natal and Zululand. *Impi yamakhanda* was the resistance by black people, principally from Natal, against the imposition of poll tax on adult black males. It was the battle (*impi*) over the poll tax paid by each male head (*ikhanda*). Bhambatha ka Mancinza, chief of the Zondi, led the resistance. For a history of the Bhambatha Rebellion see Shula Marks, *Reluctant Rebellion: The 1906–1908 Disturbances in Natal* (Oxford: Clarendon Press, 1971).
3. See NTS 3800, 2568/308 in National Archives of South Africa.
4. See Moses Muziwandile Hadebe, 'A contextualisation and examination of the *impi yamakhanda* (1906 uprising) as reported by J.L. Dube in *Ilanga lase Natal*, with special focus on Dube's attitude to Dinuzulu as indicated in his reportage on the treason trial of Dinuzulu', MA dissertation, University of Natal, 2003, p. 167. According to James Stuart, Dinuzulu was found guilty on two rather than four counts of treason, NTS 3800, 2568/308 in National Archives of South Africa.
5. Hadebe, 'A contextualisation and examination of the *impi yamakhanda*', pp. 168–169.
6. Ibid.
7. For a brief overview of Dinuzulu's incarceration and his move to Middelburg, see NTS NTS 3800 and 2568/308 in National Archives of South Africa.
8. See the district surgeon's letter to the Middelburg district magistrate, 11 October 1913, file A204 in Pietermaritzburg Archives Repository.
9. Dr Godfrey to Governor General of the Union of South Africa, 18 March 1913, GG 1540, 50/282 in National Archives of South Africa. The report that Seme received on 19 November 1912 was sent to the government some four months later, in 1913.
10. Ibid.
11. See letter from Godfrey to Seme dated 19 November 1912, which was accompanied by the report in GG 1540, 50/272 in National Archives of South Africa.
12. Seme to Prime Minister Botha, 19 December 1912, GG 1540, 50/282 in National Archives of South Africa.
13. Letter from Bok to Seme, 21 December 1912, GG 1540, 50/282 in National Archives of South Africa.
14. Seme to Prime Minister Botha, 17 February 1913, GG 1540, 50/272 in National Archives of South Africa.
15. Ibid.
16. Letter from Seme to Governor General, 17 February 1913, GG 1540, 50/282 in National Archives of South Africa.
17. See letter from Governor General to Prime Minister Botha, 1 March 1913, and from the office of the Governor General to Seme, 3 March 1913, GG 1540, 50/285 in National Archives of South Africa.
18. Dr Godfrey to Governor General, 18 March 1913, GG 1540, 50/283A in National Archives of South Africa.

19. Seme's telegram to Governor General, 15 March 1913, GG 1540, 50/283 in National Archives of South Africa.
20. Governor General's telegram to Seme, 18 March 1913, GG 1540, 50/283 in National Archives of South Africa.
21. Prime Minister Botha to Governor General, 20 March 1913. GG 1540, 50/283 in National Archives of South Africa.
22. Letter from Governor General to Secretary of State for the Colonies, 2 April 1913, GG 1540, 50/287 in National Archives of South Africa.
23. Ibid.
24. See Seme's letter to Harriette Colenso, 15 April 1913, and Dower's letter to Colenso, 29 December 1913, file A204 in Pietermaritzburg Archives Repository.
25. Telegram from Native Affairs Department to Chief Native Commissioner's office in Pietermaritzburg, 18 October 1913, CNC 144, 1818/1913 in Pietermaritzburg Archives Repository.
26. See telegraph from Chief Native Commissioner for Natal to the magistrates, 18 October 1913, CNC 1818/1913 in Pietermaritzburg Archives Repository.
27. See letter from magistrate of Nkandla division to District Native Commissioner of Zululand, 30 October 1913, and letter from Natal Chief Native Commissioner to Zululand District Native Commissioner, 5 November 1913, CNC 144, 1818/1913 in Pietermaritzburg Archives Repository.
28. 'UDinuzulu Aseko', Ilanga lase Natal, 18 October 1913.
29. Ilanga lase Natal, 31 October 1913. In the case of Dinuzulu, his izibongo extolled his bravery and his prowess in war.
30. I am grateful to Cassius Lubisi and Hlengiwe Nkonyeni for their assistance with the translation of this verse.
31. Translated by the author.
32. See telegram from Native Affairs Department to the magistrates of Mahlabathini, Nongoma, Melmoth, Nkandla and Louwsburg, 19 October 1931, CNC 1818/1913 in Pietermaritzburg Archives Repository.
33. See telegram cited in letter from Vryheid magistrate to Natal Chief Native Commissioner, 22 October 1913, CNC 144, 1818/1913 in Pietermaritzburg Archives Repository.
34. See letter from Natal Chief Native Commissioner to Secretary for Native Affairs, 4 November 1913, CNC 144, 1818/1913 in Pietermaritzburg Archives Repository.
35. See 'Isidumbu Sisuka eVryheid', Ilanga lase Natal, 31 October 1931.
36. I am grateful to Bongani Majola for his translation of this song.
37. See report by assistant magistrate, Babanango, to Natal Chief Native Commissioner, 23 October 1913, CNC 144, 1818/1913 in Pietermaritzburg Archives Repository.
38. Chief Native Commissioner to Secretary for Native Affairs, 3 November 1913, CNC 1818/1913 in Pietermaritzburg Archives Repository.
39. 'UDinuzulu Aseko', Ilanga lase Natal, 18 October 1913.
40. Although unsubstantiated, Nicholas Cope states that Seme supported Solomon's claim; see To Bind the Nation: Solomon ka Dinuzulu and Zulu Nationalism, 1913–1933 (Scottsville: University of Natal Press, 1993), pp. 39–40.
41. As alleged by Ngwenya ka Zibhebhu in a report compiled by two messengers from the office of the Natal Chief Native Commissioner, Nongejeni and Socwatsha, 28 November 1913, CNC 144, 1913/1818 in Pietermaritzburg Archives Repository.
42. 'Use Bekiwe uZulu', Ilanga lase Natal, 21 November 1913.

43. Letter from Natal Chief Native Commissioner to magistrate of Nongoma division, 6 November 1913, CNC 144, 1913/1818 in Pietermaritzburg Archives Repository. See similar letters from the Commissioner to the magistrates of Vryheid, Eshowe and Mahlabathini, in the same file.

44. Vryheid magistrate to Chief Native Commissioner, 12 November 1913, CNC 144, 1913/1818 in Pietermaritzburg Archives Repository.

45. Magistrate of Nongoma to Natal Chief Native Commissioner, 12 November 1913, CNC 144, 1913/1818 in Pietermaritzburg Archives Repository.

46. Acting magistrate of Mahlabathini to Natal Chief Native Commissioner, 12 November 1913, CNC 144, 1913/1818 in Pietermaritzburg Archives Repository.

47. The grandfather of Jacob Gedleyihlekisa Zuma, who became president of South Africa in 2009.

48. Zululand District Native Commissioner to Natal Chief Native Commissioner, 5 August 1914, CNC 144, 1913/1818 in Pietermaritzburg Archives Repository.

49. Chief Native Commissioner to Secretary for Native Affairs, 9 January 1914, CNC 144, 1913/1818 in Pietermaritzburg Archives Repository.

50. Seme to Dr Bok, 8 December 1913, GG 1540, 50/282 in National Archives of South Africa.

51. Mnyayiza ka Ndabuko was a son of Ndabuko, who was a brother of Cetshwayo, Dinuzulu's father. As such, Mnyayiza was Solomon's uncle. When Dinuzulu, Mnyayiza's cousin, died, Mnyayiza was the most senior male in the Zulu royal house, and so he took care of Solomon and the rest of Dinuzulu's family.

52. Situnzi 'Tunzi' Zuma was an elder brother of Nongejeni, also an official in the Chief Native Commissioner's office. Both were sons of Chief Mnyakanya Zuma and MaZondi of Nkandla.

53. See record of meeting, 19 February 1914, CNC 144, 1913/1818 in Pietermaritzburg Archives Repository.

54. See record of meeting, 18 December 1913, CNC 144, 1913/1818 in Pietermaritzburg Archives Repository.

55. Ibid.

56. Bishop of Zululand to Zululand District Native Commissioner, 1 December 1914, CNC 144, 1913/1818 in Pietermaritzburg Archives Repository.

57. 'Solomon ka Dinuzulu', Ilanga lase Natal, 16 January 1914.

58. Letter from Dower to Colenso, 27 March 1914, file A204 in Pietermaritzburg Archives Repository.

59. Secretary for Native Affairs to Natal Chief Native Commissioner, 4 January 1915, CNC 144, 1913/1818 in Pietermaritzburg Archives Repository.

60. For Dube's view, see 'The Teaching of Solomon', Ilanga lase Natal, 20 February 1914.

61. Prime Minister Botha's private secretary to Seme, 12 August 1914, GG 1544, 50/480 in National Archives of South Africa.

62. Ibid.

63. See the letter to the Secretary for Native Affairs from the Natal Chief Native Commissioner, 2 December 1913, CNC 144, 1913/1818 in Pietermaritzburg Archives Repository.

64. Natal Chief Native Commissioner to Secretary for Native Affairs, 2 December 1913, CNC 144, 1913/1818 in Pietermaritzburg Archives Repository.

65. Notes of an interview granted by Prime Minister Botha to Solomon ka Dinuzulu, 25 November 1916, GG 1568, 50/1359 in National Archives of South Africa.

66. Solomon to magistrate of Babanango, 11 November 1914, CNC 144, 1818/1913 in Pietermaritzburg Archives Repository.

67. Seme to Governor General, 28 May 1915, GG 1544, 50/480 in National Archives of South Africa.
68. Seme to the Minister of Native Affairs, 28 May 1915, NTS 3800, 2572/308 in National Archives of South Africa.
69. After the destruction of the Zulu kingdom, the colonial administration created various pro-government chiefdoms. The term 'monarchs' is used to distinguish between government-appointed chiefs and those of the Zulu royal house.
70. 'uSeme no Mntwana uSolomon', *Ilanga lase Natal*, 17 November 1916.
71. 'UMntwana noSeme', *Ilanga lase Natal*, 24 November 1916.
72. Seme to Solomon, 6 January 1917, NTS 7601, 6/328 in National Archives of South Africa.

CHAPTER 6: DAGGAKRAAL

1. For a discussion of the circumstances behind the passing of the Natives Land Act, see Harvey Feinberg, 'The 1913 Natives Land Act in South Africa: Politics, Race, and Segregation in the Early 20th Century', in *The International Journal of African Historical Studies*, 26(1), 1993, pp. 65–109.
2. Ibid., p. 67.
3. NTS 3440, 56/308 in National Archives of South Africa.
4. See *Abantu-Batho* report, NTS 3440, 56/308 in National Archives of South Africa.
5. Chairman of the meeting to Minister of Native Affairs, 22 August 1912, NTS 3440, 56/308 in National Archives of South Africa.
6. Assistant magistrate, Wakkerstroom district, to Secretary for Native Affairs, 15 August 1912, NTS 3440, 56/308 in National Archives of South Africa.
7. See letter, NTS 3440, 56/308 in National Archives of South Africa.
8. Seme to Secretary for Native Affairs, 11 September 1912, NTS 3440, 56/308 in National Archives of South Africa.
9. Seme to Bell, 15 August 1912, NTS 3440, 56/308 in National Archives of South Africa.
10. Letter from Secretary for Native Affairs to Sub-Native Commissioner: Volksrust, 31 August 1912, NTS 3440, 56/308 in National Archives of South Africa.
11. Sub-Native Commissioner to Secretary for Native Affairs, 27 August 1912, NTS 3440, 56/308 in National Archives of South Africa.
12. I.W. Schlesinger was an American who made his fortune in the financial sector in South Africa and eventually gained a reputation for his involvement in the film industry.
13. See letter from Colonial Bank and Trust Company, NTS 3440, 56/308 in National Archives of South Africa.
14. Ibid.
15. Secretary of the Daggakraal Natives Association to Native Commissioner, Wakkerstroom (undated), NTS 3440, 56/308 in National Archives of South Africa.
16. Ibid.
17. For the terms of the sale, see letter from Attorney General to Secretary for Native Affairs, 19 February 1917, NTS 3440, 56/308 in National Archives of South Africa.
18. See Chief Moloi's letter of 23 April 1915, NTS 3440, 56/308 in National Archives of South Africa.
19. See memorandum of agreement, NTS 3440, 56/308 in National Archives of South Africa.
20. See Lakage's affidavit, NTS 3440, 56/308 in National Archives of South Africa.
21. See Seme's affidavit, NTS 3440, 56/308 in National Archives of South Africa.

22. See judgment in NTS 3440, 56/308 in National Archives of South Africa.
23. Reverend W. Francis Hill to Native Affairs Department, 29 March 1916, NTS 3440, 56/308 in National Archives of South Africa.
24. Secretary for Native Affairs to the Attorney General, 5 March 1917, NTS 3440, 56/308 in National Archives of South Africa.
25. Bowman and Gilfillan to Secretary for Native Affairs, 23 February 1917, NTS 3440, 56/308 in National Archives of South Africa.
26. Cyril Kershaw Barry to Secretary of the Native Farmers Association, 3 November 1918, NTS 3440, 56/308 in National Archives of South Africa.
27. Bowman and Gilfillan to Secretary for Native Affairs, 3 June 1918, NTS 3440, 56/308 in National Archives of South Africa.
28. Hobbs to Schlesinger, 3 March 1919, NTS 3440, 56/308 in National Archives of South Africa.
29. Schlesinger to Native Affairs Department, 4 March 1919, NTS 3440, 56/308 in National Archives of South Africa.
30. See company letter to Reuben Dhlamini, 19 June 1919, NTS 3440, 56/308 in National Archives of South Africa.
31. See signed agreement, NTS 3440, 56/308 in National Archives of South Africa.
32. Mr L. Ham to Secretary for Native Affairs, 24 August 1920, NTS 3440, 56/308 in National Archives of South Africa.
33. See Stephen Moloi's affidavit, 29 March 1922, NTS 3440, 56/308 in National Archives of South Africa.
34. See Seme's letter to Stephen Moloi, 17 August 1922, NTS 3440, 56/308 in National Archives of South Africa.
35. See letter from Sergeant P. Henderson of the South African Police at Amersfoort to the resident magistrate, 20 March 1922, NTS 3440, 56/308 in National Archives of South Africa.
36. L. Ham to Secretary for Native Affairs, 24 April 1924, NTS 3440, 56/308 in National Archives of South Africa.
37. See Article 3(b) and 3(c) of Memorandum and Articles of Association, GNLB 339, 67/22 in National Archives of South Africa.
38. For information on the Native Farmers' Union, see GNLB 380, 4/326 in National Archives of South Africa.
39. See GNLB 339, 67/22 in National Archives of South Africa.
40. See record of court proceedings, TPD 105/27 in National Archives of South Africa.
41. Ibid.
42. See TPD 204, 184/1919A in National Archives of South Africa.
43. For Boshoff's claim, see NTS 3440, 56/308 in National Archives of South Africa.
44. See H. Selby Msimang's reminiscences about Seme in the John Aitcheson Collection, University of KwaZulu-Natal, Pietermaritzburg.

CHAPTER 7: BETRAYED TRUST

1. See biographical sketch of Seme in *Imvo Zabantsundu*, 25 November 1961.
2. Seme to Locke, 6 March 1911, in Locke Papers.
3. Seme to Locke, 1 September 1911, in Locke Papers.
4. Seme to Locke, 24 January 1912, in Locke Papers.
5. Ibid.
6. Seme to Locke, 27 January 1913, in Locke Papers.
7. See T.D. Mweli Skota, *The African Yearly Register: Being an Illustrated National*

Biographical Dictionary (Who's Who) of Black Folks in Africa (Johannesburg: R.L. Esson, 1930), Vol. 1.

8. Ibid.
9. See https://www.theguardian.com/artanddesign/gallery/2014/sep/15/hidden-histories -the-first-black-people-photographed-in-britain-in-pictures (last accessed 8 March 2017).
10. Ibid.
11. Frances Seme to Pixley Seme, dated 'Monday', WLD, 85/1917 in National Archives of South Africa.
12. Seme did not doubt that the child was his own.
13. Frances Seme to Pixley Seme, 12 February 1917, WLD, 85/1917 in National Archives of South Africa.
14. See court decision, WLD, 85/1917 in National Archives of South Africa.
15. For a brief sketch of Skota's life, see Skota, *The African Yearly Register*, Vol. 1.
16. The information about Princess Phikisile's name comes from her daughter, Helen Mamama Seme, in an interview she gave to Phiri at Unit C Ulundi, date unknown. Available at https://www.youtube.com/watch?v=Eymp4u81xy4 (last accessed 8 March 2017).
17. Ibid.
18. See Tim Couzens and Charles van Onselen's interview with Zwangendaba George Seme, 29 April 1977, Ladysmith, Natal, AG 2738-75 in Wits Historical Papers.
19. See James Stuart's interview with Seme in C. de B. Webb and J.B. Wright (eds), *The James Stuart Archive, Volume 5* (Pietermaritzburg: University of Natal Press, 2001), pp. 267–279.
20. Seme to Locke, 9 March 1923, in Locke Papers.
21. Seme to Locke, 8 December 1922, in Locke Papers.
22. Ibid.
23. Seme to Locke, 10 April 1923, in Locke Papers.
24. Seme to Locke, 22 May 1923, in Locke Papers.
25. 'Dr. P. Ka I. Seme L.L.D.', *Abantu-Batho*, 14 June 1923.
26. Information provided by Tewodros Abebe, Senior Archivist at Moorland-Spingarn Research Center, Howard University, via email correspondence, 10 August 2016.
27. Information provided by Jocelyn K. Wilk, Associate University Archivist at Columbia University Rare Book and Manuscript Library, via email, 22 August 2014.
28. Seme to Locke, 4 February 1924, in Locke Papers.
29. Seme to Locke, 6 February 1923, in Locke Papers.
30. Ibid.

CHAPTER 8: '*THULASIZWE* OF THE BLACK RACE'

1. See *Cape Times*, 22 April 1930, and *Umteteleli wa Bantu*, 26 April 1930.
2. The terms 'radical' and 'moderate' are used with circumspection. Most reports at the time used moderate to refer to the old guard in the ANC who preferred an accommodationist response to the political exclusion of black people in general and to oppressive laws in particular. The radicals, who were often referred to as communists, argued for mass mobilisation, protests, and other forms of militant response to the oppression of black people.
3. Ndobe and Tonjeni were both leading figures in the Western Cape ANC; before being ousted by Professor Thaele, Ndobe was secretary. Communist Party of South Africa delegates numbered four, with the rest being ANC members (mainly from the

Western Cape) who held radical views regarding the response to oppression and/or supported Josiah Gumede for re-election. See *Umteteleli wa Bantu*, 3 May 1930, concerning the composition of the delegates.

4. *Umteteleli wa Bantu*, 3 May 1930.

5. *Umteteleli wa Bantu*, 26 April 1930. See also H. Selby Msimang, 'Why Mr Gumede Failed', *Umteteleli wa Bantu*, 31 May 1930. Msimang, the youngest delegate at the ANC's founding conference in 1912 and a member of Gumede's executive committee, decried Gumede's influence through 'outside people', i.e. the Soviet Union and the Communist Party, declaring: 'I have no sympathy for him for I think that his blunders are unforgivable.'

6. After being forced underground by its banning in 1950, the party changed its name in 1953 to the South African Communist Party (SACP).

7. See *Abantu-Batho*, 1 May 1930, which also mentions Reverend J.L. Dube as a nominee.

8. *Cape Times*, 23 April 1930.

9. Two people were appointed 'organiser of chiefs', which may have been Seme's attempt to accommodate factions by dispensing positions to the leading figures.

10. *Abantu-Batho*, 1 May 1930. See also *Umteteleli wa Bantu*, 3 May 1930, as well as Seme's letter to A.W.G. Champion, A.W.G. Champion Papers, A922, Ea1, Wits Historical Papers.

11. *Cape Times*, 24 April 1930.

12. Thema later claimed that those who believed this were short-sighted, *The Bantu World*, 6 May 1933.

13. *Umteteleli wa Bantu*, 16 December 1933.

14. Seme to Champion, in William Ballinger Papers, University of Cape Town, BC 347 A5.V.6.3. I am grateful to Peter Limb for drawing my attention to this letter.

15. See Limb, *The ANC's Early Years*, Ch. 6. See also Phillip Bonner, 'The Transvaal Native Congress, 1917–1920: The Radicalisation of the Black Petty Bourgeoisie in the Rand', paper presented at African Studies Seminar Series, 10 March 1980, University of the Witwatersrand.

16. For a detailed analysis, see Bonner, 'The Transvaal Native Congress'.

17. See Limb, *The ANC's Early Years*, Ch. 6.

18. See Bonner, 'The Transvaal Native Congress'.

19. See Walshe, *The Rise of African Nationalism*, Ch. 8.

20. Ibid., p. 193.

21. Ibid., p. 172. It was Maduna who moved that members of the ICU executive should not be communists, a decision overwhelmingly endorsed by the ICU conference the following year, in 1927.

22. Ibid., p. 174.

23. Ibid., p. 169.

24. See S.P. Bunting Papers, Collection A949, item A1.4, Wits Historical Papers.

25. *Cape Times*, 7 January 1930.

26. Gumede subsequently disputed the claim that he had resigned, and questioned Mapikela's legitimacy as acting president. See *Ilanga lase Natal*, 11 April 1930.

27. The Natives Taxation and Development Act No. 41 of 1925.

28. See Native Administration Act No. 38 of 1927.

29. See section 7 of the Act.

30. *Abantu-Batho*, 22 May 1930.

31. Walshe, *The Rise of African Nationalism*, p. 182.

32. Limb, *The ANC's Early Years*, p. 320. Although Makgatho returned to lead the TNC in 1928, the divisions continued well into the first half of the 1930s.
33. For an explanation of the delay in policy announcements, see H. Selby Msimang in *Umteteleli wa Bantu*, 7 June 1930.
34. *Cape Times*, 20 July 1930.
35. *Cape Times*, 12 July 1930.
36. See *Umteteleli wa Bantu*, 24 January 1931. The Non-European Conference was a forum that brought together non-European organisations for the purpose of pooling resources in the struggle against white minority rule. Reverend Z. Mahabane had initiated the forum when he was president of the ANC, and the first conference was held in Kimberley in 1927, bringing together prominent leaders such as Dr Abdurahman of the African People's Organisation.
37. Ibid.
38. Ibid.
39. Ibid.
40. Ibid.
41. *Umteteleli wa Bantu*, 23 May 1931.
42. See F.A.W. Lucas Papers, AD1769 in Wits Historical Papers.
43. For Seme's evidence, see F.A.W. Lucas Papers, AD1769 in Wits Historical Papers.
44. *Ilanga lase Natal*, 5 and 12 April 1929.
45. *Umteteleli wa Bantu*, 14 November 1931.
46. *Umteteleli wa Bantu*, 21 May 1932.
47. Ibid.
48. *The Bantu World*, 9 July 1932.
49. For Kimberley convention, see *The Bantu World*, 16 July 1932.
50. See pamphlet in DCAS Acc 385, D.D.T. Jabavu Collection, University of South Africa.
51. See *Umteteleli wa Bantu*, 26 April 1930 and 20 May 1933. The newspaper's preoccupation with the demise of the ANC should be put in context. Its editorials were largely influenced by the newspaper's ideological leanings. It had been formed by the Chamber of Mines in 1920 to act as a moderate alternative to *Abantu-Batho*, which had become a voice of the radical wing of the ANC.
52. See pamphlet in DCAS Acc 47, D.D.T. Jabavu Collection, University of South Africa.
53. Ibid., p. 4.
54. Ibid., p. 9.
55. Ibid., p. 4.
56. The number refers to the black population at the time. Editorial, *The Bantu World*, 6 May 1933.
57. See pamphlet in DCAS Acc 47, D.D.T. Jabavu Collection, University of South Africa, p. 4.
58. Ibid., pp. 7 and 8.
59. Ibid., p. 11.
60. Ibid., p. 9.
61. Ibid., p. 5.
62. *The Bantu World*, 19 November 1932.
63. *The Bantu World*, for instance, printed Seme's conference call on its front page on 26 November 1932, and on 3 December it printed a Setswana version. Seme also published several articles in *Umteteleli wa Bantu*. One such article was published on 26 November, titled 'The African National Congress', while another with the same title appeared on 10 December 1932.

64. See, for example, *The Bantu World*, 24 December 1932, and *Umteteleli wa Bantu*, 31 December 1932.
65. *The Bantu World*, 24 December 1932.
66. *The Bantu World*, 14 January 1933.
67. *The Bantu World*, 22 April 1933.
68. The ANC constitution referred to the position as 'speaker' rather than 'chairman', as in the British Parliament and American Congress, thereby reflecting Seme's notion of the ANC as the parliament of the people.
69. *The Bantu World*, 22 April 1933.
70. *Umteteleli wa Bantu*, 16 December 1933.
71. *The Bantu World*, 29 April 1933. It was in reaction to his presidential address that *The Bantu World*, in its editorial of 6 May 1933, called Seme '*Thulasizwe* of the black race'.
72. See *Umteteleli wa Bantu*, 8 July 1933 and 6 January 1934.
73. See *The Bantu World*, 13 May 1933, 22 July 1933 and 29 July 1933.
74. *The Bantu World*, 28 October 1933.
75. See F.A.W. Lucas Papers, AD1769 in Wits Historical Papers.
76. *The Bantu World*, 16 September 1933. Seme remained undeterred regarding the matter of a black National Church, despite opposition from a large number of black church leaders.
77. *Umteteleli wa Bantu*, 13 January 1934. The Transvaal ANC was split between S.M. Makgatho, and S.P. Matseke and his dissident faction.
78. *Umteteleli wa Bantu*, 6 January 1934.
79. *Umteteleli wa Bantu*, 10 November 1934.
80. *Umteteleli wa Bantu*, 14 April 1934.
81. *Umteteleli wa Bantu*, 16 June 1934.
82. *Umteteleli wa Bantu*, 21 July 1934.
83. *The Bantu World*, 18 August 1934.
84. Ibid.
85. *The Bantu World*, 22 September 1934.
86. *Umteteleli wa Bantu*, 5 October 1935.
87. The nomination of Moroka is surprising as he was not known to be a member of the ANC or associated with it at the time. Nelson Mandela later revealed that the ANC Youth League had to enrol Moroka as a member of the ANC in 1949 before putting him forward as a candidate for president general against Xuma. See Nelson Mandela, *Long Walk to Freedom* (London: Abacus Publishers, 1995), p. 131.
88. *Umteteleli wa Bantu*, 5 October 1935.
89. *Umteteleli wa Bantu*, 2 February 1935.
90. *Umteteleli wa Bantu*, 9 March 1935.
91. *Umteteleli wa Bantu*, 20 April 1935.
92. See http://www.sahistory.org.za/topic/timeline-land-dispossession-and-segregation-south-africa-1900-1947 (last accessed 8 March 2017).
93. *The Bantu World*, 8 June 1935.
94. *The Bantu World*, 15 June 1935.
95. *The Bantu World*, 8 June 1935.
96. *The Bantu World*, 24 August 1935.
97. *The Bantu World*, 31 August 1935. Although the government-sponsored meetings did take place and were attended by several black leaders, they were unsuccessful in achieving their aims. Chiefs who attended one such meeting in Mafikeng from 13 to 14 September 1935 rejected the suggested abolition of the Cape native franchise and

resolved instead that full citizenship rights should be extended to all black people in South Africa (see *The Bantu World*, 21 September 1935).

98. *The Bantu World*, 1 June 1935.

99. *Umteteleli wa Bantu*, 15 June 1935.

100. *Umteteleli wa Bantu*, 18 May 1935.

101. Ibid. For a discussion of the Joint Council Movement, see Willan, *Sol Plaatje: A Biography*, p. 152.

102. *The Bantu World*, 18 January 1936.

103. *Umteteleli wa Bantu*, 4 January 1936.

104. *Umteteleli wa Bantu*, 11 January 1936.

105. *The Bantu World*, 18 January 1936.

106. *The Bantu World*, 1 November 1936.

107. *The Bantu World*, 25 December 1937.

108. Robert R. Edgar (ed.), *An African American in South Africa: The Travel Notes of Ralph J. Bunche* (Johannesburg: Witwatersrand University Press, 1992), pp. 273–274.

109. Ibid, p. 275.

110. Ibid.

111. Ibid., p. 281.

112. See, for instance, Mary Benson, *South Africa: The Struggle for a Birthright* (Johannesburg: Mayibuye Books, 1985), p. 23. See also http://www.sahistory.org.za/archive/founder-ambiguous-figure-chris-saunders (last accessed 8 March 2017).

113. Carter-Karis Document Collection, DA14 in Wits Historical Papers.

114. Ibid.

115. Benson, *South Africa: The Struggle for a Birthright*, p. 55.

116. Prince Arthur Mshiyeni ka Dinuzulu to Native Commissioner, 20 March 1940, NTS 7601, 5/328 in National Archives of South Africa.

117. See Alan Gregor Cobley, *The Rules of the Game: Struggles in Black Recreation and Social Welfare Policy in South Africa* (Westport, Conn.: Greenwood Press, 1997), pp 107–108. See also http://www.sahistory.org.za/archive/founder-ambiguous-figure-chris-saunders (last accessed 8 March 2017).

118. Ballinger Papers, A410, C2.3.7, ICU file 4 in Wits Historical Papers.

119. Harriette Colenso to Seme, 4 December 1913, Colenso Collection, file A204 in Pietermaritzburg Archives Repository.

120. M. Basner, *Am I An African: The Political Memoirs of H.M. Basner* (Johannesburg: University of Witwatersrand Press, 1993), p. 26.

121. Report of T.D. Mweli Skota, January 1930, in M.L. Faison, 'Pixley ka Isaka Seme, President-General of the African National Congress, 1930–1937: A study of the impact of his leadership and ideology on the Congress', thesis submitted to the History Department of the Graduate School of Arts and Sciences, Columbia University, 1983.

122. 'The African National Congress: Is it Dead?' in D.D.T. Jabavu Collection, University of South Africa.

123. Walshe, *The Rise of African Nationalism*, p. 223.

124. *Ilanga lase Natal*, 17 May 1929.

125. Walshe, *The Rise of African Nationalism*, p. 242.

126. Limb, *The ANC's Early Years*, p. 361.

127. See *The Bantu World*, 27 August 1932.

128. See Sibongiseni Mkhize, '*Umfelandawonye, Umendo Wenkululeko*: Selby Msimang's vision of African economic emancipation, 1930s to 1950s', paper presented at NRF Chair Seminar, University of the Witwatersrand, 23 April 2014.

129. This change was a mere whim, designed to win the support of the ascendant radical wing of the ANC. All along Gumede had been part of the political mainstream in the ANC, which was moderate if not outright conservative. His sudden change was nothing less than cynical.

CHAPTER 9: FALL FROM GRACE

1. Petition of John Moffat addressed to Governor General of the Union of South Africa, 27 November 1918, and letter from Pretoria magistrate to Attorney General, 17 August 1923, both in NTS 366, 6/56 in National Archives of South Africa. Frank McIntosh subsequently sold his shareholding in the firm to Moffat, which made Moffat sole owner of the land.
2. Ibid. See petition of John Moffat.
3. See record of proceedings in *Rex* v. *Seshele*, TPD 8/706, 676/1932 in National Archives of South Africa.
4. Ibid.
5. W.F. du Plooy's letter to Acting Commandant of Police, 12 July 1928, NTS 366, 6/56 in National Archives of South Africa.
6. See record of proceedings in *Rex* v. *Seshele*, TPD 8/706, 676/1932 in National Archives of South Africa.
7. The distance was eleven kilometres. See petition of John Moffat, 27 November 1918, NTS 366, 6/56 in National Archives of South Africa.
8. Pretoria magistrate to Secretary for Native Affairs, NTS 366, 6/56 in National Archives of South Africa.
9. Letter of Transvaal Provincial Secretary, 3 July 1920, NTS 366, 6/56 in National Archives of South Africa.
10. F. Glen Leary to Pretoria District Commandant of the South African Police, 29 August 1923, NTS 366, 6/56 in National Archives of South Africa.
11. Town Clerk to Pretoria magistrate, 26 August 1920, NTS 366, 6/56 in National Archives of South Africa.
12. Secretary for Native Affairs to Native Sub-Commissioner, 20 January 1928, NTS 366, 6/56 in National Archives of South Africa. The signed petition is in the same file.
13. See Minister of the Interior to Minister of Native Affairs, 15 October 1921, and the reply of the Minister of Native Affairs, 21 October 1921, both in NTS 366, 6/56 in National Archives of South Africa.
14. Sefako Makgatho to Minister of Native Affairs, 8 November 1922, NTS 366, 6/56 in National Archives of South Africa.
15. Secretary for Native Affairs to Sefako Makgatho, 8 December 1922, NTS 366, 6/56 in National Archives of South Africa.
16. Sefako Makgatho to Minister of Native Affairs, 11 December 1922, NTS 366, 6/56 in National Archives of South Africa.
17. Secretary for Native Affairs to Sefako Makgatho, 5 February 1923, NTS 366, 6/56 in National Archives of South Africa.
18. Secretary for Native Affairs to Attorney General, 17 November 1928, in NTS 366, 6/56 in National Archives of South Africa.
19. Petition of the women from 'the white townships surrounding Waverley' to Minister of Native Affairs (undated), NTS 366, 6/56 in National Archives of South Africa.
20. Pretoria Sub-Native Commissioner to Secretary for Native Affairs, 24 July 1928, GG 50/696, 1548, NTS 366, 6/56 in National Archives of South Africa.

21. Secretary for Native Affairs to Attorney General, 17 November 1928, NTS 366, 6/56 in National Archives of South Africa.
22. Attorney General to Deputy Commissioner of Police, Commanding Transvaal Division, 10 December 1928, NTS 366, 6/56 in National Archives of South Africa.
23. Secretary for Native Affairs to R.T. Brown, 5 September 1928 (? illegible), NTS 366, 6/56 in National Archives of South Africa.
24. Secretary for Native Affairs to Pretoria Additional Native Commissioner, 24 December 1928, NTS 366, 6/56, 1548 in National Archives of South Africa.
25. Private Secretary to Innesdale Municipality Town Clerk, 30 May 1930, NTS 366, 6/56 in National Archives of South Africa.
26. Secretary for Native affairs to Commissioner of Police, 5 June 1930, NTS 366, 6/56, in National Archives of South Africa.
27. See affidavit submitted by Tom Ntuli to the Transvaal Supreme Court in the matter of *The Incorporated Law Society of the Transvaal* v. *Pixley ka Isaka Seme*, TPD 8/706, 676/1932 in National Archives of South Africa.
28. See record of the proceedings in the Pretoria Magistrate's Court, TPD 8/706, 676/1932 in National Archives of South Africa.
29. See affidavits of Murray and Liebson, TPD 8/706, 676/1932 in National Archives of South Africa.
30. See Liebson's affidavit in the matter of *The Incorporated Law Society of the Transvaal* v. *Pixley ka Isaka Seme*, TPD 8/706, 676/1932 in National Archives of South Africa.
31. Letter from Seme to Messrs De Beer and Liebson, 5 August 1931, TPD 8/706, 676/1932 in National Archives of South Africa.
32. De Beer and Liebson to Seme, 11 August 1931, TPD 8/706, 676/1932 in National Archives of South Africa.
33. See affidavit of the Incorporated Law Society of the Transvaal, TPD 8/706, 676/1932 in National Archives of South Africa.
34. Seme to De Beer and Liebson, 5 August 1931, TPD 8/706, 676/1932 in National Archives of South Africa.
35. See Ntuli's affidavit, TPD 8/706, 676/1932 in National Archives of South Africa.
36. See Seme's affidavit, TPD 8/706, 676/1932 in National Archives of South Africa.
37. Ibid.
38. See Transvaal Law Society's affidavit, TPD 8/706, 676/1932 in National Archives of South Africa.
39. See *Seme* v. *Incorporated Law Society*, TPD 8/706, 676/1932 in National Archives of South Africa.
40. Ibid.
41. See Seme's affidavit, TPD 8/887, 260/1938 in National Archives of South Africa.
42. See affidavits by Makgatho, Marema and Mayabas, TPD 8/887, 260/1938 in National Archives of South Africa.
43. See Judge Solomon's decision, TPD 8/887, 260/1938 in National Archives of South Africa.
44. Ibid.
45. Seme to Vilakazi, 21 March 1917, GNLB 230, 290/19 in National Archives of South Africa.
46. See file GNLB 230, 290/19 in National Archives of South Africa.
47. KJB 363, 13/524A, National Archives of South Africa, Pretoria.

CHAPTER 10: IN FROM THE COLD

1. Seme to Rheinallt Jones, Thema and Baloyi, 19 October 1937, AD2186-Ga3 in Records of the African National Congress, Wits Historical Papers.
2. Provincial structures of the national organisation were named thus, according to each province.
3. Seme to Mahabane and other members of the ANC National Executive Committee, 8 April 1939, AD2186-Ga8 in Records of the African National Congress, Wits Historical Papers.
4. Seme to Chief Native Commissioner for the Northern Areas, 7 August 1939, AD2186-Ga13 in Records of the African National Congress, Wits Historical Papers.
5. Ibid.
6. Ibid.
7. Seme's notice was in the form of a letter to chiefs, dated September 1939, AD2186-Ga15 in Records of the African National Congress, Wits Historical Papers.
8. Seme to Rheinallt Jones, 20 September 1939, AD2186-Ga19 in Records of the African National Congress, Wits Historical Papers.
9. Ibid.
10. Seme to Xuma, 3 September 1942, AD843-FaF1 in A.B. Xuma Papers, Wits Historical Papers.
11. Seme to Calata, 9 December 1942, AD843-FaF3 in A.B. Xuma Papers, Wits Historical Papers.
12. Ibid.
13. See http://www.anc.org.za/content/africans-claims-south-africa (last accessed 9 March 2017). The Atlantic Charter was a statement that arose from a post-war meeting between US president Roosevelt and Prime Minister Winston Churchill of Great Britain envisioning a new world order. It was supported by South Africa as well as other countries that had fought on the side of Allied forces. Because the charter's vision of equal rights had no application in South Africa, the ANC produced the African Claims document, which sought to extend the rights enshrined in the Atlantic Charter to black people throughout the African continent.
14. Prince Mshiyeni ka Dinuzulu to Nongoma Native Commissioner, 20 March 1940, NTS 7601, 5/328 in National Archives of South Africa.
15. See Seme's affidavit, TPD 8/1026, 177/1942 in National Archives of South Africa.
16. Ibid.
17. Ibid.
18. Ibid.
19. See *Johannesburg City Council v. Monongoaha and Others (1946 WLD 509)*, p. 518.
20. Nicholas Lembede to Native Commissioner, 10 October 1947, KJB 166, 476/47 in National Archives of South Africa.
21. Seme to Native Commissioner, 14 August 1947, KJB 166, 476/47 in National Archives of South Africa.
22. Nicholas Lembede to Native Commissioner, 26 December 1948, KJB 166, 476/47 in National Archives of South Africa.
23. Seme to Nicholas Lembede, 11 September 1947, KJB 166, 476/47 in National Archives of South Africa.
24. This dispute foreshadows that of Seme's family a few years later, with his heirs believing his estate to be far larger than it proved to be.

CHAPTER 11: 'WE ARE ONE PEOPLE'

1. Princess Phikisile's affidavit, 4 September 1951, KJB 610/N1/4/3-385/51 in National Archives of South Africa.
2. See letter from Bank Manager, 7 March 1952, KJB 610/N1/4/3-385/51 in National Archives of South Africa.
3. Tambo to Native Commissioner, 25 June 1951, KJB 610/N1/4/3-385/51 in National Archives of South Africa.
4. Goss to Native Commissioner, 21 August 1951, KJB 610/N1/4/3-385/51 in National Archives of South Africa.
5. Native Commissioner to Lipkin, Jankelowitz & Stein, 4 December 1951, KJB 610/N1/4/3-385/51 in National Archives of South Africa. It should be noted that the commissioner's reference is to white lawyers, since Tambo had already made himself available.
6. KJB 363, 13/524A, National Archives of South Africa, Pretoria.
7. Princess Phikisile to Native Commissioner, 25 July 1951, KJB 610/N1/4/3-385/51 in National Archives of South Africa.
8. Princess Phikisile to Native Commissioner, 22 August 1951, KJB 610/N1/4/3-385/51 in National Archives of South Africa.
9. See letter detailing Seme's assets, 9 September 1951, KJB 610/N1/4/3-385/51 in National Archives of South Africa.
10. The motto of the Union of South Africa was 'Ex Unitate Vires' (Unity is Strength). There is, of course, a bitter irony in this.
11. 'Passing of a great pioneer', *The Bantu World*, 23 June 1951.

Bibliography

Basner, M. *Am I an African: The Political Memoirs of H.M. Basner.*
Johannesburg: Witwatersrand University Press, 1993.

Benson, M. *South Africa: The Struggle for a Birthright.* Johannesburg:
Mayibuye Books, 1985.

Bonner, P. *Kings, Commoners and Concessionaires: The Evolution and
Dissolution of the Nineteenth-Century Swazi State.* Cambridge: Cambridge
University Press, 1983.

———. 'The Transvaal Native Congress, 1917–1920: The Radicalisation of
the Black Petty Bourgeoisie in the Rand'. Paper presented at the African
Studies Seminar Series, University of the Witwatersrand, 1980.

Boyce, A.N. 'Swaziland Concessions and their Political Consequences
(1876–1908)'. Dissertation submitted in fulfilment of the requirements
of Part II of the examination for the MA degree in history, University of
South Africa.

Cobley, A. *The Rules of the Game: Struggles in Black Recreation and Social
Welfare Policy in South Africa.* Westport, Connecticut: Greenwood Press,
1997.

Cope, N. *To Bind the Nation: Solomon kaDinuzulu and Zulu Nationalism,
1913–1933.* Scottsville: University of Natal Press, 1993.

Crummel, A. *The Future of Africa: Being Addresses, Sermons, etc Delivered in
the Republic of Liberia.* New York: Negro Universities Press, 1862.

Davies, R., D. O'Meara and S. Dlamini. *The Kingdom of Swaziland: A Profile.*
London: Zed, 1985.

Edgar, R. (ed.). *An African American in South Africa: The Travel Notes of
Ralph J. Bunche.* Johannesburg: Witwatersrand University Press, 1992.

Etherington, N. *Preachers, Peasants and Politics in Southeast Africa, 1835–1880:
African Christian Communities in Natal, Pondoland and Zululand.*
London: Royal Historical Society, 1978.

———. 'Religion and Resistance in Natal, 1900–1910'. In A. Lassoni et al
(eds). *One Hundred Years of the ANC: Debating Liberation Histories
Today.* Johannesburg: Witwatersrand University Press, 2012.

Faison, M.L. 'Pixley ka Isaka Seme, President-General of the African National Congress, 1930–1937: A study of the impact of his leadership and ideology on the Congress'. Thesis submitted to Professor Graham Irwin of the History Department of the Graduate School of Arts and Sciences, Columbia University, in partial fulfilment of the requirements for the MA degree, 1983.

Feinberg, H. 'The 1913 Natives Land Act in South Africa: Politics, Race, and Segregation in the Early 20th Century'. *The International Journal of African Historical Studies*, 26(1), 1993, pp. 65–109.

Gills, H. *The Kingdom of Swaziland: Studies in Political History*. Westport, Connecticut: Greenwood Press, 1999.

Green, J. *Black Edwardians: Black People in Britain, 1901–1914*. London: Routledge, 1998.

Guy, J. *The Destruction of the Zulu Kingdom: The Civil War in Zululand, 1879–1884*. Scottsville: University of Natal Press, 1979.

Hadebe, M. 'A contextualisation and examination of the *impi yamakhanda* (1906 uprising) as reported by J.L. Dube in *Ilanga lase Natal*, with special focus on Dube's attitude to Dinuzulu as indicated in his reportage on the treason trial of Dinuzulu'. Thesis submitted in fulfilment of the requirements for the award of the MA degree in historical studies, University of Natal, 2003.

Harris, L and C. Moleswort. *Alain L. Locke: The Biography of a Philosopher*. Chicago: University of Chicago Press, 2008.

Healy-Clancy, M. *A World of Their Own: A History of South African Women's Education*. Scottsville: University of KwaZulu-Natal Press, 2013.

Hughes, H. *The First President: A Life of John L. Dube, Founding President of the ANC*. Johannesburg: Jacana Media, 2011.

Killingray, D. 'Significant Black South Africans in Britain before 1912: Pan-African Organisations and the Emergence of South Africa's First Black Lawyers'. *South African Historical Journal*, 64(3), pp. 393–417.

Kuper, H. *Sobhuza II, Ngwenyama and King of Swaziland: The Story of an Hereditary Ruler and His Country*. London: Gerald Duckworth, 1978.

Lambert, J. *Betrayed Trust: Africans and the State in Colonial Natal*. Scottsville: University of Natal Press, 1995.

Limb, P. *The ANC's Early Years: Nation, Class and Place in South Africa before 1940*. Pretoria: Unisa Press, 2010.

———. (ed.). *The People's Paper: A Centenary History and Anthology of Abantu-Batho*. Johannesburg: Witwatersrand University Press, 2012.

Macmillan, H. 'A Nation Divided? The Swazi in Swaziland and the Transvaal,

1865–1986'. In L. Vail (ed.). *The Creation of Tribalism in Southern Africa.* Berkeley: University of California Press, 1991.

Mandela, N. *Long Walk to Freedom.* London: Abacus Publishers, 1995.

Marks, S. *Reluctant Rebellion: The 1906–1908 Disturbances in Natal.* Oxford: Clarendon Press, 1970.

———. *The Ambiguities of Dependence in South Africa: Class, Nationalism and the State in Twentieth-Century Natal.* Johannesburg: Ravan Press, 1986.

Mashamaite, M. *The Second Coming: The Life and Times of Pixley kaIsaka Seme, the Founder of the ANC.* Pretoria: Chatworld, 2011.

Matsebula, J. *A History of Swaziland.* Cape Town: Longman Penguin, 1988.

Meli, F. *A History of the ANC: South Africa Belongs to Us.* Harare: Zimbabwe Publishing House, 1988.

Mkhize, S. '*Umfelandawonye, Umendo Wenkululeko*: Selby Msimang's vision of African economic emancipation, 1930s to 1950s'. Paper presented at the NRF Chair Seminar, University of the Witwatersrand, 2014.

Mokoena, H. *Magema Fuze: The Making of a Kholwa Intellectual.* Scottsville: University of KwaZulu-Natal Press, 2011.

Moses, W. (ed.). *Classical Black Nationalism: From the American Revolution to Marcus Garvey.* New York: New York University Press, 1996.

Ndlovu, M. *Cosmopolitanism and the Seeds of Nationalism: the Making of Pixley ka Isaka Seme, a Zulu Intellectual Leader of the Early Twentieth Century.* Thesis submitted in partial fulfilment of the requirements for the degree of Master of Science in African Studies at the University of Oxford, 2014.

Odendaal, A. *The Founders: The Origins of the ANC and the Struggle for Democracy in South Africa.* Lexington: University of Kentucky Press, 2013.

———. *Vukani Bantu!: The Beginnings of Black Protest Politics in South Africa to 1912.* Cape Town: David Philip, 1984.

Rive, R and T. Couzens. *Seme: The Founder of the ANC.* Trenton, New Jersey: Africa World Press, 1993.

Roux, E. *Time Longer Than Rope: A History of the Black Man's Struggle for Freedom in South Africa.* Madison: University of Wisconsin Press, 1967.

Saunders, C. 'Pixley Seme: Towards a Biography'. *South African Historical Journal,* 25(1), 1991, pp. 196–217.

Sherwood, M. *Origins of Pan-Africanism: Henry Sylvester Williams, Africa and the African Diaspora.* London: Routledge, 2011.

Skota, T.D. *The African Yearly Register: Being an Illustrated National Biographical Dictionary (Who's Who) of Black Folks in Africa.* Johannesburg: R.L. Esson, 1930.

Walshe, P. *The Rise of African Nationalism in South Africa: The African National Congress, 1912–1952.* Berkeley: University of California Press, 1970.

Webb, C. de B. and J.B. Wright (eds). *The James Stuart Archive, Volume 5: Of Recorded Oral Evidence Relating to the History of the Zulu and Neighbouring Peoples.* Pietermaritzburg: University of KwaZulu-Natal Press, 2001.

Willan, B. *Sol Plaatje: A Biography.* Johannesburg: Ravan, 2001.

Wood, A. *Shine Where You Are: A Centenary History of Inanda Seminary, 1869–1969.* Alice: Lovedale Press, 1972.

Index

Do you have any comments, suggestions or feedback
about this book or any other Penguin titles?
Contact us at **talkback@penguinrandomhouse.co.za**

Visit **www.penguinrandomhouse.co.za** and subscribe
to our newsletter for monthly updates and news